ADVENTURES

OF AN

H-BOMB MECHANIC

The Story of a Top Boomer

BY:

ALEX GABBARD

Memoir

Published by:

GPPress
P.O. Box 22261
Knoxville, TN 37933-0261

Cover and text photos courtesy of the National Archives
and the private collection of the author.

Cover design by Alex Gabbard
Book design and layout by Alex Gabbard

Dear reader,

This compilation is forty years in the making and recalls a time from my youth, a time when all things were possible, the 1960s, a time when my beautiful wife, Mary, and I lived every day to the fullest. Memories and collected "stuff" from those times have been drawn upon to reconstruct the events and places of our adventures brought on by induction into the Armed Services. That change from college life into uniform put us on new paths to exploits and destinations beyond our wildest dreams. Each set of orders sent me deeper into the US nuclear arsenal to locations that we experienced together during shore assignments and separately when shipboard duty sent me to the Mediterranean Sea and Mary back to her rural home. That cruise on the USS Forrestal fulfilled my greatest interests in seeing the places of ancient and modern history that I had studied in high school and college, then learned more about when visiting them. My cruise as ship's company with "my rich uncle's yacht club" fulfilled the sailor's enduring slogan, "Join the Navy and see the world." I did just that, seizing every opportunity to see everything, go everywhere, do everything possible during shore liberty that was sometimes only a few days, sometimes a week or more, and other times re-visits to the same port-of-call, while always keeping thoughts of Mary with me. The stories woven into this book are just part of more than four years of our adventures kept hidden away for so long among all the "stuff" that we collected along the way. Revisiting our exploits while compilng this book has been another pleasure, another adventure for me to recall the good times. Thanks.

Alex Gabbard

January, 2005

To Mary
My Co-adventurer

Chapter 1

The Russians and Me

The sky was blue, a nice fall day, November 22, 1963, as I sat on the steps of Surry Central High School. No differences from the day before were apparent while I looked skyward for the Russian missiles that I was certain would be leading the invasion. News of President Kennedy's assassination changed that day from just another school day to sad and somber as each of us young students, inexperienced in the workings of the world, wondered what was going on and why. Why kill the most popular President we had known? Why kill our young and dynamic leader? He was a war hero with a beautiful wife who had breathed a new spirit of youthful vigor into America. Why kill President Kennedy?

I was certain that I knew the answer: the Russians were coming. Nikita S. Khrushchev, blustering Premier of the USSR and World War II general, had said they would. Back in the mid-1950s he had brayed to the world, and particularly to America, "Whether you like it or not, history is on our side. We will bury you!"

I was also certain that I knew what he meant: war. I sat by myself on the granite steps of my newly built rural high school building waiting for the contrail of a missile to appear in the sky.

And there it was. I watched its slow progression high in the sky, a streak of white on blue, and my imagination soared on scenes I had seen on TV of a blinding white flash and everything at the end of the missile's path turned into a nuclear fireball, a detonation that I would get only the glimpse that distance permitted before vanishing, never to be seen again, as would everything for miles around. I waited to be evaporated and envisioned the brick and stone structure behind me being swept from the face of the earth with the homes of little Dobson, North Carolina, its courthouse... everything gone, leaving heaps of burning rubble where life had once flourished.

Then, slowly, the path of the contrail was joined by another. Two missiles were coming! The contrails crossed the sky as I sat expecting the inevitable, while contemplating the whys of assassinating our young President and a foreign leader proclaiming his way of life better than mine. I waited for changes that would twist the world around me into charred wreckage.

I watched the shadow in front of me grow longer, made by the sun advancing toward the western horizon. The day moved on. Small white clouds in the sky drifted lazily along as they always did. They stayed white and the sky stayed blue. The contrails slowly drifted apart from their narrow paths to diffuse into indistinct clouds across the sky. Another and another appeared, all heading eastward. Birds kept up their twitter. Cool breezes continued to flow by me. The grass stayed green. Nothing changed. I thought about the ancient Greeks we were studying in World History and began putting the pieces together into a different puzzle of life than I had known before. As I watched the world around me, the thought emerged in my mind that the missiles were going the wrong direction. They were moving eastward. Russian missiles would be coming from the east, the opposite direction.

The puzzle pieces began to make a bigger picture. Those ancient Greeks had days of blue skies and fluffy white clouds that came and went, the total comprising their civilization that lasted for a time, rising and falling long ago, the latter resulting from war when an invading leader and his army overran the home army and its leader, the victor always proclaiming his way of life better as proven in combat. His gods were proclaimed superior to the adversary's gods, otherwise, he would not have prevailed. Simple but circular logic. The idea of superior gods favoring the victor quickly exploded in my mind as I thought about how many gods have existed in the ancient world and the fact that every great civilization that rose also fell, their gods forgotten in time.

I wondered about that. What do gods have to do with war, anyway? I imagined that, without people, the world would go on each day just as days always do, just as I was witnessing this day of anticipated profound change that did not arrive as expected. The ancient Greeks had gods, lots of them, and when their civilization rose, was it because their gods smiled upon them or was success the product of combined efforts toward a common goal, a better life for all when people worked together? When their civilization fell, was it because their gods turned their backs on them, or was it the result of common goals losing to special interests that never protect or defend the larger good as well as they do narrow interests? We were studying these very topics, and I came to the conclusion that gods are inventions of the human mind to support what is wanted and answers to unanswerable questions such as the meaning of existence: the "why" questions. I concluded that when a victor prevails, the gods of his conviction prevail as well, and professors of the faith emerge as the priests who provide answers that rise from those convictions. When the civilization collapses, the gods and their priests collapse as well, and what was once so important to believe is no longer important at all, replaced by new gods, new images, new professors of the new faith, all supporting the same notions but pitched in different names and forms.

Forgotten and covered by the dust of time, artifacts of lost civilizations become the fascinating focal points of archeologists when a new image carved from stone is found and imaginations are piqued. I concluded that such stones were, after all, still just stone; images carved into them by stone working artisans were no more than visual connections made for the subjects of the prevailing leaders as told by the priests who point to these creations as images of god, not the actual god, but an image to help believers envision their gods and to be able to describe their superiority to non-believers. Carved in eternal stone was, supposedly, to lend eternity to their gods.

I imagined a stone more ancient than all civilizations being selected by the ranking priest of the faith who instructs carvers to shape it in particular ways. Once shaped to his approval, the stone is then placed in a prominent location that becomes a fixture of daily life around it and another anchor for adherents of the faith. When an invading army arrives and topples it, whatever significance the carving once had is reduced to insignificance, rejected by the new life around it, and lost. Time goes on, and when the stone is rediscovered it becomes a highly valued artifact of a lost civilization that our imaginations tell us was once composed of people going about their daily lives. Archeologists study the stone, and museums seek it as a valuable addition to their holdings. Once on display, spectators marvel and wonder about the people who made it and how it influenced their lives. Photographs and drawings end up in books of ancient history such as we were studying.

I asked myself some questions and answers emerged. If the stone was never discovered, forever lost, would it make a difference? No. If the Russians prevailed, would their historians of the future tell much of the United States conquered in 1963? No.

I then took a long distance view looking back at the image of a lone sitter on the steps of just another building in the broad expanse of time. If I did not exist, sitting on those steps at that moment pondering the significance of assassinating our young and handsome President, would my absence make a difference? I concluded that my existence made no difference at all. The world would go on just as it always had and the future would unfold on another course that did not include me. I recognized that time marches on, oblivious to those who contemplate its significance and that events of each day are largely the making of mankind. If so, why not live in harmony rather than amid destruction of continual wars? I concluded that the answer lay in ambition that becomes reality when a leader emerges and puts his own ambitions in motion with the resources that his people provide. That conclusion told me that choosing a leader should be done very carefully for they are the people who lead into the future, the fabric that historians will write about. John F. Kennedy was, by all accounts, a good leader. Why kill him? Was it the work of a faction that did not like the direction he was leading and chose the path of a bullet to change the course of history?

After a lengthy time sitting and thinking about the events of the day, I got up and went back inside. The hands of the clock had not missed a beat in their advance around their perpetual circles. Classes were in disarray with students sitting silently at desks or standing in small clusters talking in hushed tones. The gravity of the day was such that teachers had no need to keep order; girls were crying, guys were standing around, everyone looked at everyone else for explanations, and teachers had little more than consoling answers.

That day was different from all previous days, and, as I pondered the thought, I recognized that every day is different from all others and that those that are remembered stand out in our minds because of lasting impressions. We never know just what goes into each day because prior events shape the days to come in ways that experience alone can anticipate; only those older and wiser with the whys and wherefores of the world can make sense of it. Young minds turned to the wiser minds for guidance.

Smart people paid attention to Khrushchev's blustering, and I could never have anticipated the effects of his remarks on highly placed decision-makers in my country and how their decisions would affect me. I had difficulty putting the pieces together on the day Kennedy was murdered. The puzzle of life that I sought that day became a factor in my personality profile that was to play a role in how, with my participation, those decision-makers answered the Soviet leader. Had Khrushchev alluded to war and the destruction of America as his view of inevitable events to come? Was Kennedy's assassination the beginning of the Soviet invasion, fulfilment of Khrushchev's vision? Things far bigger than day-to-day events in my life as a teenager were taking place, and I had no grasp of them at all.

Time progressed toward our bus rides home and the evening news. That afternoon, my older brother and I capped off the brick chimney and fireplace being erected to warm the newly built study to our house. In its fresh cement we inscribed, 'Nov. 22, 1963.' During supper, little conversation was exchanged and passed in a somber mood. As I lay in bed that night, I thought about the effects that Kennedy's assassination had on my tearful friends, many of them I had known since childhood and had never seen cry before. I saw that war was not necessary to thoroughly distress a lot of people: ending the life of one man was enough, especially a life that made a difference to us.

That was the broad view brought on by the death of my nation's leader, but not a single 'why' was answered. I imagined a home in which a son or father was lost to a war's bullet and recognized the same sadness, just as much a tragedy as the death of our president but confined to that single home, friends and neighbors who answered the tragedy with talk of duty to country, a soldier's honorable death, the supreme sacrifice to further the nation's destiny. Leaders proclaim such things but don't go to war themselves or send their children; they send the nation's youth off to battle and look around for more. The results were the same, just a matter of extent, a family's loss compared to a nation's loss. The soldiers of war, the nameless fallen who fought in all the wars of man's existence and were forgotten, gather another to the fold that time will also forget. Only those of high position are remembered, especially if killed in incomprehensible circumstances.

The next morning the sun rose again, and a new day began as it always had. Each following day was the same, and with the passage of time, our Prom night and graduation arrived just as it would have in any case, except the case of nuclear destruction. After high school, each of us began new phases in our lives. I went off to college in Winston-Salem, got married the next year in a church there, and had a job with a company selling industrial supplies during the summer. Along the way, I was constantly observing life around me to determine if the America I knew had changed. I could see nothing but good times.

Terms like "Baby Boomers" had been applied to us by then, and we ran headlong into youthful exuberance expressed in good times "beach music" brought by the Beach Boys and Jan and Dean and a host of rock'n'rollers. The southern California sounds combined with fast cars that my friends in western North Carolina hill country knew well was music that held its own against the Beatles and their British invasion that swept the nation in 1964, my senior year of high school. Our "good vibrations" bolstered ever-present fascination with life. Our love affair with speed brought exhilaration when fate was tempted and we won, and tragedies when some of our classmates were killed in their fast cars. Our lives went on with endless thrills, going places in cars: Friday night football games, Saturday night dates, Sunday races. The adventures never waned. Neighborhood friends often piled into my brother's pickup truck to spend many sunny Sunday afternoons at the drag races. Several quarter-mile strips were within driving distance for such outings that were always great shows of thundering power with colorful Super Stocks, fast Gassers and thrilling Altereds that we all longed to have. Later, my girlfriend and I spent many similar Sunday afternoons at drag races, and the next year we were married. Our first summer's weekends were often spent at the races where she won trophies by shutting down the guys. I tried to win but failed. She was my California girl in North Carolina, blond, trim and beautiful.

One day during the summer 1966 after we had been married almost a year, I received a US Government letter saying I was to report for examination in preparation for military service. I had been drafted. The President of the United States following Kennedy, Lyndon Johnson, had decided it was his duty to draft young, able-bodied American males for the war in Viet Nam, able-bodied young men to perform their duty to country, a commitment made at the White House following a Tonkin Gulf attack on US Navy ships that wasn't at all clear had actually happened. But whether fabricated or actual, the President responded with military force, and by the time I was drafted I knew about war. Supper time nightly news showing body bags were common, and I was certain that sometime after October of that year, the month I was drafted, I would return from Viet Nam in one.

During the day of examination, recruiters worked the lines of similar late-teen boys, lean and strong, stripped to their briefs, in attempts to get signatures for joining the Army. If not the Army, the Marines. In my case, having scored well on tests as a result of being two years into college, I was heavily recruited to sign up to become a pilot in the Army.

"What would I fly?" I asked.

"Helicopters."

I immediately recognized the need for helicopter pilots to pose a dangerous occupation requiring a steady stream of replacements;

new Huey Cobra pilots were needed to fill the slots of downed chopper pilots that the evening news often spoke of. I declined. Next came the Marine recruiter who similarly singled me out. He read from the same script, but included the "few good men" kind of inducement that was supposed to pump me up as special among the lines of examinees. I declined again and managed to get through examination day without signing my name to anything. My future was, however, very clear. I was going into the Army and I would, most likely, be killed in Viet Nam, another name on the growing list of good times "boomers" snuffed out because our leader thought it his duty to go to war.

My older brother had been in the Navy, and, having read a multi-volume history of US Navy combat during World War II among other naval interests by then, I wanted to serve in the Navy if I was going to serve at all. When I inquired, the Navy recruiter assured me that I had no chance; all Navy billets were filled far into the future. I tried the Air Force and got the same answer. By then, further reconciled to the Army, my previous life as an early '60s "boomer" changed to resignation; a feeling of dread overwhelmed me; I would not come back alive.

I thought about war in Southeast Asia and didn't know why it was being fought. I reasoned that it was just another leader trying to prevail over an adversary, an old story I had learned in the classrooms of Surry Central High School a couple of years earlier. It was another ideological war, the West against Communism, and I was supposed to accept the thesis of America's obvious superiority, politically, culturally and philosophically, as the charter to war against other ways of life different from our own. The Cuban missile crisis had come and gone with Kennedy's leadership preventing war and causing the Russians to withdraw without a shot fired. To me, that was clearly the best way to conduct foreign affairs. I kept wondering, though: If the Communists had murdered Kennedy to start a war, they certainly had not followed through with invasion, and by now, Khrushchev was gone, too. I concluded that the Communists must not have been the perpetrators.

I wondered: If the Communists had a score to settle and did so half a world away in the jungles of Viet Nam, was it a feint to draw Americans out into an enemy's arena, an old tactic of war that I had learned from reading Civil War histories? But the Viet Nam war, or policing action as it was officially called, wasn't because of Russian Communism anyway. It was Chinese Communism, and there were American's fighting to take this hill or that hill just to fall back and give up the hills taken just to be ordered later to take them again. What kind of war was that? I was learning about politicians running a war, er, policing action, using young men as fodder for their ambitions.

Viet Nam just did not add up in my mind to anything worth fighting for, and I was about to join the fodder sent by my government to kill or be killed. I imagined myself at the controls of a helicopter gunship doing the best job I knew how to do, having trained diligently to kill people on the ground below, people I didn't know who were similar young fodder from the other side who had decision-makers telling them to put their lives and futures on the line for a cause that they did not understand, either. We fought each other for some ephemeral concept presented as duty to country. I was never able to accept that concept as a good reason for my fellow "boomers" to die, and I was certain that I was to become just another name among the growing number, thousands and thousands of young Americans like me, who died in combat for no good reason.

Chapter 2

California Sun

When I received my draft notice, it was a sad day, but the departure date was not specified. Mary cried. I saw it as the beginning of my end; I was destined to become just another of the multitudes of anonymous soldiers killed in battles that time across the centuries has collected. My emotions ran rampant; my life was just getting started with a beautiful wife, and every scenario I imagined did nothing more than count down each day toward a meeting with a bullet or shrapnel or an explosion that would send me back home in a body bag. With each sunrise after that notice, my day of departure and my end drew nearer. Notice of my departure date for US Army basic training arrived; I was to leave on a Friday, and both Mary and I were saddened by our thoughts and imaginings that neither of us spoke of. Then, early Tuesday evening prior to that Friday, the phone rang. The Navy recruiter I had spoken with wanted to know if I still wanted to go in the Navy.

"YES!" I told him.

Well then, could I be at the recruiting station at seven the next morning to meet the bus?

"YES!" I assured him.

He told me that one of his recruits had been in a car wreck and was unable to fill his billet. Since I had the highest scores on the examination tests, he offered the billet to me first. If turned down, he would go to the next name on the list.

"I'LL TAKE IT! I'LL BE THERE!" I exclaimed with a sense of relief. Just as suddenly, my gloom evaporated. I was going in the Navy after all. However, Mary and I were left with only that evening to say our good-byes. We dressed for my farewell dinner at a nearby restaurant, but neither of us was in any mood to celebrate. What would we celebrate? I was leaving. Even though I was going in a direction of my choosing, it was a somber evening for Mary. My leaving to wear either an Army or a Navy uniform meant that I was leaving, a sad evening for her in either case.

Events unknown to me were, however, at work that changed my direction into the shadows of international politics as a practitioner of war's darkest weapons, and Mary's life would change as well. It was my personality profile, the type that certain people were looking for:

farm boy, never been anywhere, never done anything, good student, a couple of years of college. The first revelation to me that anyone had noticed anything unique about me came in boot camp.

After waving goodbye to tearful Mary from the window of the bus on that October day in 1966 and taking that ride toward my introduction to Navy life, I arrived in San Diego to begin what would unfold as the strangest set of encounters I had experienced in my young life. International intrigue, with the silver screen's James Bond as the model, was to become the track I was on, and I didn't know it. My destiny wasn't Huey Cobras and the jungles of Viet Nam; I was to become my country's answer to "We will bury you!" In a short time, the products of my hands could bury the Russians, all of them. No, not "bury the Russians," evaporate them.

The first of strange things to come arrived with a letter from Mary. Enclosed was another letter; the US Army had classified me AWOL and I was being charged with the offense to the extent that, if I didn't report for duty, I would be arrested by Army MPs and imprisoned as a deserter. I couldn't help but smile: the right hand didn't know what the left hand was doing. Dispatched the next day to confer with the Training Center's legal department, I spoke with a Navy lawyer, telling him the story of how I got in the Navy, and he chuckled. He would let the left hand know that I was dutifully serving in Uncle Sam's Navy. I never heard from the Army again, but when Mary wrote telling that she had answered the door to our Winston-Salem apartment to find two MPs there to arrest me and how they thought her story that I was in the Navy was a concoction, I chuckled. She wrote saying that it took some convincing them that I was, in fact, in San Diego in US Navy basic training. When they left, neither of us heard from the Army again.

The flight from Chicago to San Diego was my second time in any sort of aircraft, and I pondered the point that in the Army, in just a few months, I would be flying a helicopter. The Boeing 707 I was on, a giant jet plane of the day, didn't seem particularly far removed from my imagined Army flying and gunnery of jungle targets as a military pilot, except for the stewardesses on this civilian flight. This particular United Airlines flight began with a prop plane from North Carolina to Chicago, my first time on an airplane. My window seat was beneath the right side wing with the engine on it roaring at a deafening pitch. The prop whirring through the air as it beat its way off the ground and into steady flight was a new and dubious experience. I dubbed the plane a "Thunderbox Airline" because of the noise and vibrations that pulsed incessantly at near-one second intervals throughout the flight. When I stepped down the ramp off the plane in Chicago, I noticed that my ears were ringing. They haven't stopped since.

The smooth and quiet United flight exposed me to the best that commercial flying had to offer; I knew that because of the great difference from the previous "Thunderbox" and having the most beautiful stewardess that could ever exist. I watched her throughout the hours to the Pacific: trim, blond, stunningly attractive and with every movement, everything about her a display of perfection that made this country boy witness to a world never imagined. Perhaps my tuning in to her every movement was no more than lonely insecurity due to the combined events that put me on that flight, but I have remembered that stewardess to this day, without having learned her name or anything about her. Just a memory of beauty and perfection.

Arrival in San Diego was arrival in a magic land. I was thoroughly saturated with California beach music, and, having not once imagined actually being there, I was in the midst of it: one day from Tobacco City to sunny southern California. The sky was a rich blue seen only occasionally in North Carolina, and a cool ocean breeze blew with the most comfortable temperatures I had yet experienced, dry. All my life in the South had been with summer temperatures made less bearable by high humidity. While October back home was the most pleasant of months, I learned about humidity in San Diego. I learned that bright sunlight need not be laden with moisture. While daytime highs got only into the low 80s, being cool and dry was a first for me, and everything about my new location felt good. I liked southern California.

My introduction to boot camp was from a uniformed sailor who collected all the incoming trainees arriving by air. He pointed toward a grey US Navy bus, and, one by one, each of us stepped up its rubber mat steps to take our places on plain brown seats much like those of the buses I had ridden during my school days. The drive from the airport to the training center took us through San Diego traffic and within sight of an aircraft carrier and other warships anchored in the distance. They piqued my interests, and I wondered if they might be famous warships I had read about and seen during TV broadcasts of "Victory at Sea."

Back in 1964, my older sister, Cookie, had bought a cabinet model HiFi and a large selection of long playing albums. Every night we went to sleep with a stack of LPs playing the world's greatest music. I especially liked the rolling score of "Victory at Sea" that fired my imagination and sent me off to sleep. As we rode through San Diego I had no idea what lay ahead, but I was comfortable and excited about being a sailor largely because I was fascinated with the Navy. Why I identified with Navy rather than Army lay, perhaps, with my older brother, Johnny, being a sailor before me; perhaps it was because of my fascination with sailing ships.

We new arrivals formed a new training company, No. 638, and the uniformed sailor who gathered us together at the airport turned out to be the new company's training assistant whose job was to shape us into sailors. He was assistant to a Chief Petty Officer, a gruff but unthreatening career sailor who was our surrogate father for the next few months. His assistant was the man who spent the most time with us.

From the receiving building where all of us in every sort of civilian attire milled around, a sudden barked order got our attention. "FALL IN!" went unanswered. We didn't know what to do and looked around blankly at each other. Our trainer had seen it all before and began aligning us dummies by putting one after another in lines of six, shoulder-to-shoulder, one line after another, ten lines deep. Sixty young men lined up to form the new company of trainees, and not one of us knew the other. Even so, we were to live together for the next three months learning how to be sailors while getting acquainted with the person, the real human beings, inside the uniforms around us.

We began our first step toward new lives with "FORWARD, MARCH!" Off we lurched, this mish-mash band of raw recruits having to figure out how to get in step and stay in step so that we didn't tread on the heels of the guy in front of us or have our heels stepped on by the guy behind. In our unskilled fashion, we marched off under the direction of our trainer completely trusting in his leadership since none of us had any idea where we were going.

By now, the California sun had set and the sky was dusky with magnificent colors. I had never seen such beauty in a sunset. Points of light began showing all around and an occasional prolonged bellow of a harbor horn rolled through the evening. Then, sounding of bells in a pattern of regular double beats told the time in a way that I recognized, having previously gotten acquainted with the sea-going 8-bell time-keeping method. Since I was well steeped in marching, having been a member of the award winning Surry Central High School Marching Band, nothing so far was a challenge, and I tended to sight-see.

"COMPANY, HALT!" brought us to a stop at an intersection where we had to go either right or left. When our trainer commanded "ROAD GUARDS, POST!", no one moved. Our trainer halted his march alongside the recruit on the outside of the third row, the same row I was in on the opposite end, and told him to go out into the incoming lane of traffic, stand at parade rest, showing him how it was done, then return to the company once the group had made its turn. Then he walked through in front of the third row and pushed me out into the opposite lane. "You're a Road Guard. Post your position at parade rest like this." I had it down pat at first teaching and did my duty, now with my first assignment as a guard after no more than a couple of hours in the Navy. From then on, whenever "ROAD GUARDS, POST!" was commanded, the two of us double-timed it into the road and blocked oncoming traffic, permitting the remainder of the company to advance in formation. Once the turn was made, the two of us double-timed it back into formation and marched on. We marched to the mess hall and had a good supper served through a fast-moving cafeteria line where I was treated to fragrant aromas that piqued my tastebuds. Outside, we formed up again and marched through the night to our barracks, old World War II wooden structures lined up two-story by two-story adjacent to the US Marines training center just across the fence.

I remembered the Marine recruiter trying to get me to sign on the dotted line, and my reluctance to do so. In a few days, I was to see the wisdom of my decision as I and my company of Navy recruits were witness to the harshness of Marine basic training.

For the first time, we had the opportunity to get acquainted and did so with bunkmates first, then those in the bunks on either side of us. In a few days, we got to know each other by first names, where we were from, and what we looked forward to in the Navy.

Our training began the next day with a battery of papers to fill out. Each of us was interviewed by US Navy personnel; my interviewer was a WAVE, a rather good looking <u>Lieutenant, JG (Junior Grade).</u> She hardly looked up as she went down the list of questions, filling in, checking boxes here and there. When she asked, "Have you ever taken drugs?" my positive response drew her attention. She looked up at me with a prolonged stare. Having told the truth, I just looked back at her.

"Where did you get your drugs?" she asked.

"From the drug store."

My interrogator displayed a tone of aggravation as if I was toying with her. It was the truth.

"What drugs?" she asked sharply.

I had to think about specifics since I had not been sick in a long time. "Aspirin, I guess," I answered. "And poison ivy lotion." I couldn't think of any others.

"Aspirin?"

"Yes, I haven't been sick since... I guess... I don't remember the last time, except for poison ivy. I get it every summer. And when I had my tonsils taken out. And adenoids. That was when I was 10 or 12."

"Poison ivy?" she asked.

"I get it every summer."

She seemed momentarily stymied and unsure of how to proceed. "I mean, drugs," she said.

Other than drug store medications, I didn't know what she meant. After all, I was a North Carolina country boy who didn't know that there were other "drugs" in the world. All I knew of were those obtained from drug stores when people were sick. She waggled her pen back and forth in thought, then made some notes and went on.

"SN-JC."

"Yes ma'am. The recruiter signed me up for my two years of college: Seaman-Junior College."

She made more notes.

And so that day went, and days following as my company and I went to various assignments and classes in the sorting out process to see where we best fit the Navy's needs. Just how I was selected for the Color Guard remains unclear to me but seemed to result from scoring well on the various tests and, presumably, requiring less training than other recruits. Since I was well skilled in marching, and already a Road Guard, I apparently made an impression sufficient to be a member among the recruits who were selected from each company to practice the graduation exercises over and over in order to perform the ceremony flawlessly. After our three months of training, graduation day was to be conducted with the military flourish and pomp of marching before the Commanding Officer who conferred graduation status upon us. Afterwards, our dispersal into the fleet took us in directions that were worked out during boot camp.

To begin preparations, on the first day of Color Guard about a week after arrival in San Diego, we went through various parade type maneuvers, and I sufficiently impressed the Petty Officers running the show that I was ordered to report to the keeper of the banners and sabers to receive a saber. On that day, I became Regimental Commander of the combined graduation parade that would be filled with dozens of companies in precise formation, each with its RCPO (Recruit Chief Petty Officer), a recruit staff bearer with each company's number flag flying as Guide-On for marching and to identify each company among others on parade grounds, and each company's yeoman, the records keeper, also a recruit. At the head of the formation was the Regimental Commander and his entourage of staffman who presented the assembled recruit graduates to the Brigade Commander. Mine was a voice part, and as we marched daily in the warm California sun practicing for graduation day when we timed maneuvers to *Anchors Away*, we rehearsed our formations and I rehearsed my lines. At precisely the timing of the downbeat, I yelled

"Officers and Guide-Ons,
"Forward, Guide Center,
"March!"

Timing was such that our first step was always with the right foot and final step was with the left foot. When the appropriate distance had been stepped off, I commanded,

"Officers and Guide-Ons,
"Halt!"

That "Halt" command had to come with the correct timing so that right feet hit the pavement followed by the left foot, all in unison, producing a sharp "whack" amplified by the hundreds of feet that came to a halt on the same stomp.

The graduation ceremony told the gathered that duty to country was our purpose in uniform and that we were well trained to become the newest sailors in the fleet. Once again, *Anchors Away* blared as we marched in front of the command podium and gathered visitors on another glorious southern California day, then marched off the parade grounds to our barracks. I toyed with the idea of changing the commands a bit, to

"Ocifers and Di-gons,
"Warford, Cuide Genter,
"Charm!"

But I didn't follow through because I suspected that all eyes and ears on me during my bit part would produce far more problems that a moment's reward for humor. I saw little humor in the proceedings of the parade and opted to stay on the straight and narrow.

Our second and third weeks of boot camp involved training that began sorting each of us into future directions, classes and test results being the method. We marched to and from everything and became quite good at formations and timed maneuvers. I was having great fun, like being on vacation in a place of wonders that fascinated me, but other recruits were not of the same mind set. As an example, our marching took us over inlets of water occasionally, each with a sturdy wooden bridge of rather massive construction, all in Navy grey and blue and arched from bank to bank. In order not to set up vibrations in the bridges, we were always ordered to "BREAKSTEP, MARCH!"

when approaching a bridge. On one occasion, a recruit bolted from our company and dived off into the inlet in an apparent effort to swim back home. I watched in disbelief; each stroke took him toward the bay and anchored warships in the distance. If escape was on his mind, where could he possibly think he was going?

Later, he returned to our company to become our "sad sack," so distraught and homesick that each day was misery for him. Nothing any of us said or did helped at all, and a few weeks later, during his watch one night, he tied his bedsheets together, quietly slid a bunk over to an open window, crawled out holding the end of the sheet, and jumped from our second story barracks. We were awakening by his screams, having broken his legs in the fall rather than climbing down the sheets. Being whisked off for medical attention removed him from our company.

One of my fondest memories of Company 638 was how helpful each of us proved to be for those among us who adapted more slowly to Navy life. Every day was inspection day with everything about our bunks and lockers required to be in precise order, exactly alike. No contraband was permitted, and when Mary sent me a small transistor radio, I had to insure that it was sufficiently hidden to never become a problem. It became our only connection with the outside world and was equally prized and protected by each of my fellow recruits who listened to it.

Each of us learned early on that when one of us got in trouble, the entire company was in trouble; that was the Navy's way of teaching the value of comradeship and the importance of interdependence among sailors. We quickly learned that striving for excellence in everything we did was the easiest way through each day.

I was, however, rather astounded that simple things like properly making a bunk was so elusive to some among us, and what a chewing-out it received. With pity for a recruit across the center aisle of tables and attached stools who just could not get it, three of us took it upon ourselves to alternate in going over and over the routine with him, then checking his work just prior to inspection. While finally getting that task controlled, he had similar problems making his locker inspection-worthy.

One day while helping to properly fold and stack his uniforms, I discovered that he had a box of candy hidden inside his locker. Inspection was certain to find it, and he would get another chewing-out that would embroil all of us. He had to get it out of his locker, so he agreed to flush the contents down a toilet and dispose of the box to prevent its discovery. Instead, he chose to secretly eat all of the candy. When inspection came and he was commanded to roll out his pockets, the candy stuck to them rolled out as well. Down we went for more pushups, but rather than being harder on him, we paid closer attention to details and helped him become a better sailor who fit the mold that inspections demanded. We quickly recognized this strategy to be effective; after a time or two of finding his failings, inspectors tended to focus on him, and we all suffered. By helping him make the grade, camaraderie developed, just what our trainers aimed for.

I enjoyed basic training as a vacation in sunny San Diego. Being a southern farm boy accustomed to long, hot, humid days of labor in the tobacco fields followed by tossing bails of hay on a wagon, then from the wagon into the barn, nothing was challenging, either physically or mentally, and marching hither and yon in the company of guys I slowly got to know was just more adventures. When drill was called off for being too hot, the mid-80s, I rejoiced with the pleasures that came with it, such as barracks time to get to know my fellow recruits better, sea breezes through open windows, the California sun, and fresh, crisp apples.

To go anywhere outside the barracks, we had to be in company or have a "walking chit" signed and approved for a specific destination and return. "Walking Chit" was a misnomer; we didn't "walk" at all. Everywhere we went had to be double-time, a substantial running pace. My Color Guard "Walking Chit" allowed me to be anywhere inside the compound, and with it I was able to legitimately make runs for contraband. We had spied vending machines at particular locations on the base, and being fond of apples, I introduced my company to those huge Washington apples, both Red Delicious and Golden Delicious, available in refrigerated vending machines. A quarter was all it took, and I was soon making regular afterhours runs to return laden with apples that were received with delight by their purchasers.

During training, our trainer taught us marching by the cadence method, calling out a cadence as,

"Gimme your left!" We'd stomp our left feet in unison as we marched on.

"Gimme your right!" We'd stomp our right feet in unison.

"Gimme your left, your right, your left!" And we'd stomp each foot in time.

And then came other cadences, "I don't know but I've been told..." and all sorts of similar drill enhancing maneuvers that molded us into a cohesive marching machine of recruits bellowing in unison the answer to each "Sound Off!"

My "vacation" in southern California came to Christmastime that year, and the Training Center went into holiday mode. Regular Navy personnel, such as company commanders and trainers, took time off, and to maintain organization with a skeleton crew, our company and an adjacent company were combined under the command of those who remained on duty. Our company commander was to take leave for a couple of weeks, and with agreement from the company commander of the joining company, our recruit staff (RCPO and yeoman) were placed in superior positions to those of the joining company. The other company's RCPO, a tall, well spoken negro, believed himself to deserve seniority due to being RCPO of the company my company moved into. He also claimed seniority due to having arrived for training earlier, thus senior by virtue of a day longer in the Navy. Heated exchanges took place in the company commander's quarters just down the hall in the barracks, and our commander resolved the situation with a strong right hand belt to the RCPO's mid-section. Bent double with pain, he recognized the futility in persisting or challenging senior authority, and

RCPO - Recruit Chief Petty officer

relented.

Our training shaped us into competence for assignments in the fleet, and Christmas slack time gave us several days to assess where we thought we might be going and to get better acquainted. When Mary's "care package" arrived, a white fruit cake, it was consumed on the spot with the gusto of the hound dog by recruits hungry for any kind of home cooking. As we shared more of who we were and our ambitions, each of us faced many unknowns ahead, and most looked forward to being in the Navy. Still, Viet Nam loomed over our thoughts, and we knew that some among us would be going that direction. If I were to, so be it, I decided. But I knew I was clearly better off on any kind of ship than tromping through the jungles with an M-16 or handling the stick of a helicopter gunship, except for the Swift Boats. We didn't know much about them, but the stories of their engaging the Viet Cong along the Mekong Delta rivers, always open to hostile fire from hidden shore positions, hung as a cloud of dread over us because rumor had circulated that our entire company was to be detailed to Swift Boat duty.

Each of us was given three choices for Navy jobs with a first choice that we hoped would be our route into school, then assignment. When asked my first choice, I told of hoping to be assigned to the Naval Research Lab in Washington, DC because I wanted to advance my education along scientific lines. I didn't know how to make such a quest become reality, but each time I was asked, whatever the circumstances, I gave the same answer as my goal. Unbeknownst to me, people were noting my interests.

After Christmas, with only a few weeks to graduation, I wasn't at all certain where I was going. Others talked of volunteering for the Swift Boats to beat being "drafted" into that service, their "gunfight at OK Corral" imagery being fulfilled in modern form along jungle waterways. Others wanted to ride destroyers, cruisers, aircraft carriers, submarines, and all kinds of ships were to receive us after training as mechanics, radiomen, radarmen, communications technicians, electricians, boilerman... every need the Navy had. We would train for these duties by first being assigned to A-schools across the country. I was assigned to GMT training, Great Lakes, Illinois.

When I was assigned to Color Guard soon after arriving in San Diego, my days were mostly filled apart from my company, and, since I had scored out of various tests, I spent much less time getting acquainted with my fellow recruits than those who spent each day together. The few I got to know included the yeoman who happened to have an aunt living in San Diego. When Christmastime rolled around and training abated for a couple of weeks, he arranged 2-day off-post passes for himself and three of his friends, including me. Do's and don'ts while on liberty were firmly laid down with Mexico strictly off limits. Well, being close to the border and with a friend whose aunt just happened to have civilian clothes we could wear, we did just that. Off we went to auntie's house, visited, consumed quantities of good food, made phone calls, and off to Tijuana, Mexico we went. What a different world awaited me.

I had never been out of the country before, and crossing into

Mexico was just a walk across a long stone bridge controlled by gates and guards. Within a few steps from US soil, I began to notice differences that I could never have imagined.

The bridge spanned a broad riverbed wash in which the river itself was a narrow ribbon of water with gravely, dirt banks and no vegetation on either side. The banks were hemmed in with concrete walls about twenty feet high that contained end supports for the bridge. As my friends and I walked toward the Mexico side among a host of people going both ways, I saw my first poor people. Some would say that the rural tobacco farm life in Appalachia that I knew was poor, but my background was filled with riches compared to what I saw that bright day: poor as expressed in utterly destitute lives.

The concrete wall along the Mexico side of the wash as far as I could see in either direction was lined with row upon row of paperboard shanties, lean-to upon lean-to cobbled together from whatever was available to make a roof to shield from summer's blazing sun. Throughout my youth, I had seen tar-papered shanties in the mountainous coal country of Kentucky and Tennessee and backwoods shacks in the inner reaches of North Carolina's mountains, each providing some protection against wind, weather and cold, but these Mexican shanties were without any form of structure that would support walls and roofs. None had chimneys or even stove pipes, telling me that they had neither stove to cook on nor source of warmth to ward off winter's chill. The occasional drift of smoke told of an open fire, a hearth in the earth like campfires I had built during backwoods outings I had enjoyed as a youth.

If a strong wind should blow, I was certain that their shanties would topple like dominoes. If a heavy rain swelled the river, I was equally certain that the rush of water would sweep everything with it leaving the concrete walls bare to attract another shanty-town.

With those thoughts in mind, I stopped for a moment as my friends went on and we became separated; a young girl about eight or nine years old emerged from one of the shanties, walked barefoot over to the edge of the river, pulled the hem of her tattered dress up as she squatted down and did her business in the dusty gravel. With dozens of people on the bridge in clear view of her, she acknowledged no one, stood up and walked straight back to the shanty that she came from. I then began noticing other people among the shanties, feet and legs here and there, no one on their feet, and I recognized their derelict lives offered no opportunity to improve, or even change, in surroundings that gave no hint that they would even survive the day. And the next day would surely bring more of the same.

I imagined a fierce storm and rushing water wrecking their village, and the little girl grimly washed away to her death, a death like so many others that my imagination confirmed would go completely ignored by the rest of the world. These were people who breathed the same air as I did but literally had nothing. I concluded that the little girl with the stringy hair, grim and dirty-faced, likely had one possession in the world, the frayed dress she had on, and it was, most likely, a hand-me-down that she might not outgrow.

Like everyone else, I walked on and soon caught up with my friends. As we wandered through markets filled with colorful touristy things, clothing, toys, food, mementos in stacks and heaps, hanging everywhere begging to be exchanged for money and hawked by incessantly bantering sellers, with commerce bustling along every street and in every shop, I kept thinking of the shanty people just beyond the wall of Tijuana. Real people lived there, lots of them, but they were unwelcome and kept separate in their own country.

My first encounters with Mexican salesmanship were the groups of talkative young boys hawking small packages of gum and candy as an introduction that immediately led to offering sexual favors with their mothers or sisters, all claimed to be virgins.

My introduction to Mexico was an awakening that has stayed with me, and I have always remembered the sad little girl who, I remain certain, had hopes and dreams like every other child. But, in her case and many other children like her, no hope was fulfilled and no dream came true. A nourishing meal was, I remain equally certain, beyond her reach day after day after day, each day at best no more than watching the people who walked in endless streams across the bridge of opportunity above her. Ever since then, I have had no difficulty in appreciating my American life.

Tijuana was fascinating. As a chess player, I was attracted to the various sets on display in one of the shops. They ranged in price from dozens to hundreds of dollars, but my yeoman host cautioned that none of the prices were firm and that I should haggle, turning to leave if a price was not agreed upon. I had about thirty dollars and saw all sorts of things that I could buy for Mary but recognized that I would have difficulty explaining how I got an item from Mexico into the barracks when south of the border was off limits to Navy recruits. Still, those chess sets drew my attention, and on my second return to the shop, a nicely formed set in light and dark wood with an inlaid, folding container in checkerboard of similarly light and dark wood priced $120 quickly dropped to $50. I didn't have that much, and in a gutsy attempt to keep my money, I offered $10 with the certainty that the salesman I dealt with would react in violent contempt and throw me out of his store. He didn't and seemed to be intrigued to have snared a potential customer. Back and forth we haggled for a time until I left the shop with the chess set purchased for $20.

I felt embarrassed to have "cheated" the shopkeeper so shamelessly, but my yeoman friend reassured me that no one "cheated" anyone; to do business in Mexico involved haggling for the best price. The seller would never lose money, so any agreed upon selling price was profitable to him.

I thought about the original $120 price tag; who was ripping who? My yeoman friend grinned. I thought of the little girl; $20 to her would likely be good fortune turned into filling meals and a new, better fitting dress.

Later, back on base, one of my fellow recruits became enamored with my chess set and wanted to buy it. Keeping it hidden was a liability, and, if discovered, big trouble; not only contraband in a recruit training barracks but irrefutable evidence of having left the country. I weighed the circumstances surrounding it with some relief as the offer to buy it climbed. Each passing day drew us closer to graduation and parting of ways, and my friend wanted that chess set even more than I did. When $40 changed hands, it was his. Not bad, I thought, doubling my purchase price in a matter of days, but I have since lamented selling it because it was my first purchase in a foreign country.

Later, Mary gave me another chess set that went with me throughout my Navy travels and on which many games were played in all of the countries I visited. My skills increased as I studied chess books, to the point that my fellow shipmates progressively refused to play, but I was able to find high caliber players both on the ship and at USO clubs I visited.

My "Walking Chit" for color guard was laminated and was laced onto my necklace chain with my dog tags. I used it on a number of regular excursions, such as apple gathering, in addition to the carte blanche nature of being color guard. One afternoon I was called upon to use it when notice came to me to report the next morning to a particular building. I didn't know the location of the building or what the notice was about, but the prospect of getting out into another spectacular southern California morning, whatever the reason, was welcome. At the appointed time I departed in the usual double time required of each recruit, inquiring along the way as to the location of the building a time or two, only to arrive in what turned out to be a puzzle.

Arriving at the door, another plain Navy grey building of WW-II vintage, I entered into a very different world than the austere barracks and training facilities designed for wholesale housing of recruits. The floor was carpeted; walls were painted and hung with photos and interesting scenes; comfortable chairs, a coffee table, end tables with lamps sat invitingly with an assortment of magazines. It was a spacious civilian office, and the young and attractive secretary sitting behind a desk immediately beyond the door greeted me with a smile. She was not Navy, nicely dressed and working at a wooden desk rather than the plain grey steel desk common throughout other facilities.

"May I help you?" she asked.

The fact that she asked rather than issued orders was decidedly different from all previous experiences at the Training Center. I thought I was in the wrong place. Nothing matched anything I expected, but I had come to the right building, hadn't I?

"I was told to report to this building, but I think I'm in the wrong place," I said.

"What is your name?" she asked with an inviting smile, her blond hair accenting her feminine beauty with makeup and lipstick, a presentation I had not previously seen on the base.

"Gabbard," I said.

She looked over a roster and said, "Oh yes. Mr. Smith will see you in few minutes. Just have a seat and make yourself comfortable."

Nothing like that had been said within my experience in the Navy, and I was immediately confused. I chose an easy chair among the four available, the only person in the spacious office other than the secretary, and as I leafed through magazines I wondered what "Mr. Smith" wanted with me? Had I done something to be singled out? I could think of nothing.

When the order arrived to report to this building, no other information came with it, and no one had any insight, not even our trainer, a resident on base. Sitting there leafing through magazines was a decidely uncommon act for recruits who were expected to constantly be on the move, in double-time, and I kept wondering about my pending encounter with "Mr. Smith." Would it be favorable or unfavorable?

Some time passed as I rather apprehensively waited until the secretary told me, smiling, "Mr. Smith will see you now." She motioned to the appropriate door down a corridor, and I went into another non-Navy appointed office. "Mr. Smith" stood up, extended his hand to me for a welcoming shake and said, "Mr. Gabbard. Nice to meet you."

I was at a complete loss and stumbled through greetings to take a seat in a comfortable chair. This began the strangest encounter of my basic training. We simply talked. Unlike all other encounters with seniors that involved commands and expected obedience to those commands, we talked. He wanted to know about me, my background, where I came from, what my interests were, where I thought I would go in the Navy, and I told again of my interest in being assigned to the Naval Research Laboratory. He was complimentary of my scores and performance so far, and during our conversation he made notes.

After about an hour, he thanked me for my time, shook my hand again, and bid me farewell. I was thoroughly confused as to the purpose of this meeting and saw no connection with anything.

Later, after more of the pieces came together, I recognized that this meeting was the beginning of my background investigation. "Mr. Smith," having never said who he was or what he was doing, was, I concluded, a government operative who conducted personality profiles of potential inductees into particular and clandestine branches of military service requiring secrecy. He was the gatekeeper, and on his selection, candidates were allowed beyond the gate he controlled without their knowing what had happened. I had no idea what was going on.

A few days later, basic training was over, and all of us in Company 638 had orders to other destinations. We had gotten to know each other by virtue of our close proximity in barracks life, and although we were parting, each of us had new horizons on our mind. We were going in various directions, but first we were going home. The Navy granted us thirty days leave before reporting in to our new duty stations. I was soon on another jet flying back across the country.

A lengthy lay-over in New Orleans gave me time to walk the terminal and see some sights. I called Mary to say hello, not having spoken with her since my Christmastime jaunt into Mexico. I also confirmed the arrival time of my flight. We would soon be together again.

I used some of my chess set money to buy a sumptuous meal and whiled away the remaining time looking at things in gift shops and flipping through magazines. During my walks up and down the airport's corridors, I saw many young men in uniform. Their number was food for thought; so many soldiers and sailors on the move made me wonder where they were going. With time to burn, I chatted with some of them to learn that, like me, they were traveling on orders to new assignments. Some were headed for Viet Nam, and my imagination painted a ghostly image of them; I knew that some would not return alive. That image also told of how uselessly their lives would be expended; more young men to join the never ending list of history's wartime dead.

As my lay-over neared its end, I took a seat directly in front of the podium used by the boarding stewardess. My day had begun early and now stretched into the night. I was tired and looked forward to getting home. Afraid that I might fall asleep, I held my ticket in hand in plain view, leaned my head back against the wall, thinking that someone among the gathering passengers would wake me if I went to sleep, and did just that.

Later, something waked me, and I looked around to an empty boarding area. The passengers were gone. No one had waked me, so my reunion with Mary and family had to wait until the next morning for another military standby seat. Another phone call relayed the change of plans, and with the rising sun, I was on the plane and headed home.

(Arrow) That's me, Commander, 2nd and 3rd Regiments and staff during presentation of officers and colors, Graduation Day for the parade grounds filled with Companies including 638, my Company, following Basic Training during the Fall of 1966. US Naval Training Center, San Diego, CA.

Chapter 3

Basic and A-School

We were too busy in Basic to form attachments, and although I had not gotten close to any of my fellow recruits, I have wondered what happened to them, having never followed up to find out. Only Sandy, a fellow North Carolinian I met two years later, and I have maintained contact. He was a career sailor whose duty took him to much of the world while I went back to college after I got out of the Navy in 1970. I came close to choosing to make the Navy my career, too, but with no assurance of getting into what I wanted to do during that career, I opted out of the Navy to venture onto another track for my life's work. However, what the Navy exposed this farm boy to shaped me and strongly influenced the remainder of my life, and both Sandy and I shared portions of our lives at Clarksville Base. I got there by a circuitous route.

Thirty days' leave following basic training brought me back to North Carolina and Mary during January, 1967. That month went by with visitings here and there and preparation for my next duty station, A-School at the Navy's Great Lakes Training Center. During Basic, Mary struggled with maintaining our apartment on my paltry Navy income in addition to her job working in Winston-Salem, and she moved back home to cut costs. That proved to be a wise move because it made our transition to Chicago easier than having to empty an apartment.

Our transportation was a Sunbeam Alpine, a red 4-cylinder sports car with black interior. Since it was British and another within the hold of the "Prince of Darkness," it provided challenges of the most unexpected kind. Mary had managed to keep it going, a rather new car less than a year old. Along the way, we had learned some of its idiosyncracies, and overall, we liked the car to the extent that we still have it, our first purchase.

We bought the Alpine, a showroom model, while we lived in Winston-Salem during the time I was in college prior to being drafted. Mary had a job bookkeeping for a housing builder, a desk job that permitted listening to the radio. WTOB radio station just up Hawthorne Road from where we lived was holding their "Trashman" contest with $1,000 going to the listener who produced the correct answer from the clues broadcast each day. Mary listened and wrote down the clues that we studied each evening after work and school. With ideas that they generated, we drove through the city in our quest to find the "Trashman's" hideout. One day we drove by an abandoned church, and all the clues fell into place. We went back to our apartment, and I wrote our findings on a sheet of notebook paper, stuffed it into an envelope, sealed it, applied a stamp and dropped it into a mailbox about dark.

Two days later, I went to our apartment for lunch because I was broke. I had managed to get by spending 5¢ a day for a pack of nabs for lunch, but on this day I was flat broke. Mary was at work, and I scoured the shelves to find only a can of beans. If I heated them and ate a third, I reasoned, both Mary and I would have a portion for supper. It was not to be.

The front door of our ground floor apartment faced the street with a short walkway to the curb. The front and rear door's roll-out glass slats enabled flow-through ventilation when opened. The back door faced a tiny backyard and the walled-off embankment of weeds topped by the Southern Railway main line. Why the trains did not bother us as they rumbled by just feet from our back door is probably attributable to our being young with attention focused elsewhere. On this bright, sunny, fall day, the slats were rolled out permitting all the sounds of the street to come flooding in. As I stood with a cabinet door opened in each hand, looking at our lone can of beans, I heard a car stop in the street out front. Two doors slammed close, and I heard the voices of a man and a woman. The thought passed through my mind, "Wouldn't it be funny if they came to my door." Why I had such a thought, I don't know, but the knock at the door startled me. They did come to my door, and I opened it to greet a nicely dressed couple. Insurance salesmen, I thought. The woman smiled and wanted to know if I might be Alex Gabbard. I confirmed, and she asked with a huge grin, "How would it feel to win a thousand dollars?"

I thought the irony of the preceding moments, her excited demeanor, and her question to be some sort of joke, and responded to the impossibility of such a notion, having completely forgotten the contest in my moment of hunger. Afterall, I was fresh from eyeing the only can of food in my possession.

"Well, you did," she said excitedly, pulling my letter from her purse.

Then it struck me. POW! And I reeled off on a slow mental escapade of disbelief. Time slowed down. Of course I could come to the station now. Sure, I'd be happy to appear on the radio and have pictures taken of me receiving a check. I went with them and did all that, then told of our last can of beans. The woman was particularly pleased that their prize was going to a "needy" recipient.

I returned to school just prior to my next class beginning, and in that few minutes, I simply could not assess all that had transpired in less than the one hour preceding. And when I mentioned that I had won the "Trashman" contest saying where the "hideout" was, my classmates stared in disbelief. Everyone, it seems, was tracking that thousand dollars, and when I pulled out the check, Mr. Basham, our instructor, called off the next class to celebrate and talk of money management, investments, the stock market and what to do with a thousand dollars.

I don't recall the remainder of the day because of the euphoria brought by such improbabilities, but when I got home wearing an irrepressible grin, with Mary digging through her purse looking for pocket change that might have fallen into bottom reaches, something to help get us to payday, I delayed showing our prize until just the right moment. She didn't have time to think I was perpetrating some kind of sick joke because the check with WTOB on it instantly grabbed her attention. With equal disbelief, we sat down with sighs of relief. We could make it now.

Our first purchase was a Magnavox black and white TV that traveled with us for years to come, given away still working when we moved to our first color TV. Our second purchase was a new car that we really didn't need, but being young and excited by our treasure trove, we looked at all the new sports cars from the E-Type Jaguar we really wanted, though far beyond our means, to the Datsun Fairlady that neither of us liked. Between were several British roadsters, MG, Triumph and Sunbeam becoming the three we would choose from. At the Sunbeam dealer sat a white Tiger that spoke to me. Beside it sat a red Alpine that spoke louder to Mary. "I've always wanted a red sports car," she said, and that was that.

The Alpine was our first purchase, and with a portion of our winnings along with trade-in of Mary's 1962 Oldsmobile F-85, a car with no pizzazz but one that would have served us well for years to come. The $2,624 list price meant manageable payments. We could have bought a new Volkswagen for $1,250 and had no payments, but neither of us turned our eyes far from sports cars we liked and settled firmly on the Alpine.

During the summer and fall of 1966, our new Alpine gave Mary and me many pleasures of going places, such as drag races, where she won trophies, to mountain excursions that top-down driving permits. For some reason I don't recall, during my leave after basic training, we were driving from Wilkes County where Mary had returned home to somewhere in Winston-Salem. Dusk fell around us as we approached the city, and I flipped the switch to turn on the headlights. The engine died. Startled, I flipped off the lights and the engine began running again. I flipped the switch on again, half expecting the car to fall apart, but only the engine died. I pulled into a service station and demonstrated such unusual behavior to the mechanic on duty. He wiped his hands and said, "That there car come from across the water."

Well, I knew that. What I wanted to know was simple enough; did he have any idea what was causing the car's engine to die when the lights were turned on? I raised the hood to reveal the engine, running just fine as long as the lights remained off, and he walked around looking things over. After a few minutes of thought, he said, "I 'spect the wirin' harness'll have to be pulled. There's somethin' wrong with it. I can get to it, maybe, Monday mornin'."

We couldn't stay the weekend waiting for service that he "might" be able do days later. Besides, the car ran perfectly well with the lights off. We'd just have to drive back home carefully. I had a suspicion that the problem was something simple that did not require the enormity of pulling the wiring system from the car. Everything worked just fine, except the combination of engine and lights. I was certain that I knew more than the mechanic. I thanked him, thinking that, at worst, we would be confined to driving in daylight.

We made it back home that bright moonlit night, and the next day I started with the battery and took everything out of the electrical system one piece at a time, everything that would come off, cleaned each part and replaced it, one part to the next, tuned the engine, then tried the deadly combination again. The car ran perfectly. I was dumbfounded; what I did to correct the problem completely eluded me.

Mary and I began packing the car for our northward journey and set off on an early February day, wintertime in the south with a chill in the air, but not a difficult day for traveling. As we drove further north, the weather steadily worsened; cold with snow in Kentucky and worse further on. We stopped to visit with relatives, the Devere family of Berea, the town where I was born, and was treated to a sumptuous spread of the best home cooking anyone could ever sit down to. "Little Ed" Devere was my age and a grand host who wanted to show me the farm and more than time permitted. His great-grandmother and my grandmother were sisters, and we had visited on occasion when I lived with my father in his family home in Berea during the 1950s.

With winter looking harsher as the day progressed, our visit was shortened to permit additional time to make our scheduled overnight with my sister, Michaela, and her husband, L. B., in Lexington. I planned to get back on the road early the next morning, hoping the grey skies would hold off on what they could do. By the time we rolled into her driveway late in the day, having cut short our visit with the Deveres, the ground was snowy white with promise of more during the night. More did fall, lots of it.

I hoped to reach Chicago by nightfall the next day and ahead of heavy snow said to already be on the way. More piled on by the hour. Ohio had snow drifts blowing across the road as our Sunbeam motored on. Snow sheets in Indiana blew fiercely as traffic was sparse, and heavy plows pushed snow off the road in steady streams of dull grey mush piling up along roadsides. Our Alpine's heater proved more than a match for the weather, keeping us toasty inside as outside windborne temperatures became increasingly bitter the further north we went. We crossed Illinois in steadily increasing snowfall that kept our speed well down, and by late in the day we were in Chicago traveling through tunnels of snow, headed toward North Chicago and the US Navy Training Center. Plows kept at least one middle lane of the Bypass open by blowing accumulated snow into the outer lanes. I had never seen so much snow before, and driving through the open lane tunnel seemed unending.

The engine in our Alpine purred right through it all, eight feet tall mucky snow banks on the left and right. Few cars on the highway made our trek easier, and those that were moving did so with lights muted by snowpack over them. I had driven with lights on all the way and wondered if turning them off would cause the engine to die. I kept my finger off the light switch; I wasn't about to take that chance.

With the light of day in its last grey before darkness, we drove up to the gate of the Navy Training Center. I presented my orders and was told to report to a particular building. With Mary along, I must have presented a problem because no space was available for us on base. A phone call rerouted us to Fort Sheridan back in Chicago where the Guest House there had accommodations for us. When we arrived in darkness and stepped out of the car, the most bitter cold winds imaginable cut through us, a phenomena we would become unpleasantly accustomed to in the Windy City.

Fort Sheridan was our base for a couple of weeks until an apartment came available on the Navy base. That first night we discovered the effects of bitter northern winters on southern cars; the oil in the crankcase thickened with the low temperatures and turned into gooey gum that the starter could not work through. Next morning, the car would not start, and I could not make my first day of duty on base. We had to have the car towed to Fort Sheridan's garage where a change of oil solved the problem. Within a few days, Mary had gotten a job with the Fort's PX, so once we were located on the Navy base, she drove back and forth each day between the military bases where I attended school and she worked.

Once on the Navy Base, we received two parking tickets a day for the first several days, and about the evening of the sixth day, she came in late, cold, shivering, and crying, the victim of insulting verbal abuse. Our Base pass had been revoked for parking in unauthorized spaces. Since our apartment had no garage or driveway, and we were not told where parking was permitted, we parked our Alpine in front of our walkway like all the other cars, not knowing that snow crews worked the streets at night and our car prevented moving the snow. I failed to note that other cars were relocated late in the evening leaving the street free of cars, except for our Alpine left perched on frozen snow pushed from the street. Mary's ordeal resulted from being reported to the Base Provost Marshall, and she had taken the brunt of his abuse and insults, then handed over our pass. Our Alpine was expelled from the Navy Base.

Having to park off base that evening, Mary pulled the car off the street into an area near the railroad tracks that paralleled the fence of the Naval Training Center and left everything on that could be left on, except the engine. Her lengthy walk through the blowing snow was challenging enough, but by the time she regained her composure and warmed a bit, and we made it back to the car in the incessant, icy cold winds, the battery was dead as a hammer. I tried pushing as she drove, but we could not get the car to start, and we left it to return in the morning. Returning the next day as soon as I could, our Alpine was gone. Checking around, I discovered that the city had impounded the car as abandoned and required a fee to be retrieved. That paid, we then needed maintenance, a new battery, and, once winterized, our faithful Alpine ran superbly.

The issue of the revoked pass remained and required Mary to walk the considerable distance around the fence that excluded us from our Alpine on her way to and from work each day. That problem was solved when she explained our plight to her boss, the Procurement Officer of Ft. Sheridan. He was friends with the Fort's Provost Marshall who was so moved that he wanted to bring his counterpart on the Navy base up on charges for abusing a civilian. Not wanting further trouble with the Navy, Mary chose to drop the subject. Instead, he issued a US Army sticker, and from then on, we drove on and off the Navy base at will, although being careful not to park in unauthorized spaces, having learned that we had a garage located down the street.

After our troubling initiation to life in the Navy, we fared as well as others, made some acquaintances with neighbors, but little time and the incessant winter encumbered what little time was available to socialize. Within a month or so, we responded to an invitation from L. B.'s sister to visit her and her family in Chicago. Our infrequent visits in the coming weeks proved a welcome break from being enclosed in winter's cocoon as we ventured into Chicago from time to time.

Upon arrival at their apartment building one evening, a small complex of up-scale accommodations, I noticed that smooth lumps of snow along the street hid parked cars buried deep within them. Rather than cleared side streets, snow was simply packed; we drove about two feet above the pavement and had to drive down off the snow-ice pack of side streets at intersections onto main streets that had been cleared. As we arrived on our first visit, a neighbor was taking soundings with a broom handle, and while we visited, he dug out his Austin-Healey 3000 from its snowy encapsulation. The perfect negative imprint of the right side of his car left in the snow was an interesting winter image that stands out in my memory to this day.

My studies were classroom instruction in the Training Center's Gunner's Mate building, a structure of about four stories high completely enclosed in green glass. Upon first reporting in, I looked at the gun emplacements and wondered why I had ended up a Gunner's Mate Technician rather than something of a scientific nature that I requested, preferably at the Naval Research Laboratory in Washington. Now in Gunner's Mate school, I resolved, I would make the best of it and learn how to operate the various gun mounts that sat on the perimeter of the classroom block. The first days were introductions to the Navy, and our instructors were all seasoned career sailors assigned to training rather than the fleet. My classmates, about fifteen of us, began our training with generalities that progressed into introduction to the 3-inch 70 caliber rapid fire gun, the 5-inch 54, and others. When our instructor told us to learn the operation of these guns because it was to be our cover, each of us new students was stunned to silence.

"Cover!?" The idea reverberated in our minds as we looked at each other with big eyes wondering what he was talking about.

When our instructor said, "Don't ask any questions, just learn everything," we recognized that our lives in the Navy had taken a turn into the unknown, and, although initially fascinated, I became a bit uncomfortable with the sense of having my life controlled by others without my knowledge. I wanted to be better informed and tended to hang around after class talking with instructors who, invariably, shed little light on the unknown. I concluded that these men were highly adept at keeping secrets and were operatives in clandestine military exploits that I had been inducted into. I resolved that I would soon be like them.

My classmates and I speculated unendingly on what we were training for. Studies were rather unchallenging, topics of problem solving using applied mathematics for which my two years of college had prepared me well enough to emerge as a top student. We studied mechanisms, such things as synchros, the Navy's use of electro-mechanical devices for control at one point in a ship from the bridge. Studies of electronic tubes and circuitry was a new experience, a challenge because of my lack of electronics knowledge, but I learned quickly. Over all, I did well enough in A-School that I graduated top in my class and was told that I scored the highest ever achieved. A small plaque was presented to me, and it is still hanging on my wall.

Near the end of A-School, some of us were so curious that we asked increasingly inquisitive questions of our instructors. What would we do next? Where would we go? Our training had not connected in our minds with anything, and our trainers had not revealed what we wanted to know. GMT; what did that mean, Guided Missile Technician? That couldn't be; we had not studied missiles at all, just basic classroom work from books. No, we were Gunner's Mate Technicians. "What is that?" we asked a Chief Petty Officer instructor. Rather than explain anything, he said, "You're next duty station will be out in the desert. You'll go to the appointed place at the appointed time and a big door will open. You'll go inside, and the door will close. You'll be in there for the next six months."

We were dumfounded. He hadn't given us any new information, but he certainly kicked our imaginations into high gear. Crossed gun barrels of the Gunner's Mate insignia was our "cover"; we had learned the rudiments of Navy shipboard guns sufficiently to talk in detail about them, but we had not set foot on any gun mount. We were headed toward an undisclosed location in some unspecified desert, and we would be removed from the face of the earth for months on end. And, we were firmly and seriously told, not a word of any of this was to be mentioned to anyone. That part was clear; we had been thrust into the shadows of military operations, and we were certainly intrigued, but nothing connected with our future except that we would be guided by others while we could say nothing, ask nothing, just do.

"Shaken, not stirred, Mr. Bond?" took on new implications for us, but discussion amongst ourselves revealed no new insight into anything. We tried to make GMT into something comprehensible, but nothing convincing emerged. Were we new recruits into National Security? Spies in training? Undercover operatives? Navy moles to be? Although fascinated with the prospects, sinister overtones came with such thoughts as "cover." It was also clear that whatever we had been studying had little to do with where we were going, and we began to suspect that our A-School was another sorting-out process, that we had been subjects of study to determine various factors about our capabilities. "Sinister" applied to being guinea pigs, observed by the unobservable, and we suspected that each of us was, unknowingly, competing with the other, the result of sorting us into what the Navy had need for and acquired by sorting those deemed suitable for the job.

As events unfolded, not one of us had it figured out. Security was doing its job, but I suspected that my interview with "Mr. John Smith" while in basic training had something to do with the route I was on.

Service School Command

U.S.N.T.C.
Great Lakes Illinois

Honor Graduate

This is to certify that

William Alexander GABBARD
Seaman Apprentice, U.S. Navy

has satisfactorily completed a course of instruction in

Naval School, Gunner's Mate Technician, Class "A" Phase 1

standing FIRST *in his class on*

and was graduated with DISTINCTION   *Final Mark* 94.7

this 21st *day of* APRIL 19 67

V. H. FIX, Lieutenant Commander, U.S. Navy
Officer-In-Charge, U.S. Naval School,
GUNNER's MATE

J. F. HEALD, Captain, U.S. Navy
Commanding Officer, Service School Command

9ND-NTC-1650/13 (10-64)

Chapter 4

Great Lakes

That piercing winter surrounded and penetrated everything Mary and I did, which wasn't much because of restricted income. Early on while in the Ft. Sheridan Guest House, which housed about a dozen military transients and their companions, we were introduced to thievery.

Although accommodations included a shared bathroom and shared kitchen with all appliances and utensils furnished, each of us was responsible for our own food. I had regular military privileges at the Navy Mess at the Training Center, but Mary did not, so we made our own way. Having small means during our transition into the frozen north, Mary and I made careful selection of provisions that included a package of sandwich meat that went into the communal refrigerator. It was placed there to await our return with the same respect that I applied to all the other food; if it isn't mine, don't touch it. We learned that our anonymous companions did not adhere to that philosophy when we opened the refrigerator the next day to discover our supplies were gone. We went without our planned dinner and had to resupply ourselves with what meager funds we had left, a box of cereal and a gallon of milk we kept on the window sill where it remained cold. Another modest selection of sandwich preparations and peanut butter gave some variety, and this time I kept our supplies in the bag from the store and wrote on it, "FOR THIEVES ONLY". Thereafter, our bag and its contents remained where we left it.

Fort Sheridan was a small complex of interesting, prairie style architecture in buff brick construction presenting an elegant, military country club air that I assumed was meant to provide a quiet sort of duty. When entering the Fort, the Nike-Hercules missile standing erect to the left of the entrance spoke to me as rather odd; what did GMT mean - Guided Missile Technician? I was beginning my Gunner's Mate training in the Navy and living on an Army Fort whose mission was coordinating missile defense of Chicago and the upper Mid-West. There seemed to be a connection, but nothing came of it. Mary liked the installation as well and quickly found her job with the Post Exchange enjoyable, and the people she worked with contributed to favorable experiences. We were southerners introduced to a most ferocious winter, worse than we could have imagined, but the Chicagoans didn't let the snow and the cold hamper their lives.

Our adjustment was slow. However, Christmastime in the city was still everywhere, and we discovered the decorations from that time of year continuing the spirit of getting out and enjoying the wintertime. In the towns of Highwood, Highland Park and Lake Forest surrounding the Fort back-to-back along the way between Ft. Sheridan and the Navy base, we noticed what we thought was rivalry between them to display the best yuletime decorations that gave each location a festive quality, unlike downtown Chicago that was drab and bitterly cold.

During one of our first days in the Guest House, Mary came across a newspaper ad for Vogue magazine. The person she talked with said they were looking for models, and her phone call received sufficient encouragement to schedule an interview. On the appointed evening, dressed in the highest fashion she had but far from warm, we drove our Alpine between the tall buildings of the city to the prescribed location, took the elevator to the prescribed floor, and went into the prescribed office. Elegance surrounded us in decor we had seen only in movies and in magazines, but, most importantly, the offices were warm. It took time to put pink back into her chilled body, and while I, in my dress blues and peacoat, read magazines in a waiting area, Mary's interview went well. She was favorably impressed with the prospects, and later, she told that her California girl look with southern charm was warmly received, but when it was noted that she was the wife of a transient sailor, the prospects turned to thanks but no thanks. Unless she was willing to stay in Chicago long term, Vogue was not interested. We talked about her prospects, but Mary said that she was with me and we would be in the area only into spring when I finished training, then on to another assignment. Her future as a high fashion model came to nought.

During the following weeks, on our way back and forth between Ft. Sheridan and the Navy base, an Alfa-Romeo dealership attracted my attention. Stopping in one day, I was drawn to a Formula-2 racing car. I returned several times to look closer at various aspects of the car, a current world class competitor in the second tier of Grand Prix racing. Its highly polished 4-cylinder engine behind the driver, brilliant red, yellow and green coloring throughout, and its invitation to great fun handling the small diameter steering wheel while roaring through high speed curves in the manner of Grand Prix racing, shifting gears, watching the tach needle wind toward its maximum as the engine behind me wailed with satisfaction, filled me with Walter Mitty-ish imaginings. Ten thousand dollars. That's "all" it cost to fulfill my every dream of racing. I think I had $1.10.

Nothing came of my ventures into that dealership when, admiring the F-2 car one day, a young Navy officer in uniform dressed me down for being out of uniform. I was in uniform, as far as I knew, but I had on a work jacket not to be worn off Base. I didn't know that. It was part of my issued Navy uniforms, blue colored jacket of nice fabric, clean and worn with distinction. I thought I looked entirely presentable, but for fear of encountering that officer again, I never returned to the dealership and left my favored Alfa-Romeo F-2 behind as a memory.

February and March slowly turned from bitter winter to just plain winter. We got out more and more, and while driving by Northwestern University one day, our Alpine slid on ice and bounced to a perch on top of a snow bank along the street, stuck solid. Walking onto the campus to make the necessary phone calls, I noted its grounds and stately buildings although snow covered everything. Students in heavy coats lugged books as they hurriedly went their way. Everything spoke to me; I wanted to do that, go to college, and I liked the looks of Northwestern, but the winter meant enduring similar winters to come, and that dimmed my interests in college in the north.

Only the earliest vestiges of spring were evident by March, and during April, Mary and I got out to see more of Illinois and Michigan, driving here and there. Up and down Lake Michigan brought us to new and interesting sights that helped make memories of the frigid winter and our troubled first couple of weeks fade, although never to leave my recollections and forever remaining reasons not to live in the north: miserable winters.

Everywhere along the lake, signs of spring began to appear in response to April's prolonged sunlight and warmth that brought the most profound change of scenery in my experience; seemingly in just days, frosted over windows that confined us indoors cleared to an emerging world of budding greenery and first hints of flowers. Colorful crocus contrasted the snow and brought reassurances that winter really did end in the north. Mostly confined to driving and sightseeing at a distance, the three of us, Mary, me and our Alpine, made the most of afternoons and weekends when I did not have duty.

After a couple of weeks in Fort Sheridan's Guest House, our Navy accommodations became available, the duplex apartment mentioned earlier, and we furnished it with a roll-away bed, a card table and four plastic chairs. We used only the living room, kitchen and bath, keeping the other two rooms empty and doors closed. Our roll-away served us for both sleeping and a daytime couch, and when occasional visitors dropped by, they were offered a pillow, plastic chair or a corner of the roll-away. We entertained very little, our most lavish being a southern style meal that a couple we met wanted to sample. We kept largely to ourselves as young people with paltry incomes tended to do. For this evening, Mary's excellent cooking was more than our guests could have hoped for, but when they called an hour before it was to be served to say that they could not make the engagement, we were faced with a sumptuous supper far beyond what we could consume.

Another of my basic training buddies, Hershel, had arrived at Great Lakes for training when I did, although in a different area of training, and we had stayed in touch. Mary suggested having our lumberjack friend over, and when I went to his barracks, I found him sleeping. The invitation to a hot meal roused him, and hungry he proved to be. By the time the two of us arrived, Mary was pulling her homemade biscuits from the oven, their fragrance whetting our appetites further.

The three of us sat down to baked chicken, mashed potatoes and gravy, buttered corn, green peas and dumplings, and those melt-in-your mouth biscuits, coffee and milk, followed by apple pie.

Mary prepared bowls of food in the southern tradition, and our card table with its checkered table cloth sat laden with inviting, steaming hot fixin's. Of the six chicken breasts, one apiece for Mary and me was all we could handle; Hershel ate four. Potatoes and gravy, corn, peas and biscuits went a round or two between us; Hershel was encouraged to eat all he wanted, and each bowl was dutifully emptied. The plate of biscuits, more than a dozen, dwindled to a few crumbs. Luscious apple pie with its thick, sugar and spice crust went a round apiece for us; Hershel went two, with coffee. To watch this man eat was a pleasure, testimony to the tradition of southern cooking and a lumberjack's appetite, but how he was able to pack so much away remains a mystery.

As graduation from A-School neared, I faced assignment to an isolated, undisclosed desert somewhere with a persistent question on my mind; What would happen to Mary? She and I faced additional questions as well; Take our furnishings or leave them? Closing out our apartment would be simple if we took everything with us, and we wondered if my next duty station would offer another unfurnished apartment. If so, we would have to buy everything again. After considering our meager funds, we chose the smallest rental trailer and tow bar for our Alpine, then headed for Albuquerque, New Mexico.

"A big door will open in the desert..." echoed through my mind as I imagined Mary alone for days on end. Going to Albuquerque was heading into the desert, and I reasoned that the Nike-Hercules missiles of Fort Sheridan were just indications of the Fort's mission, not my track. What my A-school instructors told about, secret things to come, seemed to be correct; next came the desert just as we were told. As ordered, I did not discuss my Navy duties with Mary, and with confidence that the Navy would take care of her in my expected months of confinement from the southwestern sun, I could not help but wonder what Navy facility would be in the desert. Navy meant ships and water to me; Albuquerque was a most unexpected assignment but was accepted as more adventures to come in a part of America that I wanted to see.

Our first leg was from North Chicago through the city toward St. Louis to overnight with my sister, Cookie, and her husband Ron. The day, Friday the 21st of April, was densely cloudy as we readied our Alpine. Our belongings in a little trailer tagged along behind as we turned out of the Naval Training Center for the last time. Back we went onto the inner-city loops that retained the last vestiges of shadowed snow in grimy black coatings, remnants of the high banks that rose above our heads on our trek in three months earlier. I anticipated more carefree motoring as we settled in for the long drive ahead, Route 66. The clouds had blackened considerably by the time we drove through Chicago, and once onto the flatlands southwest of the city, the band of white just above the horizon did not connect with anything in our experience, so we drove on. I noticed that the highway was almost empty of traffic, and I assumed that travel through this part of the country was infrequent and made no particular note of it. The sky was heavy and dark. I switched on driving lights in mid-day, having confidence that lights-on no longer killed the engine. Still, I sensed nothing unusual, except that I was unable to go as fast as I thought our Alpine should. Everything before us was new and different, and we just kept on going toward the band of bright at the horizon. It spread as far as we could see, and I concluded that our trailer in tow was a drag, never thinking that a stiff headwind might be impeding our progress. With such unusual conditions still not registering and our Alpine purring onward, we were well out into rural flatlands when I looked over at Mary and saw a tornado funnel beside us, not so far away. Exclaiming the surprise to her, we looked to our left and saw more funnels; behind were still more: seven, eight, the sky was full of tornadoes whipping all around us. We had never seen a tornado before, or the conditions of their making, so this sight was startling; tornadoes were everywhere except in front of us. We kept going, and I kept wondering what might have happened if we had left Great Lakes just a few minutes later and had driven into them instead of just leaving them.

The remainder of our drive to St. Louis was uneventful as we passed through town after town, stopping for fuel and lunch along the way but no sight-seeing. Both Mary and I marveled at the rapid disappearance of winter the further southwesterly we drove. Out of Chicago, winter's snow faded away into the stark beauty of leafless trees and greyed undergrowth we knew so well in southern winters. Our arrival in St. Louis was to warm sunshine and the spreading of springtime's light green in new leaves breaking free of their snug winter cocoons to stretch themselves toward the sun. A short visit and the evening news brought sobering revelations; Mary and I had told of our encounter with the tornadoes, and we learned from the TV news that we had driven through the worst tornado destruction in Illinois history. The final toll was 59 deaths with over a thousand injuries from funnels that suddenly appeared giving little warning. Damage stretched for miles and laid waste to every town in their paths. Later on, I learned that year's number of tornadoes was 40, up from an average of 26 a year, and those of April the 21st roared through with category-4 winds up to 260 mph. A feeling of dumb luck came over me.

Our overnight with Cookie and Ron put us on the road again, and we planned to reach Amarillo for our next overnight.

Since our life experiences were mostly Appalachian Mountain terrain, the thrill of traveling Route 66 made famous in the early-1960s TV program of that name motivated us to look for sights along the way, perhaps some that we had seen. New sights and new adventures greeted us with each passing mile as we traveled the path of the stars who drove a Corvette roadster and had time to do things that turned the program into real life adventures told in each episode. For Mary and me, traveling Route 66, also in a sports car but with a trailer tagging along and only four days to make the trek from North Chicago to Albuquerque, sightseeing adventures were not possible. Most of our time was spent on the road.

Missouri's forested hill country and farmland rolled up and down under us with few curves, so the drive through Rolla and on to Joplin along with other small towns along the way was no more than "just passing through" for us. Exiting Missouri toward Tulsa, we rolled into our first toll booth leading onto the Will Rogers Turnpike, the beginning of several in a row that Oklahoma put before us. At its end on our approach to Oklahoma City, we left the exit toll booth to an unexpected flat tire. Pulling over onto the broad apron, I unloaded the trunk and changed the flat for our spare. Now without a spare, Mary and I felt uncomfortable about venturing further into the vastness of the southwest that our maps indicated lay ahead of us, so we decided to stop in Oklahoma City to have the flat repaired. A clean, modern-looking service station came into view.

The reason that the establishment looked so clean was that it was new. I exchanged pleasantries with the only person on duty, the owner as it turned out, and learned that he was a newly retired US Navy commander of a nuclear submarine. Our conversation was interesting, but I did not associate "newly retired" with lack of experience in the service station business. All his equipment was new, and he had never used the tire changer. I knew how to handle the machine, and between us we set to removing the tire to repair the flat.

Assembly of our Alpine's wire wheels comprised the outer rim and inner hub held in position by 72 wire spokes in tension at precise angles. A thick inner band of rubber over the interior of the wheel covered the screw heads of the spokes as a protective barrier for the inner tube. The tube had lost air, and once the hole was repaired, we would be on our way. Only one problem; among all the new, unused equipment was no device for changing a wire wheel, only standard American steel disc wheels. To hold the wheel securely so that air pressure could force the separator around the outer rim to free the bead of the tire from the wheel rim required forcing a pin as large as my thumb into the wires to hold the wheel firmly. I didn't like the prospects of the pin putting so much strain on the spokes, but with no alternative, we went ahead, removed the tube, found the hole, repaired it, and Mary and I were on our way. I wondered if the $4 paid to the owner were his first earnings in civilian life. He had no other customers while Mary and I were there.

Replacing the spare on the car with the newly inflated repair, we were back on the road. Not more than five miles later, another flat had us parked on the side of the highway in Oklahoma City; the same tire. Off it came and on went the spare again, then we wheeled into the first service station we came to. This one, well used and grimy, was less inviting, but the young man who worked on the spare knew exactly what to do. Once the tire was separated and the tube removed, he pulled out a lead wheel weight from inside the tire that had gone undetected during the previous change. Neither the captain nor I thought of removing the weights prior to separating the tire, exactly the sequence that my experienced attendant performed, and one of the weights had fallen unseen into the tire and wore a hole in the tube. Once repaired again and reinstalled, Mary and I were on our way, for $5 this time.

Overcast, grey skies and scrublands waking up from winter with a flourish of greenery and flowers was welcome scenery. In two days, we had driven from Chicago's winter to Oklahoma's springtime that spread to the horizon as flat as a table top in all directions. As we drove from the Turner Turnpike onto another one, exiting a toll booth, we were greeted with a thump, thump, thump as we rolled away. I stopped our rig and walked around looking for a flat tire. None were flat, and I was mystified as to the origin of the sound. Pulling away once again, we heard the same thump, thump, thump. I stopped again and took a closer look to discover that the right rear wheel had collapsed; not a flat this time but several broken spokes in a tangle that was no longer capable of holding the wheel and tire concentric to the hub.

I remembered the thumb sized pin the captain and I had used to hold the wheel in place as we broke down the first flat. My suspicions at that time were confirmed as I looked at the damage; the pin cracked the spokes and they broke when carrying the weight of the car. Replacing the failed wheel with the spare again put us back on the road once more without a spare, and the wide open spaces of the southwest loomed before us. Our Alpine motored on toward Amarillo along Route 66 where we made our first and only Texas overnight.

Mary and I didn't know the highway we traveled out of Chicago would one day be called the "Blues Highway" and the portion we were on the "Main Street of America." We saw on our maps that Route 66 was known by segments of the turnpikes on which we would have to pay to travel, the Will Rogers, the Turner and other segments. Decades later we saw Route 66 described as the "Mother Road of America" as well. Why the latter I never learned, but to us, Route 66 was simply the most direct highway from St. Louis to Albuquerque. The fact that it was famous was of no importance other than the satisfaction of traveling the route made famous in the television series.

I was vaguely aware that this highway was the migrant route that John Steinbeck wrote of in *The Grapes of Wrath*, but having come from a background of work-every-day farmlife and making do, I didn't associate our modern rig of belongings heading west with those hard-timers who packed up everything they could carry and headed toward California three decades earlier on this same highway. They were "Okies" trying to find a better life while we were young and adventuresome and on the best tour of your lives.

The terrain west of Oklahoma City was dotted with short, flat topped trees of a decided easterly bent, their new foliage pointing in the same direction. They were our introduction to the stiff, always-from-the-west prairie winds that pushed every growing thing into a similar shape. Our experience with trees grown tall and erect in Appalachian forests could not have prepared us for what surrounded us; no forests, no tall trees, nothing but scrub growth and the occasional tree beaten into submission by the wind. This was a different land.

We crossed the border into similar but progressively dryer Texas terrain as we drove further west. Sprawling Amarillo slowly rose out of the horizon ahead of us. Springtime in the desert brought every growing thing that could be green and in bloom into clumps of color or shoots of blossoms along tall spires of desert plants. The flat scrublands around us was waking up from winter while last year's bent-over and broken dry grass, brown shrubs and the occasional tumbleweed rolling along at the behest of the never-ceasing wind were fascinating. After miles and miles of the same, our interest faded and we were reduced to staring into the horizon. We were hungry and tired from our travels and the day's unexpected events that took both time and a portion of our travel cash, so we were not interested in sight-seeing upon arrival mid-way of the Texas panhandle. In spite of setbacks, we had kept to our plan and made Amarillo before dark. The day remained gloomily overcast and cool all the way, good for traveling in a car without air conditioning.

Upon selecting a roadside motel, we were soon able to shower and rest before dinner. Along the way we had seen signs of a restaurant that offered a 72-ounce steak free, if it could all be eaten, and we decided that was the place for us. It was a Texas-size restaurant with its large parking lot full of big rig trucks. Inside, the establishment was open, a beehive of activity with cowboys and cowgirls seemingly straight out of TV and movies. Boots, western hats, weathered blue-jeans, checkered shirts, wide leather belts with big silver buckles were the norm for the guys, and I suspected that our "back east" look was noted by the regulars: Tourists. The atmosphere was brash and loud and the place rough hewn with longhorns on the walls, steer hides, branding irons, too, and alive with cowboys who had come to eat; and did the steaks pour out of the kitchen! Plate after plate of thick, steaming hot steaks, baked potatoes or heaps of french fries, enough to feed a table full was a meal for just one. We had never seen such huge meals, but none among those we observed displayed signs of over-eating, and no one was trying to put down a 72-ounce freebie, either. That was for tourists. The patrons were working men, regulars mostly, who needed meals that would stick to their ribs. I imagined them to be ranchers and cowhands whose long days out on the range on horseback was rewarded with a trip to town and a favorite watering hole to feast on steak. Big steaks were the ticket while Mary and I opted for lesser fare, served with Texas-size grilled toast, icy cold tea in tall glasses of pitcher-sized proportions; salads for us and smaller portions. For a few bucks, this was good eating, but still too much to eat.

NEW MEXICO

The
Longhorn Ranch
on Route 66

Chapter 5

Albuquerque

Up early the next morning, we greeted the faint light of the new day and overcast sky in summer wear. The sunrise to come shrouded by heavy clouds would not drench us with sunshine as I had hoped, and with jackets to ward off the cool Texas morning, we set off for breakfast. We had traveled from winter's penetrating cold to summer's warmth in three days, but looking around the landscape, I saw little haste in welcoming spring; cool nights and brisk winds still dominated the season. This day would take us to Albuquerque, and I wanted to get underway, but I had heightened concern about the door that would open in the desert. What would become of Mary? I had no clue and trusted the Navy. She had no clue what I was thinking and trusted me.

Breakfast like back home was more than enough to hold us to Tucumcari, our planned mid-day break, and once our Alpine was topped off with fuel, Mary and I were ready to hit the road. Around us the dusty, gravel parking lot slowly emptied as truck after truck belched smoke from their stacks and lurched onto Route 66. With our Alpine and trailer among them, the day's highway train formed to continue our straight shot through Amarillo. Not far out of the city the traffic dwindled off to mostly trucks as our small 4-cylinder engine hummed on song with the pavement in what proved to be the dullest portion of our adventure: flat scrublands and oceans of prairie grass again in drab hues of browns and dull greens under threatening clouds. The morning hours passed in the drone of our westward passage, a stop for gas and a stretch somewhere along the way, and little else. This part of Texas wasn't much to see, but as we neared New Mexico, my interests perked up.

I kept looking into the far distance in hopes of seeing mountains along the horizon. With the idea that changing terrain from table top to foot hills indicated nearing the Rockies, our merging into so different a landscape the further we went came ever so slowly. I was certain that fascinating things lay ahead; my own interests with New Mexico as the heart of the Spanish southwest inspired all sorts of imaginings, and I wanted to get there. Ahead was the land of gunslingers and outlaws like Billy the Kid, the Santa Fe Trail and wagon trains, big science at Los Alamos and world shaping secrets, wondrous Albuquerque and lots more; all places I wanted to see. They would come, but that Texas morning passed with the gait of the tortoise.

When we finally got to the border, Route 66 disappeared into the horizon straightaway ahead of us. I pulled off onto the gravel to capture the moment on film. Stateline, New Mexico. The rustic wooden sign of stubby timbers inset with a yellow panel sat low to the ground. Boldly written on it in red were the words; "Welcome to New Mexico" and underneath "Land of Enchantment." I was already enchanted even though Stateline was no more than a dusty stop with a few trees for shade and an adobe building for tourists among a few smaller out-buildings that the locals lived in. The sign above the door of the largest building stood out against the background of ominous black clouds ahead that spoke of heavy weather. More tornadoes, I wondered?

Pulling off the dirt and gravel back onto Route 66 again, what-ever the day was to bring, we were headed into it. Then, as the morning warmed, the sky opened into increasing blue overhead with dark-bot-tomed clouds billowing high into the sky, their tops boiled up into pic-turesque white pillows highlighted by the brilliant sun, their moisture laden bottoms flat and parallel with the desert. The sunlight bright-ened both the land and our senses of adventure, and as we motored on we noticed an especially dark cloud off to the right ahead. It was dumping its contents onto a swath of desert, a ribbon of moisture pouring onto the thirsty desert, another new and interesting sight. I speeded up a little. The cloud was on a southwesterly path that would cross Route 66 ahead. Could I get past its rain? I speeded up a little more. Our paths drew to a focus in the distance, and as we watched the cloud move across the desert beside us, our race with it took on comical proportions, another fascinating New Mexico adventure.

We rolled along in perfect conditions of warm southwestern sunshine getting ever closer to converging with our cloud. The faster I pushed our Alpine the more I realized that the cloud would win. It did. At that focal point in the distance, the downpour suddenly turned on and dumped an intense shower on us. Our respective paths crossed, then separated, and just as suddenly, the downpour turned off. Our cloud moved on southwesterly as we drove westerly from under it back into the marvelously sunlit day with its blue sky and billowing clouds of fluffy whites with their flat, dark bottoms. New Mexico was indeed enchanting. As the morning warmed further, the sky became a deep blue accented with white fluffies floating lazily along in the dazzling sunlight. Our introduction to New Mexico became a long enduring memory.

Arriving in Tucumcari some time later was like opening a new chapter of adventures. Legendary Tucumcari: I still don't know why I considered it legendary. My mental image of it was a dusty desert oasis made accessible by a spur off the Santa Fe main rail line known as Six Shooter Siding, a town on the edge of the Bad Lands with desperados and saloons, imagery that remains with me to this day. I suspect that such thoughts formed in my mind from a forgotten western movie or a TV program I had seen. Instead of rough cowboys and quick draw gunslingers, smoky saloons and double dealing card sharks, Tucumcari was a quiet town of wide gravel streets intersecting Route 66 from the south and north, each street interspersed with the occasional motel and restaurant in southwestern or Indian motif, whitewashed and with brightly colored, eye-catching signs pointing the way for tourists. The real Tucumcari was a sleepy desert town with a few cars parked around and with long haul trucks rolling through. Still, I was fascinated to be there.

The enormity of the sky with clear views to far distant horizons gave proportions of vastness to these ancient lands in ways I had never before seen. I imagined the land changing so little over time that when I envisioned indigenous tribesmen trekking its soil eons ago, followed by Spaniards seeking golden riches in the Seven Cities of Cibola, then wagon trains of settlers rumbling slowly along, and finally Mary and me in our Alpine heading the same direction, the scene did not change. New Mexico was timeless.

The horizon before us seemed to go forever, but far away the shadowy outline of distant mountains began to appear. The terrain along this portion of Route 66 was still mostly flat, but we seemed to be going up hill all the time among prairie grass dotted occasionally by a few trees and scrub bushes. With no need to stop, we motored through the towns of Montoya and Santa Rosa slowly to gather more of the flavor of New Mexico. Everything about the day was beautiful with desert life so very different than anything we had known, perhaps accentuated by recollections of Chicago's confining winter.

From Santa Rosa, the whole world seemed to be flat and never ending, but ever so slowly the mountains ahead loomed larger. We came to a huge sign describing Clines Corners as THE place to stop on Route 66. Mary and I decided that it looked sufficiently inviting to do just that. More miles of dry grass went by, then another huge sign about Clines Corners sailed by. OK, we'll stop. Miles and miles more droned by, and another huge welcome to stop in Clines Corners emerged from the landscape. We began to muse; Clines Corners must be some place, but how far away is this place?

Finally, after what seemed to be hours, Clines Corners stood before us. With all the billboard hype, I expected far more than a tourist stop, but there it was, Clines Corners, a large building with exterior tourist-inviting graffiti dominating the landscape among a few scattered companions. That was all. Clines Corners claimed to be halfway between Santa Rosa and Albuquerque, the best place to stop and stretch, and that we did. But, while we sauntered through the racks of t-shirts and touristy trinkets thinking that Albuquerque was just ahead, Mary and I chose to buy nothing more than gas.

Albuquerque was just ahead, but in New Mexico terms. It was a long way to go in real terms. Moriarty came first and with it a long remembered surprise, the Longhorn Ranch. Our introduction to the "Old West" of our imaginations was just a turn off Route 66 into a parking space. The day could not have been more perfect, but I was surprised that so few cars were parked there, almost a ghost town. In no hurry, Mary and I strolled through the "town" and settled in at its restaurant for a lunch of sandwiches, fries and cold drinks. After refreshing a bit, we walked the "town" to discover the assembly of stuff to be just like a movie set; each "establishment" was stocked with everything any set would need, a saloon that fit every notion of a dry gulch barroom, a general store museum stocked floor to ceiling with 19th century needs, a Wells Fargo office, everything straight out of the "Old West." I was amazed at the quantity of items on display and the effort all of it must have required to collect.

At the General Store "Museum," I encountered an artifact of the real "Old West" that was a singular throwback to the law and lawless as practiced in the late 19th century that focused my attention to remain a lasting memory ever since. Sitting on a glass-topped counter filled with all sorts of interesting items, mostly old and dusty but interesting just the same, sat the strangest pair of brogan type work shoes I had ever seen. They were made of an eerie, translucent kind of leather that I could not identify. With no other patrons in the "store," I struck up a conversation with the "proprietor" who was filled with southwest lore and enjoyed the opportunity to tell me about this item or that, another historic piece here, a fascinating tale there, and the lives of famous characters entwined with the displays. He was loaded with fascinating facts of the era, and my inquiry about the strangely pale shoes brought a smile to his face. I could tell that a favorite story was about to be told.

His tale began by describing a despicable character with a pronounced nose. Big Nose George Parrott was not just a gunslinger, he was a bandit of malicious intent wherever he went, a man who dispensed the same contempt for civility on whoever crossed his path. Two lawmen faced him and died, and the peaceful citizens of the Black Hills territory southward into Wyoming came to fear not only his presence but his name as well, and no one felt safe if Big Nose George was even hinted at being nearby.

The time was the "Old West," the 1880s, a time when action was swift and decisive and carried in the holsters of those who kept their fast draw hands near six-guns. Their barrels of cold steel dispensed final authority in those parts, and George used his sidearms to further his path of lawlessness with stagecoach holdups. He and his gang filled their pockets with loot taken from other people traveling the unprotected stage routes.

Big Nose George was a desperado known to shoot up the place and make off with whatever he wanted. His notoriety spread far and wide at a time when verbal descriptions of outlaws and sketches of them on wanted posters were about all anyone had to go by for identification unless they were photographed, which was rare. Such anonymity protected outlaws, but George's nose was a dead give-away; he could not hide among the anonymous. People knew him on sight, and word spread fast.

When Big Nose George and his gang of cutthroats rode up, trouble was in the making. His was the sort of lawlessness that caused great contempt for him among the honest citizenry to the extent that when he was captured, the populace readied themselves for a hanging;

but George cheated them and death by escaping. During 1881 he was back in the Dakota Black Hills where he was captured again. Extradited to Wyoming, the local people were determined to prevent another breakout and to finally rid themselves of him. An angry mob stormed the jail. George was taken to a nearby telegraph pole and strung up. Frontier justice was served by the hands of the frontiersmen themselves.

Among the witnesses was the town doctor, a future governor, who recovered the body, skinned George and cut him into pieces. Parts of him went in various directions while his hide was tanned. Among the items made from it were two pairs of shoes, one for a lady and one for a working man, the brogans on display at the Longhorn Ranch. The legacy of Big Nose George Parrott remained among the dusty relics of the General Store and its "museum" some eighty-five years later.

I was thoroughly engrossed as the narrator completed the tale matter-of-factly, leaving me with a clear image of "Old West" life and times that transcended all the movies and TV shows I had seen. This was real, a tale of an outlaw and his fate that I had never heard before. I looked closely at the shoes in an attempt to identify what part of George's body they were made from, but could not. Showing wear, their craftsmanship seemed similar to other brogans I had seen; nothing special but their strange color and their story. How they came into the Longhorn Ranch collection went untold, but when the old man mentioned that the doctor carried his medical instruments in a tote bag also made from George's hide, I could not help but wonder what other pieces of Big Nose George Parrott might exist elsewhere among dusty relics of the "Old West" that were subjects of more tales told to tourists or stuck back somewhere and forgotten. I wondered who else might have had a similar fate, now lost in times long past.

After walking the breadth of the Longhorn Ranch and seeing everything open to us, Mary and I piled back into our Alpine and headed for Albuquerque. Out of Moriarty the terrain became rocky and hilly. Route 66 actually made some noticeable curves, and as the highway approached a pass between two ranges of abrupt hills ahead, a surprise awaited us.

That day was perfect, warm, sunny and filled with adventures among new and fascinating terrain. Then, as we rounded that last turn, behold, there in the valley before us lay the most beautiful city we had ever seen. "Spectacular" fit nicely; both Mary and I uttered a "Wow" each. Then the thought of that door in the desert presented itself.

How was I to find Sandia Base? The destination of our journey was that elusive door, a secret door in the desert. How was I to find it? My first thought was simply to stop at the first service station, fill up our Alpine and inquire, certain that none among those I would encounter had ever heard of Sandia Base. Once pulled to a stop at the pumps, a young man trotted out to our rig and provided service, this being a time before self-service. Casually, I inquired if he knew how to get to Sandia Base.

"Straight on into town and take the third left."

I was stunned. How could a local service station attendant know of things so secret? Now more confused than ever, I drove back onto Route 66 to the third left, went a few blocks and drove into the entry lane of Sandia Base.

Long, nicely prepared matching plinths of sand colored stone on either side of the entry rose from near the ground to about head high and extended back toward a guard shack between the in and out lanes. No sentry was on duty; no one was there to provide directions to the secret door in the desert. Tall trees lined the entry way as I drove slowly past the empty guard shack with its large sign proclaiming Sandia Base, U.S. Army, expecting at any moment to have gun-toting MPs jump from hiding to thwart my incursion onto the Base. I kept going slowly looking for anything suggesting directions. Beyond the entrance, the military installation took on the air of others I had seen as I recognized WW-II structures, barracks and buildings with Army personnel going about their day on foot and in drab green vehicles. Civilian vehicles of many varieties were among them, and nothing at all seemed secret. Then, off to my left, I noticed in the distance down a street another guard shack with a gate and tall chain link fences. This was surely the entrance to the secret door in the desert.

I turned my little red Sunbeam Alpine and its trailer onto the street and traveled nearer to the guard station when a uniformed guard emerged and flagged me down. I handed him my orders.

"You're in the wrong place," he said. "You need to turn around and go to the Navy barracks."

With his directions, I re-routed our path to the appropriate barracks and took my orders inside. I was a day early, expected to arrive on the 25th of April, but the duty yeoman knew exactly what to do. I was expected, with my wife, and quarters were available for us, an apartment on base. The remainder of the day in the bright southwestern sun was spent getting oriented to Sandia Base and into our new quarters, a second story 4-room flat. Our apartment was conveniently located in the two-story building across the street from the NCO Club. Mary was to spend the summer at its poolside to achieve the most beautiful New Mexico tan anyone could hope for. Trim and blond, she was to have a glorious summer while I kept an eye out for that elusive secret door in the desert. By now, my suspicions of being duped in the Great Lakes kept me from inquiring of such things. I was among sailors with experience and responsibility who would keep me informed of where to go and what to do to complete the second phase of my GMT A-school. If that door existed, they would show me the way.

For the next four months, Sandia Base was our home and operations center for venturing out to see Albuquerque and beyond. Every day brought new adventures for Mary and me that melded into a fabulous adventure among all sorts of things to do and places to see.

My introduction to the secret things that I suspected to be in my future was immediate assignment to barracks duty. Mary and I had just gotten moved in and had not even stocked our apartment with food when I had to report for duty on the first day of my new assignment. Left alone to handle whatever was needed, she had a new task; our Alpine took that day to stop running. I could not assist, but being of the do-it-herself type, Mary changed into work clothes, stuffed her golden hair under a cap, raised the hood, and starting searchng through the engine to repair what had stopped working. She knew what to do. We had become increasingly tuned in to the idiosyncracies that the Prince of Darkness had bestowed on our car and was forced to learn how to keep it running.

The starter, for example, would occasionally stop at a dead point. The next time the key was inserted to start the car, nothing happened. Our trick was to use the lead hammer used to knock the spinners on or off the wire wheels to tap on the starter. A few taps, and it usually started. Those times it didn't start required a few more taps to get it to work again. When the car would not start even with the starter engaged, I had learned that the distributor points needed attention. We carried service tools with us along with spare parts, such things as gap gages for spark plugs and feeler gages for the points and emery cloth to clean the points. Cleaning everything and resetting the points usually did the trick in getting going again. If not, once sure that the engine had spark to the plugs, it was clear that the carburetors needed adjustment. With dual sidedraft Stromberg single throat carbs that required synchronous movement for the engine to run properly, we carried a flow gage and spare jets and used our feeler gages to set the throat pistons at similar points to insure that each carburetor was doing its job. If after all this, it still didn't start, we knew that the Prince of Darkness had struck again.

On this, our first day in Albuquerque, Mary was under the hood when an MP rolled to a stop beside the car.

"Hey buddy," he called. "Need some help?"

Mary raised up, her blonde hair falling to her shoulders, grease smeared on her cheek. "No. Thanks anyway. I can fix it."

Well now, that unexpected turn of events was sufficient for the MP to get out of his pickup. "Let me take a look."

"No thanks," Mary told him. "It just takes...."

As his chivalrous heart warmed to the occasion, he would not hear of failing to come to the aid of this damsel. He tinkered here and there, tried this and that, but could not get the car to start. "I'll have to call a tow truck," he said.

At that, Mary tucked back under the hood, tapped the hammer on the starter a few more times, went around and slid in under the wheel. Turning the key, the Alpine fired and purred perfectly. She smiled at the MP's chagrin and explained that the starter gets stuck some times and needed only a few taps to make it work.

Not more than a couple of days later, the engine died when the lights were switched on, and I racked my memory trying to recall what I had done the last time that happened. I could not remember anything other than spending a day going through every electrical connection from the battery to the dash and the engine. Beginning again, but this time trying the ignition each time I did something, I soon discovered a secret of the Prince of Darkness. Cleaning corroded battery terminals did not solve the problem, but when I cleaned the battery cable connection to the body of the car, the ignition worked perfectly with the light switch on or off. The Lucas electrical system tied the entire electrical network to that single connection, and when it corroded just enough to permit only sufficient electricity to flow to support the engine, turning on the lights drew more power than the corrosion permitted to pass, and the engine died. From then on, I knew what to do.

Defense Atomic Support Command patch
DASA, Field Command Headquarters
Sandia Base, Albuquerque, NM

Chapter 6

Sandia Base

Albuquerque held adventures in every direction that Mary and I investigated in my off-duty hours, afternoons, evenings and weekends. Rising with the sun for my first day of duty, I so enjoyed the crisp New Mexico morning that I walked from our apartment to the Navy barracks, leaving the Alpine for Mary. Even though daytime temperatures got into the 80s, perhaps low 90s in direct sunlight, that day and those following melded into a succession of bright, sunny days that were spectacular. On each of my morning walks thereafter, I took a different route to see more. Off to the east rose Sandia Peak with the Monzano Mountains stretching southward to the horizon. Surrounding Sandia Base was Kirtland Air Force Base, and on the back side were the runways with all sorts of jet fighters and military aircraft. One morning I noticed in the distance the low silhouette of a long fuselage and thin wings much longer than usual. It was a black, droopy winged airplane, my first U-2. It sat just out of its hanger while being serviced for launch. It fulfilled my image of the legendary gooney bird: lumberingly slow on take off, but capable of graceful soaring flight at exceptionally high altitudes for exceedingly long distances, just the sort of spy plane that the CIA used to overfly the Soviet Union, another answer to Khrushchev's "We will bury you!" With U2s soaring near the stratosphere, our eyes in the sky were watching his every move with high definition cameras from such high flyers and others posted around the world. In the days to come, I noticed that the all-black U-2s were guarded and kept at a distance from the other planes that took off and touched down with regularity.

After a few days of orientation, my group of new trainees assembled one morning to begin our introduction, another answer to Khrushchev. "Now," I thought, "we are going to that secret door in the desert."

With a Chief Petty Officer introduced as our instructor and roll called, we then marched to a massive red brick building, squat with a flat roof and no windows. It sat behind chain link fences with rolled razor wire on top, interrupted only by a guard station with a turnstile permitting one person at a time to pass. The building was part of the fenced-in complex I had driven to when first arriving on Sandia Base, except to another guard station. The size of the complex was impressive, and I wondered what went on inside. I also wondered about the secret door in the desert: was this the way?

I was still trying to figure out what was going on, but I knew that this building could not be secret. Everyone passing by could see it, and it looked to have been built sufficiently long ago to have been the subject of innumerable conversations. Secrecy, I was learning, was really nothing more than isolating those to be kept ignorant from those who were not. Windowless buildings, fences and guards accomplished this compartmentalization in physical terms very well while maintaining "Need to Know" accomplished similar division in human terms.

The path I was on would soon fill me with secrets I had to keep from everyone, my compartment, my "Need to know." The pieces I had at that time clearly began with "Mr. John Smith" back in boot camp and came to this guard station and its turnstile outside this red brick building on Sandia Base during early May, 1967. Without my knowledge, my background had been investigated during training at the Great Lakes. I came to realize that A-School there was more of a holding time while the FBI checked out each of us, and only those who were accepted advanced to Phase-2.

I first learned of this qualifying investigation when my grandmother displayed great contempt toward me. She was angered by her conclusion drawn from the men in suits who canvassed my home neighborhood of Little Richmond, North Carolina asking questions about me. That signaled to her that I was up to no good, that I was taking money from the Government for being married when I was not. Those thoughts went with her to the grave; never once did she give up the idea that I was involved in something fishy and that the government was after me. The strange men who claimed to be insurance salesmen, magazine salesmen, whatever reason they gave, who converged on the people who knew me, each one going from whatever they said they were doing to asking questions about me, left her with convictions displayed when she cast a suspicious eye toward me. There was something fishy about me, but the FBI had another purpose in mind.

By the time I was on Sandia Base, everything in my background had received the scrutiny that materialized in the ID badge the guard handed to me that first day. Every day after that, the Army guard looked closely at that badge, then closely at me, then rubbed its surface between his finger and thumb before motioning me on. It was then that I noticed an embossed pattern on the picture portion of the ID, something easily missed unless examined closely but easily felt, another security measure.

The building layout was long halls with lockers embedded into walls at shoulder level alongside classrooms, each locker with a combination lock. Classrooms branched off to the right while corridors led off to the left in directions we would soon learn about. We filed in behind our instructor and took seats in a classroom laid out like a small theater. I was impressed with its high quality furnishings, solid wood paneling along the walls, carpet on the floor, comfortably padded theater style seating. Each of us wondered what was coming next. We sat for a while, talking quietly among ourselves, all young, naive sailor trainees, ignorant but trusting. When our instructor returned, he began introduction and orientation to this phase of A-School with more checking of lists, assignment of lockers, issuance of combinations, and our first action: opening our lockers. Inside each one was a pad of paper, two pencils and a pack of multi-colored ink pens. With our provisions in hand, we returned to the classroom where our instructor told us that we were never to take anything from the building. "Bring in nothing, leave with nothing, and never discuss what you see and do here."

With piqued curiosities focusing our every thought, all of us were intrigued about what was yet to come, and it began quickly. The lights were dimmed and the screen behind the stage lighted. Initial images of an introductory nature led to the first important slide, an electrical schematic with different colored lines connecting various symbols and geometric objects with cryptic names. What made the slide immediately important and riveting was the unmistakable word in bold red type on its top and bottom, SECRET. I followed the lines from what appeared to be input points through some electronic symbols I recognized to other symbols I didn't. All of them came to an end, a block with DET in it.

When our instructor said, "This is the schematic of the Mk 101 nuclear depth charge," each of us was suddenly struck with the realization that our prior and obscure training only alluded to secret things in an oblique manner. Everything was now clear. We were all eyes and ears as our instructor went on with, "You will learn the firing sequence of this weapon and recognize the components in the circuitry from initiation signal to detonator. A properly functioning sequence results in firing the detonator of a high explosive charge that accelerates the final component of high purity uranium-235 to make a super-critical mass. The yield of this weapon is 20 kilotons...."

The same thought resonated in each of us: "Holy shit!" Our track was now clear, we were James Bond's "Q" in training. We were the hardware guys. Soon divided into "hooks" of four men, we were then assigned an instructor who operated under an overall instructor when gathered together in classrooms. The back side of the building reached by the corridors leading off to the left housed training bays with weapons and support systems for each of the warheads in the fleet. From that day on, each "hook" trained on these warheads. We learned to take them apart, check components, use dedicated instrumentation to verify proper function, reassembly of each warhead, how to configure them differently, and how to perform final circuitry checks to ascertain that the warhead would operate as designed. The various configurations and modifications were taught as we learned that each weapon had multiple capabilities depending on its configuration and various settings.

Our jobs-to-be were now clear: ours were the last human hands to check out and load hydrogen bombs for delivery against whatever target they were assigned. Our hands were the last to verify that the weapon would perform as intended. Massive destruction was their purpose, the most destructive devices ever conceived. And I was troubled.

Each of us accepted our roles with differing results. While I had philosophical problems with being the gatekeeper of massive death, others were so enthralled as to forget the importance of secrecy. Our number soon dwindled by two. Rumor quickly spread that one sailor was so excited about what he was learning that he had to tell his mother. Phones were monitored, of course; his conversation had other ears listening, and he was quickly reassigned. The second among us thought he could trade what he was learning for cash from the USSR and made a phone call to the Soviet embassy in Mexico City. He was not off the phone in his chosen phone booth on base when MPs rolled up and arrested him. Those lessons were quickly learned; secrecy was of utmost importance. Later, I learned that the Mk 101 nuclear depth charge was an old, obsolete weapon used to initiate us to special weapons as the bait for anyone who might choose to disregard maintaining secrecy. It was, in fact, "Little Boy," the simplest of the World War-II weapons but modernized and maintained as both a teaching aid and a real weapon.

Our first week of intensive training set the pattern for each week to come, and a weekly exam evaluated how well we learned the material. The information quickly went into overload, too much to digest in too short a time. All of us failed that first exam. With some reservations about what we were learning, I made an off-hand comment to that effect. Other ears were listening, as I learned when my instructor pulled me aside with orders to go see Chief Petty Officer so-and-so, the head of the school. My instructor leveled his eyes on mine and told me in no uncertain terms, "You're about to throw away the best duty this Navy has to offer. Next week this time, you'll be on the first garbage scow to put out to sea if you don't say the right things."

"Right things about what?" I asked.

"The Chief heard you say you didn't like what we're teaching you. He takes that sort of thing seriously."

"Oh, I didn't mean...."

"You better say the right things or you're history, sailor."

With that admonishment, I was faced with a dilemma; follow through with my philosophical reservations about being an H-Bomb mechanic or continue on with the most fascinating exploits of my life.

The Chief was, indeed, a severe man who took his job seriously. When I arrived in his office, he was reading through my record.

"You wanted to see me, sir?" I asked.

He flipped from one page to another while pacing slowly back and forth. "You don't like it here, sailor?"

"No sir, I like it fine."

He turned to me sharply. "I heard you say you didn't like it. Do you deny saying that?"

Now I knew why I had to be careful what I said. "I probably did say something like that, sir, but I was aggravated about doing so poorly on the exam. I did well in Great Lakes, and I wanted to continue doing so."

He paced back and forth again reading my file. "Top in your class."

"Yes, sir."

He turned sharply again to me. "The Navy and the United States Government has a lot invested in you, sailor. If you have any doubts about why you are here, now's the time to say so. We can find another place for you."

Garbage scow, came to mind. "No, sir. I don't have any doubts. I just want to do well in everything I do." In the following moments when my track for the next several years in the US Navy was in the hands of the Chief Petty Officer looking into my eyes, the nagging idea of becoming a secret operative responsible for final preparations of the destruction of millions of people in a single blinding white flash festered into a conflict of conscience. What I said in the next minute would shape the rest of my life. I decided to keep that festering bit in the back of my mind.

"We're in a cold war with the Soviet Union, son, serious business, and we want only the best men who are dedicated to this country and to the purpose that we train you for. Are you the best, son? Do you have any doubt about that, sailor?"

"I think so, sir. I mean about being the best, and I don't have any doubts, sir."

He paused on the brink of decision. "I'm going to permit you back into school, but if you don't think you are up to the oath to this country you've taken, say so now."

"No, sir. I don't have any doubts."

He looked into my eyes and saw what he wanted, then dismissed me. I returned to class with a new lesson firmly learned: be exceedingly careful what I say.

That afternoon after school while walking back to my apartment, I was of a different frame of mind than that morning. This assignment held very high expectations, and I had to meet them for both myself and for the trust the Chief placed in me. He would be watching, and I might not like the idea of my duties on the last line of offense whose measure of success was the destruction of mankind and all the wonders created by the multitude of hands that shaped the world I marveled at, but there were people who would do away with my America if it were not for people in my position. I thought about the day JFK was killed and my expectation of seeing missile contrails in the sky as I sat on the steps of Surry Central High School and understood more completely how Khrushchev's conviction was shaping my life.

That early May day in Albuquerque was as beautiful as any I had ever seen, but I now saw the world with a different perspective. I walked along the sidewalks thinking, passed by the hospital, then walked onto the grass between the hospital and the street leading to my apartment. Then, I froze. My next two steps would have been onto a coiled rattlesnake who claimed that portion of ground. His tail certified his claim, a shrill chatter that got my attention. I chose not to contest the claim. Carefully, I stepped back, then around the snake, then scampered onto the street just as a neighbor boy rolled by on a bicycle.

"Watch out for that rattlesnake over there in the grass," I cautioned.

"Where?" he asked.

I pointed out the spot, and he immediately went over to capture the thing. I watched him hunker over the snake, it striking at him but missing. He had a stick with a cord around one end and managed to get it over the snake's head. Pulled tight, the snake was caught. He picked it up and held it high, as long as the boy was tall, about five feet. He then placed it in one of the saddlebag type wire mesh baskets across the back fender of his bike, and throughout the afternoon, he rode around showing his rattlesnake to anyone who was interested.

That day was filled with shaping influences that converged in my mind: the need to be ever alert to listening ears and prying eyes, to always be wary of unexpected hazards at any moment, to always guard what I said, always vigilant toward maintaining secrecy while displaying a "take charge" attitude of the most absolute kind; H-bombs and the Cold War were at hand. Rattlesnakes and spies and security were more of the mix. Life was, for the first time, full of dangers, and I had to be sure of each step.

Chapter 7

Southwest Adventures

Our range of adventures from Albuquerque to points of interest beyond this portion of the Rio Grande was limited by reduced funds and no spare tire for our Alpine. Since Mary was in town only as long as my training lasted, her transient status kept her from getting a job. So, she lounged the summer away in the glorious New Mexico sun. As our means permitted, we socialized with other couples in our apartment building, but, since there were attractions in all directions, all of us young and eager-to-the-see-the-world types tried every one of them, and that left little time to gather socially. "Just driving around" fulfilled afternoon after afternoon and many weekends, and every time we spied something of interest, we stopped or it became our next destination. Knowing nothing of Albuquerque except what we saw and read, such discoveries proved fascinating. They broadened our interests and enticed us further afield.

Just a few days after settling in, three of us couples made plans to sample the Spanish Southwest cuisine with our first venture to a local restaurant. My introduction to this type of food was overwhelming; being a southern country boy, I had never smelled anything so deliciously mouth-watering. And, knowing nothing of the menu items, I was at a complete loss regarding what was what and requested of our waitress a sample platter of typical fare - *BUT* - it had to be mild. I already knew that I could not accommodate spicy, hot flavors. The six of us were crowded into a booth just marginally big enough to hold the large, brightly colored plates that were served us, each handled carefully with a mittened hand because of their heat. I thought the heat was from the oven, until I sampled my sampler. *WOW!* Was this stuff hot! With one bite I was on fire and instantly became the laughing stock of the group who could not believe how much water I drank. One pitcher after another could not put out the fire, and I was reduced to nibbling carefully for the duration of the meal. My companions devoured their sumptuous entrees while my mouth watered in responce to the ever so enticing aromas, but I just could not eat it. With that introduction, I learned to be careful with spiced and peppered foods, another lesson well learned.

Our Alpine accommodated just two, so any ventures with companions required a second vehicle or riding in theirs if it was suitable. One neighbor couple we got acquainted with had a nicely styled Sunbeam Rapier, a four place sedan that was the Sunbeam-Talbot built companion to our Alpine. It had the same power train as our roadster, although de-tuned a bit, and it had annoying problems, too; for one, the floor mounted shifter rotated in a half-spherical hub in the transmission linkage housing, and the hub had a habit of popping out of place into the housing and locking. I learned the details of this Sunbeam problem while working on their car, our Alpine exhibiting no such behavior. Otherwise, the Rapier was an ideal car for a young couple, sporting and stylish, a small 2-door that could transport four of us while using small amounts of gas. Shared cost for fuel made our outings more economical for each of us.

One occasion took us to Blue Water Lake west of Albuquerque near Grants. Our friends liked to fish and had all sorts of tackle. Mary and I had no such equipment, and, with their offer to supply all that we needed, we were off to an oasis in the high desert. Not being a fisherman, I was, nevertheless, interested in learning the techniques offered. Long rods with spinning reels and all sorts of bait produced nothing. Neither of the guys caught a thing. My friend's wife made camp in preparation for the fish we were supposed to bring, but it was Mary who supplied the trout. She knew how to fish, and with a line around her finger and a small artificial lure, she simply walked the large rocks along the water's edge dangling her bait within arms reach and pulled out a half dozen pan size fish. With our campfire's smoke wafting among the tall trees in a camping area, the fish sizzling in the pan became a tasty meal, but Mary declined. She really didn't like the taste of fish, but she had enjoyed fishing with her father who had taught her the winning techniques. Years later, we discovered that she was deathly allergic to all saltwater seafood, less so for fresh water fish but still not something she liked.

Other outings with our Sandia Base acquaintances occupied our off-duty time when we were not out on our own. Since I was the only married man among my "hook," my three companions tended to make our apartment their home away from home, especially when Mary cooked up a tub full of spaghetti, tossed a huge bowl of salad and made heaps of Texas toast. Along with strawberry shortcake, a southern favorite of ours that was well received, my "hook" packed in the good food that Mary and I put together. They brought their own beer, and our refrigerator was temporarily stuffed. Such cook-ins and grill oriented cook-outs were the sorts of things that comprised our New Mexico summer fun with friends.

Old Town Albuquerque was a delightful discovery made during one of our first "just driving around" outings. Mary and I made it a regular destination when time was limited, and when strolling around the plaza to the varied Spanish tunes with leisure stops in the shops, fragrant southwest cooking filling the air and our sampling of tasty things such as sopapillas dripping with honey, we were further introduced to New Mexico's motto, *Land of Enchantment.* Sunsets were awe-inspiring; such vibrant color, such spectacles of beauty: Old Town at sunset was very enchanting, indeed. With darkness, lights came on amid the rapidly cooling air at such an altitude, a mile high, and each romantic evening was filled with strummed tunes and melodic voices and enticing fragrances, smiles and bright colors. Both Mary and I began thinking that Albuquerque would become our home some day. As of this writing, though, almost forty years later, that has not happened, but recollections of our summer in the southwest remain favored memories for both of us.

Occasionally, when we had enough money, we rewarded ourselves with dinner in the old La Placita Dining Rooms on the southeast corner of Old Town Plaza, a long remembered favorite of mine. Its covered walkway of broad, rustic timbers and brightly painted displays of old world Spanish motifs on adobe walls could not have been more intriguing, and inside, it was a step back in time to the days of hacienda life in the high desert.

Further afield, we ventured along paths fairly well traveled in the event of another flat or collapsed wire wheel that would require help. Consequently, all of our destinations were day trips that put us back in Albuquerque by evening. On Route 66 to Grants one day, we marveled at the lava flows. Cones of ancient volcanoes rose high above the desert, long silent sentinels that once belched massive quantities of lava into rivers of rock that we now drove through. I imagined animals and humans alike scampering in all directions when the land shook and blazingly hot liquid stone rolled toward them, burning everything it touched, subsequently to cool and freeze into the enormous fields of solidified foam all around us. In addition to the black lava stone, red lava rocks were used in all sorts of construction in and around Grants making decorative natural colors.

Most surprising of all was the ice cave. We turned south onto New Mexico Route 53 and drove through more arid terrain that became increasingly forested with juniper, fir, Ponderosa pine and similar trees. At the base of a tall volcano, we turned at a sign reading "Ice Cave" and stepped into another unexpected adventure. We learned that the Bandero Volcano ended its reign of molten destruction perhaps ten thousand years ago, and the surviving products told us just how short long ago is when talking of rocks. This inhospitable area, called El Malpias by the Spanish (bad-lands), straddled the Continental Divide along the nearby Zuni Mountains. The frozen river deep within the earth was revealed one day when the ceiling of a vast cavern collapsed making a giant depression in the earth. The collapsing mass sheared a blanket of blue-green ice that had formed during eons past. Rather than being around a hundred feet below the surface, one face of the sheared ice mass was now exposed to the morning sun and to outside weather, but it didn't melt, a fascinating natural wonder.

Our tour began with the curios in the Trading Post where we bought tickets for the next showing. With our companions and fellow sight-seers, we then walked through the forest to a long stairway leading down into the depression and to the exposed ice face. Summer wear of light shirts and shorts was just the ticket for outings in the New Mexico sun, but as we neared the ice, frigid conditions surrounding it meant that we made one step after another into air that got progressively colder. At the level of the ice, the air temperature was below freezing, about 50 degrees colder than the forest air we had walked through.

Our guide told many fascinating things about the ice cave, especially that earth scientists had climbed along its path far back into the earth and did not find its origin or the source of conditions that caused liquid water to freeze into distinct layers clearly seen in the face of the ice shelf. He told of the great age of the ice and that the conditions had remained unchanged for thousands of years. I thought it ironic: a volcano that belched vast quantities of molten rock from deep within the earth went to sleep in a way that put the surrounding earth into deep freeze. This was truly a natural wonder; earth temperature is normally about fifty-five degrees but here it was below thirty-two degrees and had been that way for a very long time. I wondered what the local Indians of past millennia thought of this strange phenomena.

Nearby was another New Mexico fascination but one of more modern proportions. Inscription Rock rose out of the El Morro Valley and became the soft stone tablet for passing peoples to inscribe their marks. Across the eons, the signs left by long forgotten native peoples, then Spanish explorers and adventurers, then wagonmasters guiding settlers and merchants along the Santa Fe Trail came to this spot and stopped their wagons to resupply water at a spring. Carving their presence into the rock left lasting impressions that Mary and I wondered about. Some names and dates were translated for us; "...passed by here... 16th of April 1605," signed by Don Juan de Onate who became the first governor of the new Spanish territory. This was my first contact with an actual "Don Juan," but unlike the tales of love told in literature, this person was settling a new and demanding land. With that notation, the English landing at Plymouth Rock in 1620 took on a different perspective. The Spanish were in this area years before them and a century earlier in Central America.

There were many other carvings, modern petroglyphs, and Mary and I wondered about the people who left them. Who were they? What were their lives like? Where did they go? We were well steeped in movie and TV westerns, and this sort of wild west was ever so fascinating. Unbeknownst to us, high above us on the table-top-like flatness of Inscription Rock, actually the cliffs of a sizable mesa, were the remains of a pueblo built by the Anasazi, the "Ancient Ones" who predated the Navajo and Zuni Indians and may be their forebears. This plateau hewn by wind and water over a vast span of time was the home of native peoples who must have known the region well, admired its vistas and amazing sunsets as we did, lived and died here, but because of the considerable distances to anywhere, they must have lived isolated lives. Our Alpine returned us to Albuquerque in an hour or so, covering a distance that many of those who lived here during ages past never achieved in a lifetime.

Off in the distance from Route 53 we could see Los Gigantes, tall stone giants standing among the bands of multi-colored earthtones of stone carved by wind, water and time. Nearby, the Zuni Pueblo, the oldest continually inhabited place on the continent, had grown into a small town. The Zuni people, known for many colorful works of art in pottery, beautifully hand crafted kachinas (Zuni dolls and gods), silver jewelry and a pace of life near stall speed told of slow days bathed in near-perpetual sun. Once, from this area and surroundings, the natives, Apache among them, rose up in revolt and drove the Spanish out, southward to around what is now El Paso, Texas and beyond. In time, though, settlers gradually returned as Spanish claims in the new world were too inviting. Ultimately, the territory of New Mexico gained US statehood in 1912.

It was on this tour that we saw our first roadrunner, a grouse-sized desert runner on long legs. We were amazed at its speed. Long eared jack rabbits were more than twice the size of Appalachian bunnies, and their long ears standing high in the desert scrub growth gave away positions that they must have thought hid them. And the coyotes lurking through the underbrush after both of them made an interesting display of high desert life. Rather than barren waste land that the word "desert" conveys, this New Mexico terrain teemed with life and dotted the landscape with plants and animals who made the arid expanse of flat-floored valleys and abrupt cliffs rising up to flat-topped mesas their home.

Water, of course, was the source of all life, and where it came from was a mystery. Still, during May, the desert was in bloom with bursts of flowering color that were new to us and made the view in any direction a treat. Some miles further along we came to Ramah Lake. We learned that its man-made dike had not held up so well, collapsing from time to time under the might of unusually heavy springtime snowmelt runoff, but its deep blue beauty against the stark red sandstone surrounding it was both a source of irrigation water and the wellspring of life from fertile soil. Where quantities of water were available, such as along the Rio Grande and other rivers that collected into lakes or bubbled up from springs, life sprang forth in profusion.

Once back on Route 66 and just for the fun of it, we crossed into Arizona and drove through the nearby Petrified Forest. Here the desert revealed another natural wonder, huge trees that once stretched their limbs toward the sun for centuries met an unusual fate; where they fell they turned to stone everlasting to give hints of their past glory to people across the ages, wanderers and wonderers of the far distant future who recognized that the towering trees of times past and the life in and around them once covered this now-barren landscape. My sense of time in the southwest took on very different perspectives with the wonders Mary and I saw on this one day of excursion into the high desert.

Another outing, this one to Bandalier National Monument to see its ancient cliff ruins, showed just what water in the desert could do: dense growth of trees, bushes, flowers, grass and everything green sprang up along the foot of the mesa into which the ancients built their stone and adobe village. All life that grew nearby or found its way to such locations existed because of the life-giving oasis. Unfortunately for us, the park was closed that day, so we were unable to tour the ruins or take trails through the area.

Our first visit to remarkable Santa Fe made it an instant favorite. This town, the oldest seat of government in the United States with the oldest house and the oldest church and oldest continually used road, Canyon Road, was filled with fascination every step along the way. And as we strolled through one historic site after another, the atmosphere so laden with the lives of peoples past took time to sink in. One man we met helped fill in the blanks and made a lasting impression, Bill Tate.

Chapter 8

Bill Tate

Racing down a curvy mountain road in hopes of making it to the hospital in time, Bill Tate lost control of his pickup and careened into a snowbank. He had run out of road and time. Stuck in the snow, he delivered his infant daughter on a cold, Christmas day.

I was intrigued by his stories, one after another, and soon realized that this bearded Santa Claus of a man had been a true New Mexico cowboy, now a great weaver of yarns. Santa Fe was his home, but his youth among dusty arroyos and magnificent vistas had become artistic with age. Paintings, drawings, and writings for sale lay about his small house, and in them I recognized that New Mexico was his heart.

Mary and I had been to Santa Fe several times and we learned the land by seeing and reading, but learning the people took insight gathered only by getting to know them. On this return, Bill Tate presented me with many intriguing insights as our afternoon wound its way through his life and times. Even though in poor health, he rose to the occasion with enthusiasm.

Just down the street from his house on Canyon Road, the San Miguel Mission Church rose from the soil from which it was made, and while visiting during our first foray to Santa Fe, I noticed the letters B T carved boyishly into one of its large wooden doors. That seemed an inconsiderate thing to do to such a venerable structure, America's oldest church, and no one I asked knew of their origin. When I asked Bill if he knew anything about those letters, he laughed heartily. The yarn he told went like this.

"I did it!" he said with a huge grin. "All the time I was a boy, my mother took me to church there. A few years ago when they installed new doors, they gave me the one with my handiwork. I've got it in the next room.

"Well now," he said. "I was a real boy back then, and if I wasn't sneaking peeks at the bosoms around me, I was trading spit wads across the aisle. It wasn't at all unusual for me to have my ear pinched by a padre who lifted me from my seat to be expelled beyond closed doors.

"And that's just what happened one spring Sunday. There I

was with my knife carving my namesake into that ancient door as the sacraments were spoken on the other side. I made quite a name for myself with that one."

What a story! I thought.

While I, a tourist, admired the Mission for its history and culture, it was just part Bill Tate's life. In more tales, topics broadened to include other parts of New Mexico he knew well, and I gained a deeper appreciation for this enchanting land and its people.

Panoramic vistas linger in my memory, and I found myself imagining what Bill Tate might have seen and done in his adventurous life. Magnificent views in every direction are the same that he knew from much earlier in the century, the same that the Spanish Conquistadors saw centuries before him as they searched for fabled Cibola, the seven cities of gold.

Having conquered the Aztec Empire in Mexico and the Incas in Peru, the Spaniards searched for a "new" Mexico with similar wealth. In 1539, a Franciscan priest, Fray Marcos de Niza, exaggerated claims of having seen vast cities of sparkling wealth that resulted in the expedition led by 29-year-old Francisco Coronado.

When sunlight glittered off flecks of mica in the mud houses of the Zuni Pueblo of Hawikah near today's Black Rock, the Spaniards thought they had reached their golden quest. Instead, they found humble Indians and their tenuous existence amid nature's arid pageantry, a slow way of life born of the earth, and stern words for Fray Marcos were likely uttered at length.

What motives drove the priest to describe the Pueblo as larger than the city of Mexico remain unexplained, but his descriptions drew Coronado deeper into New Mexico and beyond, all the way to the plains of Kansas during the next two years, only to return to Mexico with no loot.

Spaniards returned in 1582, established a territorial province, and in 1998, New Mexico celebrated its 400th anniversary as a seat of Euorpean government in the New World. Santa Fe was older than the immigrant easterners who carved out a fledgling nation a century later. Santa Fe became the capital of the Spanish southwest in 1610 and remains the oldest state capital in America. In time, a steady stream of settlers via the Santa Fe Trail and others brought the English influence that soon prevailed to fashion the tripartite basis of modern New Mexico: Indian, Spanish and English. Native Americans settled it thousands of years ago, Spaniards conquered it hundreds of years ago, but it became the 47th state of the Union in just 1912.

I learned of New Mexico as the "land of enchantment" where deep blue skies and sun-drenched days offered a broad variety of outdoor adventures laced with history, legend and natural wonders. This land of primal grandeur, of badlands and desert in the south to Aspen forests and highlands in the north, from stark poverty among Indians clinging to old ways to the most advanced science, from landscapes sculpted by nature to beautiful creations of hand-fashioned art, from magnificent sunsets to thrashing storms, offered Mary and me more adventures than we could possibly undertake.

The land beckoned to be seen; from the bustle of modern Albuquerque to quaint Truchas, the American Tibet that Bill Tate spoke of so fondly; from old in the state's many pueblos to Santa Fe's charm; from the latest science of Los Alamos to parched ruins and wild flower-strewn Alpine meadows: "Enchanting" is an appropriate but insufficient description. Sunsets filled with magnificent colors upon iridescent clouds and soft blues fading to night skies sparkling with stars are finales to each day. And Bill Tate had seen a lifetime of them.

Mile-high Albuquerque lies in the Rio Grande Valley near the center of the state. The Sacramento Range and Sandia Peak, a favorite for sunset watchers, stretches north-south to the east, and a vast flat-topped mesa lies to the western horizon. Pueblos along the Rio Grande valley are among America's oldest pre-Columbian cultures, and traveling along the valley northward from Albuquerque is rewarded with finds of exquisite Indian crafts, weaving, pottery, paintings, turquoise and silver jewelry, and remnants of Indian life as it has been lived for centuries.

The southern badlands of Billy the Kid to ghost town remains of once-bustling mining camps to Alamogordo's portal to the nuclear age are just a few of the many sites that we just did not have time to see. But just a drive in our Alpine among sagebrush and sun, blue skies and boulders, wildflowers and jack rabbits made every outing a new adventure, each one only glimpses of the terrain that Bill Tate knew well.

Conquistadors led by Coronado were disappointed with the lack of gold, but the Indians needed no gold to be part of the earth, and cowboys like Bill Tate found much more than gold. Artists have always found inspiration in New Mexico, and visitors like us have continually been drawn to this crossroads of the southwest, to its wide open spaces, its fascinating cultural diversity, some choosing to remain as Mary and I decided to do but ended up elsewhere.

Bill Tate wrote and painted and told stories of his adventures to tourists who frequented his home, but his heart was a mischievous boy's love of the out-of-doors, memories that he so enjoyed to recall. I bought several of his "books," his typewritten, photo-copied works on many topics, and gained some insight into the times that exist only in his recollections.

Around his studio off from the main room of his house was accumulated stuff from his life as a painter. And what stuff he had! On a cluttered desk sat a vase. Had it once contained an assortment of brushes, a utility piece? On closer examination, a flabbergasted "Is that a Picasso?" brought another smile to his face.

"It sure is," confirmed Bill with a hearty laugh. "He gave it to me back when we were starving artists. It's been handy to have around. And over there in the corner is a Monet." Sure enough, arrayed among oils standing on their frames stacked in the corner was another gem of the art world, an exchanged gift from the time before fame.

Bill Tate was an intriguing man with a love of life expressed from mind to hand, a man who created his own timelessness in a timeless land that he so loved.

(Above) "Little Boy" (Hiroshima: about 16 kT) and "Fat Man" (Nagasaki: about 20 kT) were A-bombs; the beginning, August, 1945. Twenty years later, "Little Boy" was a training weapon being phased out of the arsenal while "Fat Man" had been refined and reduced in size to become the small igniter of far more powerful H-bombs.

Chapter 9

H-bombs

Back on Sandia Base, just a tiny spot on the map surrounded by sprawling Kirtland Air Force Base, my fellow GMT trainees and I were taken deeper and deeper into the workings of H-bombs. After introduction with the Mk 101 nuclear depth charge, we learned about the history of "the bomb" from Los Alamos to Alamagordo and on to modern weapons. Although wartime development was no more than a cursory introduction to those first bombs, puny weapons compared to the warheads we were to work on, this history and my deepening involvement piqued my interests to the extent that I have since continued inquiry into the origins and the times surrounding the emergence of mankind's most destructive weapons.

Our instructor told of the first A-bombs, "Little Boy" and "Fat Man" of World War-II, then went on to desribe the Mk 6 as the 1950s version of "Fat Man" as the route to modern weapons, among them, the Mk 15, the first of a new generation of H-bombs employing very different concepts applied to the Mk 6 that enabled smaller dimensions and reduced weight with far greater yield. The Mk 15 replaced the Mk 17, the huge H-bomb that the B-52 bomber was designed to carry, and, although the Mk 17 was retired in the mid-1950s, for teaching purposes, it illustrated the evolution of hydrogen bomb design from the very large to the much smaller with the Mk 15 and its Mk 39 variant in the arsenal into the mid-1960s. We were introduced to these warheads only in classroom training.

Compared to the small warheads we trained on, the "strategic" Mk 17 was enormous, a cylinder more than six feet in diameter with a cone nose and finned tail enclosing the potential of fifteen megatons. The much more modern and smaller Mk 15 of just under four megatons combined both "strategic" and "tactical" capabilities deliverable by various methods rather than just the B-52 bomber. Later, we trained on the more modern Mk 53, still about five feet in diameter and weighing eight thousand pounds, and learned that making such bombs of high yield, nine megatons, enabled the same bays of the B-52 to carry more than one bomb of the "strategic" class.

Beginning with the Mk 101 nuclear depth charge, we were

taught that "Little Boy" was a gun-type warhead, then on to other applications of the same principle such as large diameter Army nuclear
shells, the Navy's Mk 23 "KT" round as well. WW-II designs had become smaller with higher yields as compact, multi-use warheads in
great variety. The gun-type design had limitations that the "Fat Man"
implosion design did not, and warheads of the "Little Boy" type, whether
bomb or shell, were being phased out.

The difference between high yield "strategic" and lower yield
"tactical" weapons was no longer a function of size; even small warheads had megaton yield, enough to obliterate many square miles of
any city. The trend to smaller designs was taught as a division of yields
into "strategic" warheads that could destroy a large city in one burst in
favor of "tactical" weapons that were deliverable by a variety of ways
depending on configuration, thus the need for GMTs. A well placed
"tactical" detonation had greater military advantage than massive destruction inflicting widespread collateral damage, and used in tandem,
smaller scale detonations in particular patterns produced more destruction than a single larger explosion. As a consequence, "strategic"
weapons were no longer needed, only improved delivery capability to
place one or more lower yield warheads where they would have the
most effect.

Within the first couple of weeks we were introduced to the ver-
satile Mk 28, the bombs of Palomares. The Mk 28 was both a strategic
and tactical warhead depending on what yield was selected and how
the weapon was configured. During January, 1968, Air Force B-28 H-
bombs focused worldwide attention when a plane load fell from high in
the sky over the southwest coast of Spain. A B-52 bomber collided with
a KC-135 refueling tanker, and both planes disintegrated in mid-air.
While little was said of the crews who perished, that incident captured
worldwide attention, and months later, deployment of H-bombs of all
types still received intense public scrutiny while we eager-to-learn trainees hardly grasped the Palomares situation and its implications.

That B-52 bomber was loaded with four B-28 H-bombs, each
Mk 28 warhead with a yield of almost one-and-half megatons. Their
tumbling back to earth revealed to the world a number of sobering
aspects of nuclear weaponry and Cold War politics. One: H-bombs were
flying onboard any number of planes in the air at any time. Two: the
range of possibilities for falling back to earth, real or imagined, fixed
public attention and raised fear of an accidental nuclear detonation.
Three: the bombs of Palomares were the first photos of actual H-bombs
the public had ever seen, and, for the first time, the public saw that
they were small. For our training, the fact that handlers somewhere
performed the final assembly and checkout of those weapons prior to
loading on that B-52 was instructive; both the technical aspects of the
warheads subjected to crash conditions and aspects of the multi-fac-
eted politics of the incident were discussed in our classes.

Perhaps the most telling result of the massive American-Span-
ish effort to recover the bombs was how both governments treated the
matter, with a massive effort indicating the seriousness of the situation. One bomb was recovered on the ground, crumpled but intact. The

high explosives surrounding the cores of two others exploded on impact, called a "single point detonation," that scattered their nuclear cores over the landscape. The fourth splashed into the ocean. While many people went about the challenges of recovering the weapon remains and cleansing the Spanish countryside of contaminated earth, subsequently returned to the US in thousands of barrels, the previously unaware public was exposed to secret operations surrounding the US nuclear arsenal flying over other nations, revealing for the first time what many believed to be narrowly missed nuclear catastrophes of unimaginable proportions. Even more sobering was learning that Palomares was just another in a long sequence of accidents and lost H-bombs, whose various circumstances and significance were played down by the government only to pop back into public view from time to time when disclosure was made, always by civilian media.

Our instructor went to great lengths to explain to us why nuclear catastrophe in the Palomares incident was not possible. The theater was dark as we studied the circuitry of the Mk 28, following his pointer along each path. With diagrams and charts, he illustrated the safety designs of the warhead and explained why they did not explode with a nuclear yield, even though two of the cores were subjected to the enormous pressures of high explosive (HE) detonation, compared to properly timed initiation of all the detonators in the HE sphere required to produce a nuclear fireball. The B-28 recovered from land proved to be highly useful for studying the shock mitigating features of the bomb's structure among impact effects on components and their assembly that survived ground impact without ignition. Many "lessons learned" were later incorporated into improved earth penetrating designs. The two warheads that exploded did so because of impact shock; their lesson indicating that less impact-sensitive high explosives were needed, and more modern warheads than the Mk 28 that we were to train on later were of the less sensitive type. The fourth B-28 required eighty days to locate and recover from the ocean, from nearly a half mile down, and it was in the news week after week.

Our instructor told of Mk 28 inadequacies revealed in the Palomares incident, a "Broken Arrow" made famous decades later in a feature film of that title but with a story line unrelated to the Palomares incident. Using the B-28 as a model to compare more modern designs, he then went on to say that warheads we would be introduced to went far beyond the Mk 28 in safety and handling features. In studying their configurations, the design sequence of each component was studied, each receiving the right signal at the right time and within the right range monitored by "watchdog" circuitry that disabled the warhead if all measures were not met, an important safety feature. Only with proper functioning of the firing sequence was the warhead capable of cataclysmic detonation, and he pointed to a particular block labeled SEP, the Strike Enabling Plug. It was, in fact, a simple plug that completed various circuits, the bottleneck that separated the core initiators from ignition signals. In addition to redundant enabling circuitry and "watchdogs," the SEP was the mechanical device that inhibited the bombs of Palomares from making far greater impacts on the history of mankind.

SEPs were not installed.

Military procedure to light off an H-bomb included GMT signoff of weapon acceptance and serviceability prior to mission loading. Preceding GMT signoff, clever designers expended great effort to keep the weapons dormant unless everything leading to ignition was exact in several modes and in proper sequence. Once onboard the plane, flight personnel did not have the necessary information at take-off. Decisions for launch were made only when the right communications in the right sequence were received with the correct identifiers issued from military command, orders that originated with presidential decision. Insufficient information for deployment was routine during flight, insufficient to enable and release a workable warhead. No person or group of people could deploy the Mk 28 to detonation without the warhead receiving the correct sequence of codes in the right range, and even then, the SEP had to be installed. Onboard B-52s, SEP installation, the final act of arming the weapon, had to be performed by a person with concurrence of a second key-holder, and among the SEPs maintained under lock and dual keys that worked only in unison, the correct SEP specific to the warhead had to be installed for it to work. The correct SEP was revealed only with arming information and instructions transmitted from military command, never onboard until authorized by highly specific communications on highly specific frequencies with verification codes that changed daily. Because SEPs were visually identical, any one would fit any Mk 28 warhead but only the correct plug allowed the warhead to work by completing specific circuitry that varied from warhead to warhead. If the "watchdog" circuitry did not receive the correct signals of the correct logic permitted by the SEP, the warhead remained dormant, the condition of the bombs in bays of the B-52 at the moment of collision over Palomares.

When the two planes disintegrated at high altitude, the B-28s configured from Mk 28 warheads with specific nose and tail fairing assemblies designated by command and control prior to loading tumbled to earth and into international news as hydrogen bombs. As the ocean recovery story unfolded in the media, the public's fear escalated from one shocking revelation after another, among them that B-28 yield was eighty-eight times greater than the Hiroshima bomb. The public shuddered with the fright of Armageddon produced from all four making over three hundred fifty times Hiroshima, a frightening holocaust by any measure. Visions of enormous destruction averted only by the grace of God were bantered around while we learned that they did not "go" because of Arm-Fuse-Fire (AFF) circuits cleverly integrated into the weapon's circuitry that kept them dormant, even in the most severe conditions of high velocity earth impact. Additional requirements for firing were not complete as well, such as the Permissive Action Links (PAL), the "black box" in the cockpit used by the pilot for receiving properly coded and sequenced launch codes with verified instructions followed by final arming of the weapon. In each case, PAL had not been activated. The combination of SEP and PAL was a design redundancy with multiple applications that varied from bays of bombers to underwing mounting on jet fighters. In the case of fighters, SEPs had to be installed at loading, making the PAL and codes the primary safety mechanisms.

Although the Mk 28 series of W28 warheads were not as sophisticated as later warheads, each of the four Palomares bombs provided severe condition test data that illuminated insights to improve designs for keeping the destructive power of these and future weapons dormant until all AFF conditions were exact. The recovered Palomares bombs went back to service depots for thorough study to determine how they performed, and collected data improved future designs.

In Januany, 1968 just a few months prior to my arrival in Albuquerque, the Thule incident occurred, but it was not reviewed in the detail of Palomares. In this case, a B-52 caught fire in flight and crashed a few miles from landing at Thule Air Force Base, Greenland. The HE in its four weapons exploded and burned leaving little to be learned. Core material spread over surrounding ice and snow, along with blazing aviation fuel that melted ice to subsequently re-freeze, making cleanup a massive effort in the bitter cold and wind. However, re-freezing helped by encapsulating the debris, aiding US and Danish military personnel who conducted cleanup and recovery operations. The Thule incident was of little study value for hardware oriented GMTs, but following the trail of radiation tracked on the shoes of officers from the crash site to various Washington offices revealed just how sensitive radiation detection equipment actually was. That was reassuring since we trainees were being introduced to all sorts of special test and monitoring equipment along with requirements to keep track of everything we did.

Our initial training during 1967 and my return to Albuquerque for advanced warhead training in the spring of 1968 taught us that H-bombs had changed from the huge size and massive weight of the mid-1950s to much smaller B-28 type weapons further improved as the much less shock sensitive warheads of the Mk 43, Mk 57, Mk 61 in just ten years or so. After the Mk 28, more modern warheads of smaller dimensions were similarly packaged for configuration with a variety of front and rear fairings for different applications. The warhead alone comprised about a fourth of the length of the assembled B-28 H-bomb seen in photos of the Palomares bomb. A rear fairing from an array of designs could be fitted, including one to contain a parachute that slowed free fall to give time for the delivery plane to get away. The weapon's radar in the nose functioned for precise altitude detonation. One of various nosecones could be fitted; radar for height sensing in the air burst configuration was typical of Air Force applications. Another was crush material in the nose for parachute assisted laydown on runways or other military installations. A third was earth penetrating snouts, one of the main applications of the Mk 43. What the public saw in photographs of the Palomares bomb recovered from the ocean was a long, silver cylinder with a diameter less than knee high. Its round nose and no fins made its appearance so unthreatening that it could have been described as a torpedo.

In fact, the packaged warhead concept demonstrated in the Mk 28 was a torpedo in a different configuration designed for submarine tube launch, giving all submarines nuclear weapon capability. Such torpedoes were designed as sub-to-sub and sub-to-surface weapons. In torpedo form and wire guided, the sealed configuration of the warhead with yield in the range of twenty kilotons was just one application of the packaged warhead concept. Later, we trained on Mk 55 SubRoc warheads, the tube launched rocket with a nuclear tip of a design both smaller and more advanced than the Mk 28. With the SubRoc, a submarine of any type was a nuclear rocket carrier. Another was the replacement of the Mk 101 with the ASRroc, Anti-Submarine Rocket, in which a small, low yield warhead launched from surface ships was the nuclear equivalent of WW-II "ash can" depth charges. The Mk 28 was among the first of the package concept; variable use warheads with multiple configurations. More advanced designs were progressively smaller while configuring, checkout and certification for deployment as War Reserve H-bombs was the job of GMTs.

The Mk 101 nuclear depth charge that began our training was a gun-type uranium-fueled weapon changed little from its Hiroshima forebear. It was the first A-bomb we took apart. The Mk 28 was the first H-bomb we took apart, a very different concept evolved from its Nagasaki forebear, an implosion weapon. In mid-60s dial-a-yield warheads like the Mk 28, Mk 43, Mk 57 and Mk 61, the reduced dimensions of the "Fat Man" core was just the spark plug used to light off thermonuclear aspects of these advanced designs.

When we moved from classroom to work bays for hands-on training, each "hook" was assigned a bay, and we saw our first Mk 28. Our trainer was configured like the Palomares bomb, and, when looking at it, I had difficulty constructing a mental image of its potential in full thermonuclear (TN) mode. The "Fat Man" type spark plug alone could produce a massively destructive blast exceeding the results that we had seen in various training films, including those showing Hiroshima and Nagasaki destruction. To think that such potential was just the trigger of the TN package, itself more than three times the yield of "Fat Man" but used to initiate a blast seventy-three times greater than Nagasaki, took some time to put into perspective.

Our training taught nuclear weapon destructive potential as surface area effects per megaton of near surface air burst; everything within a diameter of two miles would be obliterated with a blast wave and fire storm from there out to ten miles in diameter leaving massive destruction from there on another five miles around, obliteration to massive destruction eleven miles around from ground zero. A circle of destruction twenty-two miles across for each megaton could "take out" the center of any city. That phrase, "take out," was commonly used within the realm of nuclear Armageddon, and we were its trainees. As a measure to better understand such weapon potential, I recognized that one megaton was sufficient to "take out" all of Albuquerque, just one bomb, and the Mk 28 had forty-five percent more potential than a single megaton. Its spark plug alone was sufficient to destroy most of Albuquerque, and that igniter simply lit off a far bigger blast from within the same bomb. The dial-a-yield concept illustrated that warhead capability could be turned on or off even though all of the weapon was consumed within its nuclear fireball. Why full yield components did not participate in low yield detonation was contained in the various branches of AFF circuitry that had been worked out by the designers and illustrated the exactness required of conditions for nuclear yield.

We learned that the Mk 28 had several yields according to circuit selections, and yield boost was a function of several components that participated in AFF sequences moments before the HE was ignited. Full yield brought all potential into action while partial yield down to lowest yield was also determined by component participation. Various components in each package were used or not used according to a particular yield selection ranging from seventy kilotons up to nearly one and half megatons, a range from three-and-a-half Nagasakis to seventy-two-and-a-half Nagasakis, all from a single package weighing just over twelve hundred pounds. Learning the various configurations and preparing the warhead followed by verification checkouts was the nature of GMT training, and as with all subsequent warhead operations, strict adherence to procedures was maintained along with all activities conducted under the watchful eyes of our instructors, highly trained GMTs themselves. This introductory schooling was the mode I experienced throughout the remainder of my GMT years, strict oversight of work, attention to details, careful record keeping and accounting, and work always conducted in pairs.

Because I was from North Carolina and had been through the town, the most disturbing lost H-bomb incident I learned about took place in Goldsboro, the town along the route to the beach that Mary and I had been on a time or two prior to military service. Goldsboro came the nearest to nuclear holocaust of any of the accidents discussed in our training. Like Palomares, an in-flight collision began the sequence of events that produced very different effects between the two H-bombs carried onboard. One left the wreckage in freefall and slammed into the soft, marshy land belonging to a farmer near Goldsboro. The friction of its path through the earth stripped the weapon from outside in, and with the core's small size and massive weight, it simply kept going. The recovery team tried everything they could to recover the core, but the moisture laden soil increasingly inhibited going deeper. Finally, having purchased the land from the farmer, the hole was filled with concrete and the area surrounded by fences to be kept off-limits ever since.

The second warhead posed the most troubling sequence of events. Somehow, the collision produced the correct firing signal, and that H-bomb left the collision on a path toward ignition. The parachute deployed, and the warhead's circuitry sequenced correctly. Each AFF circuit received the proper signals, and at about three thousand feet, the weapon fired, doing exactly what it was designed to do. Were it not for the SEP that was not installed, Goldsboro, North Carolina would hold a very different place in history. Instead, the weapon fell to earth with parachute deployed and was recovered intact. It was studied in detail, and lessons learned were incorporated into future designs. One result was that existing weapons received modifications and alterations to upgrade their safety features, among other improvements, and the Mod and Alt numbers stenciled on the exterior casing told GMTs exactly the configuration of each warhead.

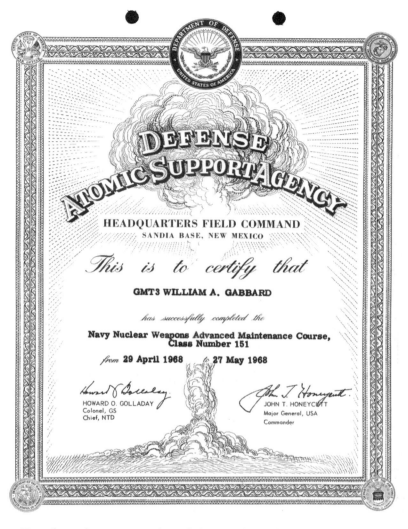

DEPARTMENT OF DEFENSE
UNITED STATES OF AMERICA

DEFENSE ATOMIC SUPPORT AGENCY

HEADQUARTERS FIELD COMMAND
SANDIA BASE, NEW MEXICO

This is to certify that

GMT3 WILLIAM A. GABBARD

has successfully completed the

**Navy Nuclear Weapons Advanced Maintenance Course,
Class Number 151**

from **29 April 1968** *to* **27 May 1968**

HOWARD O. GOLLADAY
Colonel, GS
Chief, NTD

JOHN T. HONEYCUTT
Major General, USA
Commander

Based on demonstrated proficiency, the individual named on this certificate is currently qualified to perform depot level maintenance for the following weapons pursuant to the series of the Joint Atomic Weapons Publications (JAWP) shown beside each weapon: W28-1A, W30-1A, W34-1, B43-1A, W44-1A, W45-1A, B57-1A, W55-1A, and B61-1A.

H. G. Cleland
CDR, USN
Chief, Navy Weapons Division
Nuclear Weapons Directorate

Chapter 10

DASA

While in basic training and having to choose among the Navy's billets, I learned about what I recall to have been the Aviation Cadet program for training pilots to fly WW-II era propeller driven fighters, such as the F4U Corsair. The purpose for bringing back such old planes in the jet era was to provide close-in support for troops on the ground. Although intrigued by the prospects of flying such legendary aircraft, I wondered about the sanity of going to war with antique fighters in the modern world of intense ground fire, such things as rapid fire small bore cannon, shoulder launched rockets and grenades, high tech surface-to-air missiles, and all sorts of modern armaments that did not exist when the Corsair was a mighty plane. After recalling my decision to avoid flying Huey Cobras over Viet Nam's jungles, it was just a small step to conclude the same about propeller driven fighters, and I did not pursue that option, if in fact it actually existed.

I did entertain the prospects of volunteering for Underwater Demolition Teams, the UDT, frogmen, what became the famed Navy Seals. Although the challenge of demonstrating physical excellence as an extension of my ability to swim fast and to hold my breath underwater for long periods of time, I just could not escape the nagging notion that the rest of my life after the Navy would be better spent with training having long-term benefits rather than short term gratification. That notion was, perhaps, the basis of my initial encounter with a moral decision about continuing as a GMT. That decision made and in Phase II of A-School, I was committed, and like those branches of the military that the public sees as highly trained "gung ho" young men with a get-it-done attitude, I was determined to be the best GMT that I could be while recognizing that I would remain thereafter in the shadows of Cold War politics. The public knew that people like me and my fellow GMTs existed, but without exposure, we were the silent, unrecognized warriors of secrecy. Whatever doubts I had were tucked away more firmly each day as I was exposed to, and entrusted with, more and more warheads and nuclear weapon secrets. Among many fascinating aspects of our training was explosives school.

Firecrackers had been my biggest bang as a country boy back in the North Carolina hills, and I never imagined in college what the next few years would bring. Consequently, I was continually in a state of awe as training introduced me to progressively bigger bangs, up to the biggest bang yet conceived by man. Initiation of nuclear reactions began with high explosives, and explosives school was my introduction to their effects. Conducted in the desert south of Albuquerque, Explosive Ordinance Disposal (EOD) teams were our instructors who began our training with demonstrations.

The blue sky and bright sun over the arid range on our first day was another in our gloriously continuing New Mexico summer. First came the explosives and signal generators to ignite them, then wiring, primer cord, TNT, Boracitol, Cyclotol, RDX, PB-RDX, C4, Cyclonite and others. Charges were set to demonstrate the effects of different explosives and to demonstrate the effects of different configurations. Ignitor cap use and care were major points of discussion because they were handled near the body by hands that would be lost in any discharge, accidental or intended. Proper handling of ignitors ranged from proper selection for the explosive to careful installation. Modern high explosives such as C4 and PB-RDX were quite insensitive to handling and could be shaped like clay. When a cap was embedded, lighting off the charge demonstrated the effects of how the HE was shaped and what the blast could do when it was focused.

Comparing the effects of two equal quantities from a blob of clay on a concrete wall to a shaped charge was startling. The blob made a big bang but produced little damage while the same amount of charge packed into a metal tube focused the blast sufficiently to penetrate the concrete leaving another hole in the structure. Our instructors had done this demonstration before, and showing the effect of shaped charges as a fundamental aspect of nuclear weaponry was instructive.

A length of primer cord stretched between two posts looked like a clothesline, but its length was immaterial; primer cord burned so fast, about 24,000 feet per second, that lighting off one end ignited the other end with no perceptible delay. The entire length went up in smoke with a sharp *CRACK!* In another demo, a couple of laps of primer cord around a post about the diameter of a telephone pole was a use that I was aware of from WW-II movies. A twist of the handle on the electrical signal generator ignited the primer cord that cut through the post in one blast, the same technique for felling trees that I had seen in those old movies. The utility of explosive ditch digging was also demonstrated; a line of charges set in the earth and discharged in rapid sequence laid the dirt over in an instant leaving a nicely formed ditch with its fill dirt deposited on one side.

All sorts of HE were used for training that also rid the store of excess or obsolete explosives, including a number of shaped charges from warheads. Later in my GMT duties that involved further explosives training, various charges were set and detonated. The largest was half of a Mk 28 HE sphere, something over ninety pounds that produced a thunderous blast that sent debris skyward from the earthen depression it was set in. That reach for the sky wasn't like typical bomb bursts that scattered debris upward and in all directions around; this blast shot up in a sharply directed plume that had little scatterings surrounding it, a focused shaped charge.

School was over around four in the afternoon each day, and when I didn't have evening or night duty, Mary and I were off seeing the sights. While being as touristy as we could be, I often wondered if she had any inkling of what I was doing. One day, we happened by the Sandia Base US Army Headquarters buildings, and there by the main building with wide granite steps, each on it own plinth, sat "Little Boy" and "Fat Man." They were just the outer shapes of the weapons with their names on information plaques, and Mary knew without doubt what I was doing, although we never talked of details.

While looking at these mockup A-bombs, I also learned something I had not recognized before. The small sign by the steps into the building read, "Field Headquarters Defense Atomic Support Agency" and another piece of the mystery fell into place when I pieced it together with our injunctions against wearing Navy uniforms when in public and saying anything about being in the Navy. "What's a sailor doing in the desert?" was the sort of question to avoid, a question that led to others that delved deeper and deeper into the goings-on within the Sandia-Kirtland-Monzano complex that, no doubt, had produced rumor after rumor reaching every ear, rumors always tainted with clandestine government operations of the Area-51 sort including flying saucers and aliens. Sailors in the desert was a curiosity I thought rather strange when told of that secret door in the desert, and when we were told that Central Intelligence Division operatives were throughout the area listening and watching, admonishments were taken seriously. One case involved a sailor being arrested for answering an inquiry saying, "You've heard of flying saucers. Well, we make the cups for them." The arrest was to quell ANY contribution, even whimsical, beyond the area's cloak of secrecy.

Back in Great Lakes training, such ideas were exciting, and when standing in the desert before that sign, I put DASA together with all the hush-hush and repeated admonishments against even mentioning being a sailor, and another aspect of life in the secrecy fog began to emerge. I had joined the Navy, and I wore Navy uniforms while within the confines of official duties, but I was detailed to another government agency that wanted no public display of Navy-ness at all.

When I thought about "agency" as in CIA, I recognized DASA to be another separate entity within the government, the military's nuclear weapons service that was equally cloaked in secrecy, one that was a direct response to "We will bury you!" That response was to find young men newly inducted into the military who fit a particular personality profile that background investigations confirmed. The fact that I was standing in front of the headquarters building of an agency that I had never heard of, a member of its organization and did not know it, was a lesson in how the military worked on matters of high security. I recognized that, somewhere within that building, my name appeared on official documents that were examined and controlled by people I would never know. Their decisions determined my destiny, and as long as I performed as planned and conformed as required, my name did not stand out as needing further scrutiny. I recognized "big brother" for the first time. That recognition also took some time to mature into the realization that, for the rest of my life, I was to be watched by unseen eyes to determine if my performance and conformance strayed from the requirements for retaining a Top Secret security clearance with in-depth knowledge of advanced weaponry for the last line of offense at the edge of nuclear Armageddon.

May and June passed in the glorious Southwestern sun with one nearby adventure after another, both the classified sort while in school and the tourist sort afterward. With each day, Mary and I became progressively more enthralled with New Mexico. However, without a usable spare for our Alpine, we were pinned closer to Albuquerque than we would have liked, but each of my attempts to locate a replacement for the collapsed wire wheel had failed, largely because Sunbeam was a make with fewer dealerships than MG or Triumph, both similarly small British sports cars that we had considered buying prior to selecting the Alpine. Shortly after purchasing the car in Winston-Salem, NC the year before, our dealership closed, and although the much larger dealership in Greensboro was always helpful, the additional distance and inconvenience was a disadvantage that we had not considered. Albuquerque did not have a Sunbeam dealership, and I could find no replacement wheel. So, we were hampered by our unwillingness to travel far without a spare. Every search turned up no replacement or anyone who could repair ours, and as my months of training progressed, I became increasingly concerned about driving back across the US of A without a spare.

I reconciled myself to having to mail order a wheel from the factory, and I wondered if I would have sufficient time in Albuquerque for it to arrive. Well into our stay, I was told of a local enterprise that might have such a thing, Nine Mile Hill Garage. It was located west of Albuquerque on the nine mile long incline to the mesa, a place we had passed several times. I drove in one day thinking that a greasy fingernails garage was certain not to have a Sunbeam-Talbot wire wheel, but when I went inside, I was amazed at the extent of racing hardware, photos and posters all around. This place was big and clearly not just a garage; it was a race shop of high breeding that immediately intrigued me. Stepping up to the parts counter, I told the young parts man what I was looking for and held no hope that he even knew what I was talking about. He went back into the garage and returned in short order with exactly what I was looking for, a brand new wire wheel trued and balanced. I was amazed, and the price wasn't nearly as much as I had anticipated having to pay for a wheel shipped from England.

Looking around further, I asked the parts man about the place. "This is the Unser brother's garage," he said. "You know, the Indy 500 racers."

I didn't know, but I was pleased to actually have been there, now with a purchase in my hand that I would always remember as another adventure.

Santa Fe

The oldest territorial capital in America, although New Mexico was next to last among the contiguous states to join the union.

Chapter 11

Santa Fe

Our first venture to Santa Fe was filled with fascinating discoveries. On a warm and sunny Saturday morning, Mary and I drove north from Albuquerque and discovered dusty Bernalillo. This small town just off the main highway about half way to Santa Fe seemed an unlikely place to settle. No visible farming beyond vegetable gardens and no ranching made me wonder why it existed. The town was, however, situated between two sources of water, perhaps the reason for its location. To the west running southward was the Rio Grande, rather small in its volume but constant; on the east side paralleling the highway and railroad tracks connecting Santa Fe with Albuquerque was a stream. Both sources of water originated in the mountainous north and east and produced greenery along each bank. I thought of Bernalillo as a curiosity but typical of the small-to-tiny towns sprinkled along New Mexico's few water routes. How this town managed to survive was not clear, but what it had to offer was amazing.

We turned off the highway westward, crossed the stream and railroad tracks, then turned right and drove into the heart of town. The broad central street was empty of traffic as we pulled to a stop in front of a line of old west style store-fronts with a sprinkling of cars sitting idle here and there. No other tourists were in sight, and not more than a half-dozen people stirred, mostly on sauntering walks toward their destinations on opposite sides of the street. Boots, blue jeans, checked shirts and cowboy hats set the tone for inhabitants who were in no hurry. The cool morning with its gentle breeze was the time of day for stirring about prior to the heat of the afternoon when sitting in the shade was the thing to do.

As I looked up and down Bernalillo, that breeze whipped up little dust devils that spun round and round, doing their wobbly dance darting hither and yon only to expire and deposit themselves some short distance from where they started. A few trees and their green stood above the town's skyline, mostly along the Rio Grande and the stream, and store fronts with broad glass windows were straight out of western movies. Everything had a dusty earthtone look, construction of aged lumber with its grey patina, deteriorating lettering on doors and windows, faded images on signs and hightop storefronts. As Mary and I strolled along the covered walkway, our steps making that hollow sound of walking on boards, we passed through rustic construction that made me wonder of Bernalillo's age, or was it the setting where some western saga was filmed and continued a tenuous survival since?

We went inside one of the stores to discover that the line of them facing east were connected and ran together into a long interior expanse filled with more southwestern and native crafts than we thought could possibly exist in one place. I was amazed at the quantity of brightly colored handwoven blankets and rugs, magnificent pottery in an astounding array of styles and types, ingeniously hand laced decorative baskets by the dozens, beautifully crafted sand paintings - an art form that I did not know existed. Among the huge array of fine quality paintings and drawings of southwest motifs and native life sat old photographs by the box full, along with marvelously crafted woodwork. Displayed around the place was equally finely crafted silver and turquoise jewelry filling glass-enclosed counters throughout the store, along with leatherwork from silver-tipped bolos to tooled saddles. We discovered many new worlds of New Mexico in this dusty old store.

When talking with the proprietor, an aging lady whose life interests displayed all around indicated her dedication to the artisans whose handiwork she sold at little profit, I learned that native Indians had few outlets for their work and little means of earning an income in any other form. She mentioned several Pueblos nearby with artisans that she knew by name, the Sandia Indian Reservation just south of town, the Santa Ana and San Felipe Pueblos just to the west and north, and the Santo Domingo and Zia Pueblos further northward along with the Santa Ana Indian Reservation. I then realized that Bernalillo was the trading hub for the area and provided what little contact the Indians had to the wealth of the nation far away.

As a tourist, I knew little of the realities of native life and saw it all simply as settings that invited me to visit. I did not recognize until additional outings educated me further that the enchanting terrain only tenuously supported life to just marginally above subsistence with few opportunities beyond selling of hand crafted goods. I was impressed with the collection on display, truly remarkable in its range and extent, thousands upon thousands of individually crafted products waiting for tourists to stop and buy them. But in dusty, off-the-beaten-path Bernalillo, New Mexico? In time, I gained a much better appreciation for the area's slow pace of life when I pieced together the bigger picture of the town lying along pathways long trodden by foot and hoof. I was a child of the automobile age, with machines that enabled me to go great distances in short spans of time. Bernalillo was a place that time seemed to have forgotten, a different world running on a much slower clock. Inside the store we visited were the life works of countless artisans who were, for the most part, anonymous.

Just before leaving town, I stood by our Alpine and imagined the street around me without the few cars sitting here and there, with only horses tied to hitching posts, and those few residents walking about to be cowboys; Bernalillo was a step back into the previous century, a rare experience in the fast paced, high tech world that I came from, even Appalachian back woods. Mary and I happened by this treasure trove of New Mexico on our way to Santa Fe, a destination known worldwide, but Bernalillo was completely unknown to us. We stopped only because it was close to the highway on the way to Santa Fe, and I wondered if any tourist intentionally came to Bernalillo, reasoning that only those who had previously discovered this wonder of New Mexico would make it a destination.

Unlike other tourist stops that, for the most part, sold knick-knacks, a walk among the rooms of the store and its enormous collection housed within old wooden walls, floors that creaked when walked on, doors that squeaked when opened and closed, and a dustiness characteristic of desert life, existed a museum of southwestern lore, and every piece of it was for sale. With our ambitions to purchase all sorts of things limited by little cash on hand and a day of travels ahead of us to our intended destination and return, Mary and I confined ourselves to looking things over and took home only memories.

Bernalillo was our introduction to the real New Mexico, gateway to increasing remoteness the further north we went, of terrain that varied from pleasantly green valleys where water flowed to forests girding inhospitable mountains of spectacular grandeur, to fantastic gorges and expansive caldera of extinct volcanos. Roads were few and far between but every one a drive through desert-to-mountain scenery displaying the last remnants of springtime blooms, colors that melded perfectly with the rich blue of the sky and its brilliantly white clouds floating lazily along to far horizons of eroded cliffs and mesas of reds and yellows and sandy tones visible for miles in every direction. This was Conquistador territory with remnants of 16th century heritage sprinkled among Spanish speaking towns and Spanish place names almost everywhere we turned.

All roads seemed to focus on Santa Fe for a reason: this modern city with its heart determined to continue its Spanish heritage by not permitting a hint of modern highrise architecture to spoil its skyline has been, from its inception, the hub of the entire Spanish holdings of the southwest, the capital under four flags, Spain, Mexico, CSA and USA. And here, much of its past remained for citizen and tourist alike; fascinating adobe construction nearly as old as the first steps made by Europeans into this land melded into modern lifestyles of new adobe showing Spanish, Indian and Anglo influences. Santa Fe had long been a melting pot of cultures and a living museum of real people whose respect for their heritage did not encourage change from its wonders.

On our first stroll through Santa Fe, we were introduced to different ways of living that I found particularly appealing. For these reasons, Santa Fe remains unique among all the places in America I have seen, a quietly vibrant city with a special character molded by a clear vision of its past, its future, and not the slightest inclination to become overwhelmed with the modern. The slow pace of life here gave time to breathe, to stroll among America's oldest habitation and gather perspectives from long past melded with ancient legacies maintained. We could absorb only the merest hints of the reverence that the residents of Santa Fe felt for their city and surroundings. To stand in the shade of its riverside trees along the Santa Fe Trail as others before us have, Anasazi and Indian, wagonmasters and pioneers, mountain men, Spanish, Mexican, and New Mexican alike, is to be surrounded with history and culture heaping with visual imagery. The city sits among earthern hues of the high desert out to distant vistas bathed by the glorious sun and maintains hidden gardens within. To stroll along Canyon Road is to gather a sense of its permanence and its transience, then to watch another majestic sunset close another day tells us that all who came before us saw this repeating pagentry in this timeless land of natural beauty, pure New Mexico. I quickly concluded that Santa Fe was Albuquerque's Old Town on a grand scale, not just one plaza and its surroundings, but an entire city with its "new" sculpted among its "old" in perfect harmony unseen anywhere else.

Such combinations as a Star of David over the entrance to Santa Fe's Catholic church of Bishop Lamy told of the area's melding of beliefs and lifestyles, tolerance and acceptance, and the willingness of its people to gather and enjoy that special atmosphere that is Santa Fe. Our first day wandering the old byways of Santa Fe was one adventure after another; the oldest church in America, the oldest house, the oldest street, the territorial governor's rustic home from a time long before New Mexico became a US state, and among those who had lived here was Gen. Lew Wallace of Civil War fame, author of *Ben Hur*. All of the city's storied history set in the foothills of the Sangre de Cristo Mountains is laced with Spanish and Indian heritage that preceded Santa Fe's founding in 1610. From that date, a continual lineage of people came, some to settle, others just passing through to today's throngs of visitors. Like many before and after me, I recognized the magic of this place: dry, sunny, beautiful and somehow other-worldly.

At the San Miguel Mission church, we saw the stand-alone staircase that should not be standing, then tried to make out the fading images of religious scenes painted on buffalo leather hides that hung along its high adobe walls. Outside, I noticed that low on one of the thick front doors were the letters, B T, carved incongruously into the wood, the legacy of Bill Tate told in an earlier chapter. When I inquired, no one knew their origin, and it would be more than a decade before I learned their very human nature from the man, a boy then, who carved his legacy into the outside of the mission's door while the sacraments were spoken on the other side.

At the much larger and more stately Catholic church built of stone, the same bearing the Star of David, I learned of further human connections: its Archbishop Lamy was the inspiration for Archbishop Jean Marie Latour in Willa Cather's novel, *Death Comes to the Archbishop*. The church was, from its beginning, the focus of the Royal City of the Holy Faith of Saint Francis (La Villa Real de la Santa Fe de San Francisco). With religious reverence permeating daily life, and the spirit of festival renewed annually by banishing the Zozobra (Old Man Gloom), Santa Fe lives its heritage and invites everyone to join its fiestas.

Canyon Road, the pre-Spanish route eastward to Pecos Pueblo, was lined with small homes converted into shops and studios by artists and artisans who called this ancient route home, among them Bill Tate, as told earlier, a native New Mexican, artist, writer and philosopher whom I got to know and who provided so much insight into living the New Mexico life.

On this stroll, our first along Santa Fe streets, Mary and I meandered here and there in the day's warmth, enjoying the cool breezes and shade we came to while soaking in the captivating beauty and picturesque scenes, and, along the way, Canyon Road began to take on broader implications. I sensed what was meant by Santa Fe's slogan, "One visit is not enough," and I recognized why artists continue to be drawn to it and come to stay. I did not want to leave, although knowing that our outing would be followed by more. We returned to Santa Fe later, among all sorts of other destinations that called from all directions, and always found it inviting.

Our walk around town took us under the canopy of shade trees overhanging the Santa Fe River in a park where wagon trains heading to California once stopped. Imagining what those days were like, I sensed that this site was just an introduction to abundant adventures everywhere we looked. This quiet and unassuming city has purposely grown into a cultural center of the southwest by living its past.

If time had permitted us to venture into the natural beauty of surroundings, the marvelous "outdoors" northward to Truchas and Taos, Bill Tate's favorite country, or into the Rio Grande Gorge, or in any other direction, we were sure to find adventures far too numerous for our limited summertime discovery of New Mexico. Beyond Santa Fe lay pueblos that preserved the region's Indian cultures with their own expressions in dance and celebration that I learned was going on somewhere almost every day, celebrations that we could find neither the time nor the money to attend.

On our first Santa Fe visit, a time before my discovery of the Unser Brother's Garage and purchase of a new wheel for our Alpine, we were without a spare, and my increasing concern about finding a replacement shaded every thought of driving somewhere. Even so, we ventured where we were comfortable and were richly rewarded. If only I had made the Nine Mile Hill discovery when first arriving in Albuquerque, we would have solved our spare tire problem and added more adventures further along Route 66 and to points branching off further north and south.

Chapter 12

Wind and Rain

Our summertime in New Mexico was a page out of the Wonders of the World for Mary and me, day after day of magnificent weather highlighted by blue skies and lots of sunshine, until a dark mass loomed on the horizon one day. Boiling up from the desert and riding on the wind came a vast cloud of sand, our first sand storm. We knew of nothing like it and had no knowledge of what to do, so our preparations were simply closing doors and windows. The wind wailed and blew into every crack and crevice as the dark mass rolled over Albuquerque and on into the desert leaving behind all of those cracks and crevices filled with the gritty dust of the desert.

As I thought about this new experience, I recalled watching the dance of the dust devils in the streets of Bernalillo, among many others seen in this arid region, and I recognized that those little whirlies were just fleeting whimsies of what nature had called up in a big way and sent toward us, a massive whirlwind that left remnants of its presence everywhere in its wake. This giant was not at all whimsical as it swept across the desert, testimony to the wiles of living in the southwest. The wind and sand it brought gave me a new appreciation for what John Steinbeck wrote about in *The Grapes of Wrath*. In that story, farmers saw the topsoil they depended on simply blow away and ravaged crops left behind ended any prospects of getting by. So the Oakies packed their family cars with whatever they could and headed for California, away from the dust bowl. I now understood better why they left everything behind in search of better lives in a more rewarding climate, making their way along Route 66 through Albuquerque, the very route Mary and I spent our summer exploring.

The cracks and crevices in what we thought were tight closures were filled with the most annoyingly fine sand that we had ever seen. It blew into places that we never expected, under and around windows and doors, and even left a fine deposit in the tub. How sand got there remains a mystery but showed what wind-driven dust can do. Even after thorough cleaning and re-cleaning, our apartment yielded unexpected surprises in the most unlikely places, fine grit that we could feel but could not see. Thorough vacuuming did not get it all as sand turned up here and there for days after return to blue skies and sunshine. Carpet near windows and doors offered up deeply embedded sand for weeks, and drapes drifted dust every time they were moved requiring vacuuming and washing until finally free of sand dust.

I knew from leaks while driving in the rain that our Alpine would have sand everywhere inside, and a layer of dust had sifted through and lay on the interior, none of it a surprise. But as I ran my finger through it to reveal the black seating upholstery underneath, I shook my head with disbelief at how much had gotten around rolled up windows. Lengthy vacuuming, cleaning and vacuuming again finally removed it. The blowing sand did not damage the paint or leave any visible effects other than fine grit everywhere. But that grit required hours to remove with surprises remaining in hard-to-reach areas from then on. Years later, I found sand in the wells beneath the gas tanks in each rear fender and knew exactly were it came from. Once again, I marveled at how it got there.

We soon learned that the dry, swirling behemoth of the desert had its counterpart in too much rain. When rain came it was always welcome, and the occasional storm was either a repeat of the race we had with that first rain cloud we encountered on our way to Albuquerque, or the entire sky was dark and threatening with bolts of lightening flashing across it in an immense display of nature's fireworks orchestrated with wind and torrents of rain. Back home in the Appalachians, rain wasn't at all like the fascinating southwest variety. Unlike individual clouds that deposited their moisture along a swath of earth below as often seen in the desert, my eastern variety was most often from densely overcast skies that gave us dizzles to boomers amid lingering cloud masses that often lasted for days. In the desert, the clouds and their moisture came and went with the suddenness of a new scene of a play, and like the contrasts of dry and wet, the contrasts of sunshine and dark clouds were just part of what made New Mexico so enchanting. Heavy rain was, however, a major problem for Albuquerque.

On our drives through the city, I noticed that almost every major street crossed large concrete culverts at some point, and only trickles of water ran in their bottoms. I wondered about their much oversized dimensions as clearly more than required to handle the streams feeding them until driving along after a storm one day. Crossing a culvert filled with raging mud water, the wash of the desert brought by a deluge that would have, without the culverts, flooded Albuquerque with seething goo, I was both surprised and instructed about proper planning. I had not recognized the importance of the culvert system until after seeing the rush of water crashing its way out of the hills in its mindless quest for peaceful settling somewhere.

I remembered my play while a boy when I built all sorts of dams across streams that often occupied my time while in the woods. My construction provided an overflow and a routing of flow to further my imagination. A row of tomato paste cans with top and bottom removed made a pipe through the dam that carried a stream of water, and I envisioned water wheels turning in the streams, probably inspired by the wooden dam across the Mitchell River at the bottom of

Burch Hill near the community where I grew into manhood. That dam backed up river water for mill grinding, but the mill had burned long ago, its foundation all that remained. All of the boys of Little Richmond played in the river among the slippery wooden beams of what remained of the dam. Its simple construction of massive triangles set repeatedly about four feet apart across the river with thick boards secured along their slope down to the narrow ends buried in the river bottom up stream made a fascinating but tricky place to play along an ancient rock outcropping washed over by the river for eons. Whoever built the dam and mill spent a lot of time and effort in construction, the site then becoming a focal point of the community.

My dams were simpler, constructed of available stone, mud and moss, and, when one broke, the rush of massed water set free washed over everything downstream until exhausting itself. I recognized that my boyhood quest to harness streams for fun was the same quest that Albuquerque's planners set upon by necessity, to control the wild and raging flash flood waters produced by desert storms. That was a standout lesson long remembered; planning and proper execution produce long term benefits.

Water caused a range of problems in the southwest, from too much to too little. Although I had been educated about too much when spring rains swelled and flooded the Mitchell River far beyond its banks, then Albuquerque's control of flooding, too little water gradually emerged as a long time southwest problem that Mary and I had never known.

To the east of Albuquerque along upward rising slopes of the Sangre de Christo Mountains, a water rights dispute erupted between neighboring ranchers one day when one decided to dam up a stream. I had never questioned my dam building, but his doing so to fill his reservoir reduced water flow to the ranchers down stream. Perhaps thinking that each of them could benefit from their own reservoirs, fed sequentially from higher to lower terrain, the first to do so caused a near riot of gun wielding magnitude. If he had gotten his reservoir filled, water flow would continue as before, but the time with reduced water downstream was too much for his neighbors to bear in the daily need for water. Their dispute made headline news, but being from the temperate forest of the Appalachians, I had no appreciation for just how volatile the issue of water was for people in this dry region.

Mary and I were simply enjoying our summer in New Mexico and remained naive to its challenges, a beautiful region that fascinated us to no end. On a drive up to Sandia Peak during another superb day, we came upon new views of breathtaking magnitude. What we knew were undulating Appalachian forests cast in different hues of blue from ridge to ridge, thus the Blue Ridge Mountains, and foggy mornings with days of smokey hues, the Smokey Mountains, and included spring time greens to vibrant fall colors, very different from the arid Southwestern terrain and its clear view to the horizon all around. Our first sunset seen from the Peak was nearly indescribable.

The ruggedness of the mostly barren southwest revealed the earth as it had been shaped over millennia with only scrub greenery offering any change. As a boy, I had played in mud washes in which tiny rivulets of water cut through the soft soil on their meandering way to larger pools. From Sandia Peak I saw the same sort of terrain, only on earth scale rather than mud hole scale. The similarity was striking and spoke of water long ago cutting through the soil and rock, pooling in low places, then drying away leaving parched earth behind, just what we saw in vivid colors of earthy reds to sandy tones all around. On this day, as the sun settled slowly in the west, the view of Albuquerque in the valley below was breathtaking, and I imagined a time far back when the valley was filled with water that nourished both forest and beasts around it, perhaps including barefoot humans on their perpetual hunt for food, foot prints long ago blown away in the wind.

Both Appalachian and New Mexican terrain displayed a timeless aura, but while my eastern experience was one of soothing comfort in soft forests with plentiful water, where sunlight through the forest canopy made bright, nearly spiritual beams falling upon the moist floor making patchworks of light, the brilliantly sunlit southwest fired my imagination with harsh realities of survival on the fringes of moisture, a dry and unforgiving land. But what a land! Our first sunset from Sandia Peak was unforgettable: Albuquerque slipped into darkness highlighted increasingly by its sparkling lights, with the flat mesa beyond the city to the west bathed in rich reds of softening sunlight from the horizon, then the sky going to hues of darkening blues and purples and the white of clouds highlighted with shadowed grey outlines against a background of increasing darkness. Their undersides were the day's glorious finale; lit up with vibrantly blazing oranges fading to deep reds against a background of deepening blue was beyond anything we had ever seen, and Mary and I watched the spectacle unable to utter a sound.

The scene was breathtaking, but I was thinking along different lines. The sun settling on the horizon, fattening and reddening and growing dimmer as it slowly dipped out of sight, the uppermost part of its disk shimmering in atmospheric refraction as it slid behind the horizon, that shimmer becoming a slivered fragment of red that separated and settled after the sun's disk was out of sight, then slowly vanished as well, had been repeated over and over throughout the vast reaches of earth time. That one slow sunset before us, first the fireball of the sun quietly dropping to the horizon, was the model of thermonuclear physics that I was training on, although each warhead could produce only an insignificant portion of what was going on in the sun all the time. The same processes were reproduced in the instant of ignition within the fusion portions of the Mk 28 or Mk 43 or Mk 53 or Mk 57 or Mk 61 or other warheads I trained on. The beauty of this Sandia Peak sunset was the sort of natural wonder that had focused the intelligence of inquiring minds for eons, but just a few decades earlier, the physics of the sun's energy was first postulated giving the principles of thermonuclear fusion, principles accounting for the sun's glow and showing that hydrogen isotopes forced together perpetually in the sun were the same that, compressed for just an instant, could produce a blinding white flash that unleashed great quantities of energy from devices designed for massive destruction.

While standing on Sandia Peak bathed in the rich, warm light of a magnificent sunset that had repeated itself every day since the beginning of time, then thinking of just how small a portion of its total emitted light my body intersected, I came to a much better appreciation for the prodigious quantities of energy that poured from the sun all the time, although just a modest star among the vast reaches of space strewn with stars in great variety and in uncountable numbers. Remembering the sunburns that prolonged exposure produced on my skin, I also came to better appreciate the enormity of destruction available in tiny quantities of similar fuel within each warhead I worked on that could evaporate everyone within its fireball. By learning how both the sun and warheads worked and insuring that the latter would ignite when called upon to do so, I recognized that the natural processes continually going on in the sun that produced the great spectacle of magnificent sunsets had been harnessed in nuclear weapons to mankind's peril, the understanding of both having been produced in the halls of Twentieth Century physics, halls that I would wander for the rest of my life.

Wind and rain and southwest adventures in New Mexico's gloriously enchanting spectacles of sun and terrain were memory-making exploits for Mary and me. Even with all we did, so much was left unseen and undone because we simply had neither the time nor the money to take full advantage of everything available, and I came to realize that to fulfill the wonder I felt for this land and its people, I would have to live it.

We often talked about moving back to Albuquerque, although Los Alamos was the most likely location for the sorts of scientific interests I wanted to pursue. When looking the place over, we found that laboratory town and surrounding bedroom communities completely uninviting with cost of living well into the California index. Albuquerque was more livable and much more interesting, and I wondered if the Sandia complex that I came to know well might offer other employment options that would bring us back to Albuquerque.

The Sandia complex had originally been "Z" Division of the Los Alamos World War-II A-bomb project that was established in Albuquerque when a weapon assembly site closer to Alamagordo was needed. By the time I walked its corridors and learned its mission, the facilities were a separate entity, and I wondered about working there as a way of living in the southwest. But doing so was integral to my philosophical problems with the training I was receiving, followed by my years of DASA association that gave me time to think about my future. After a Los Alamos interview and much discussion, Mary and I decided not to pursue either and never fulfilled our interests in living the southwest life.

Even so, our memorable excursions along Route 66 and throughout northern New Mexico remain favorite recollections, especially our frequent evening strolls in romantic Old Town, the heart of Albuquerque.

Chapter 13

Old Town

A little corner of the now-sprawling metropolis of Albuquerque is Old Town, founded in 1706 by Don Francisco Cuervo y Valdez. Valdez and the few Spanish families he brought with him soon planted the romantic roots of their European culture in this rich land by the fabled Rio Grande River. A new landmark in the New World was born as a farming village and military outpost along the Camino Real between Chihuahua and Santa Fe. Provincial Governor Valdez named the villa in honor of the Viceroy of New Spain, the Duke of Alburquerque. In the early 1800s the first "r" was dropped from the official spelling. They built their village in the Spanish tradition of a central plaza surrounded by the church, government buildings, homes and businesses. Across time, four national flags were to fly over Old Town, Spain, Mexico, the Stars and Bars and the Stars and Stripes, and each left its legacy making Old Town the focus of Albuquerque's heritage.

Old Town grew slowly during its first century and was plagued by pestilence and Indian raids. But the village continued to increase in importance as a trading center for corn, squash, beans and other produce, as well as handwoven cloth and blankets, and shoes and durables made from cow and buffalo hide. Such trading and commerce were important in those early days of village life, but the real center of activity in Old Town was San Felipe de Neri Catholic Church, which hadn't missed a single service for more than 250 years by 1967. Its sand-colored adobe walls rose from the earth to smooth contours that are soothing to the eye and lend an atmosphere of quiet contemplation to the structure and to Old Town. In 1880 when the railroad came to the Rio Grande, tracks were laid a few miles east of Old Town, and the area around the depot, called New Town, boomed to become Albuquerque, eventually to grow into a metropolis engulfing Old Town.

By the time of our visits, ox-drawn *carretas* no longer rattled through the streets of Old Town, but cobblestone, adobe and wood still echoed the foot-tapping music once enjoyed by those who stopped to stay a while. Collected treasures of the centuries remain in modern form; quaint shops filled with fine Indian and Mexican jewelry, candles, pottery, arts and crafts. Quiet, hidden patios, winding brick alleys with profusions of flowers, and an inviting openness that beckoned peeks into every corner. Gardens and balconies were delightful discoveries. Benches and bancos (adobe benches) invited a stop to sit awhile in the shade, take time to breath the fresh, cool air, and reinvigorate in old world style. Old Town, on the banks of the Rio Grande, the holy river of the local Indians, once garrisoned soldiers in the rambling Armijo home that still serves the aromatic foods of timeless New Mexico.

Known as the La Placita Dining Rooms, this beautiful old hacienda was for generations the property of the Armijo family that was prominent in the history and politics of the town and territory. Nothing was spared by the Armijos to make their *casa* one of the most gracious centers of social activity in the Southwest. The balls given by Don Ambrosio Armijo for the young people of the time were splendid, and for the wedding of one of his daughters, he added a second floor reached by a staircase the length of her wedding train.

The thick adobe walls, deep-set windows, the patio (enclosing a great tree growing through its roof) are typical of an early *rico* home. Each of La Placita's six dining rooms has been beautifully restored, offering a charming background for the exceptional collection of regional paintings displayed on the walls.

From La Placita's kitchens, the sweet, homespun aromas of the centuries is one of chile rellenos (stuffed green chili with cheese), enchiladas, tacos and tamales, all echoing recipes of the past. Of all New Mexico culinary treasures, chile is the flavor of choice in a great variety of delectable dishes that are not complete until followed by delicate sugar and spice sopapillas. Chile exists in two forms, red and green, and lovers of each still argue their choice to be the best with innumerable examples of good taste. I had difficulty eating either.

Sitting in the quiet atmosphere of the La Placita, Mary and I savored the ambience of Old Town's Spanish southwest hacienda life, then counted our small change to insure that we could cover the cost, an expensive outing for my feeble income as a sailor. We managed and came away with another favorite memory, then ventured back a few times before leaving Albuquerque.

As my departure date approached, we talked about where my next duty station might be and turned attention increasingly to holding on to cash for travel. Meanwhile, the problem of our Alpine's broken spare nagged us even though a replacement wheel was in Albuquerque all the time we were there. Had I simply stopped at the Nine Mile Hill Garage on one of our many excursions by the sprawling complex and bought the spare, we would not have been so limited. But then, once learning of the Unser's racing, would I have spent more time there, perhaps getting acquainted with them, at the expense of traveling, spending evenings and weekends around racing cars? Tough call.

Lack of a spare had not kept us from nearby Old Town, and we thoroughly enjoyed each stroll and occasional visit to our favorite dining room. But to this day, I still wonder how I missed the Unser brothers' garage until late in my tour of duty. Years later, I wrote a book on Indy racing that included much of their successes. I had been where they began.

Chapter 14

On the Road Again

As our New Mexico summer came to an end, Mary and I had many new and fascinating adventures to talk about, and we looked forward to traveling new roads. Having finished training and received all the security clearances necessary to become a hands-on Cold War operative with advanced weaponry, my new orders brought assignment for two years to Clarksville Base in Tennessee. Having long since discounted the "secret door in the desert" thesis as coming from the uninformed backed by active imaginations, the fact that the location of Clarksville Base was not so clear to senior GMTs returned me to the mode of our arrival in Albuquerque; once in Clarksville, I would ask a local for directions to another Top Secret base. Whether or not my seniors simply continued the secrecy inherent in work with H-bombs or actually did not know the location of Clarksville Base, the result was the same to me.

Since I was not going to sea, Mary and I looked forward to continued travels together, and, once again, we loaded our Alpine for a destination that I would have to find. Saying our farewells to Sandia Base and friends, we pointed our little red sports car back onto Route 66 early the morning of July 18, 1967 to retrace our path of several months earlier, back through familiar terrain but without the high degree of anticipation and wonder held during our previous drive in the opposite direction. A colorful sunrise greeted our new day by the time we made Moriarty, and passing by the Longhorn Ranch prior to its waking gave me a sense of the "ghost town" it was to become when Interstate 40 passed it by years later. One of my objectives upon arrival in New Mexico was to visit a real ghost town, unfulfilled by the time we drove slowly by the "Ranch," so this last parting was the closest that I came to that goal.

As the morning wore on, the drone of our Alpine's engine added to the growing heat of the summer day, and, even though we wore lightweight clothes, rising afternoon temperatures taught us a new aspect of traveling in a British roadster: no amount of ventilation reduced the "ovens" that our feet lay in. The soles of my tennis shoes melted and stuck to the carpet.

From the cool of our last Albuquerque morning, then watching our last New Mexico sunrise as we drove eastward, across the Texas panhandle in growing heat, then the long turnpikes of Oklahoma, all went well until a careless driver ran us off the turnpike. As with other long drives, we chose not to put the top down because of getting sunburned during the day's travel. Even with all vents open and windows down, the black interior of our Alpine made long distance summer travel a sweltering endeavor.

Along open highway, no speed limits in those days meant that drivers could go as fast as they chose, with the occasional law enforcer concerned only with unsafe driving and assisting the needy along the vast stretches of mostly empty highways and turnpike. With little traffic, mile after mile of flat, hot terrain tended to dull the senses. We had been on the road since early morning, always leaving so that we could watch another sunrise, then slipped into a Texas stupor from the heat and remained lulled into half-consciousness by the monotony of the Oklahoma landscape. Frequent stops to stretch and refresh were necessities. Then, on a long stretch that looked like it would never end, I glanced at the rear view mirror to see a fast-approaching car. I shook myself from my stupor when a police car went by in the left lane at such a speed that the long "fishing pole" radio antenna attached to a rear fender lay bent over straight back. Looking at my speedometer, its needle pointing to just past 85, I estimated that the police car was traveling at twice my speed, maybe 150 mph, without a single light flashing.

Well behind the police car came a new model American cruiser with its windows up; air conditioning. In my sweaty, slowly baking, stuck-to-the-seat, right foot glued to the carpet mode, I decided that MY next car would have air conditioning, too. The car whooshed by as the driver laid down the miles by following the example of the police car, though not as fast, but his companion was not pleased. She was giving him a tongue lashing and finger whipping of the first order, perhaps sufficient for him to slow down. Miles ahead, we caught up with the car, both of its occupants now in a more peaceful mood. Maintaining my speed, I moved over into the inside lane to pass just as the rear of a long haul truck loomed ahead in the distance. Seeing it as well, the driver of the other car decided to move over to pass, too, his big car pushing us onto the dusty median at 85 mph. Laying on the horn, then gripping the steering wheel to keep the car straight, our Alpine simply steered smoothly through the scrub growth as it churned up a rooster tail of Oklahoma dust and debris. Mary, suddenly roused from her stupor, gasped and grasped at anything to hold on to, no doubt envisioning our little red car going end over end to roll into a wreck on the Will Rogers Turnpike.

The advantage of a good handling sports cars lies in its low center of gravity, and keeping my foot off the brake turned the potential disaster into just another story to tell of traveling the southwest. The other driver slammed on his brakes and darted back over into the outside lane just as his companion renewed her tongue lashing and finger whipping. I steered our Alpine back onto the hard surface and looked over at the other driver, his face displaying both surprise and apology, while his companion, impassioned by the intensity of the moment, continued her finger whipping. I waved to indicate all is well and went on, never to see the car again.

Quick gas stops and sandwiches along the way made our trek to St. Louis for a return overnight with my sister, Cookie, and her husband, Ron, a long day's drive. Having made the blast furnace run across the desert, the sweltering humidity of Missouri green made the black interior of our Alpine even hotter and stickier, as if we were sitting on seats of pins, their pricks causing us to frequently squirm to new positions. Along the way, we stopped to dry off as best we could, our backs soaked, and placed towels over the wire mesh cushion seats we had bought in hopes of providing cooler seating. Then, slowing as traffic crowded in and down to a crawl in places, I concluded that I had never been so hot in my life and announced to Mary's sweat-streaked face that the Mississippi River basin in summer was the armpit of the world.

Upon arrival in St. Louis at my sister's air conditioned house, a shower to remove the day's sweat-logged grime and a change into dry clothes stands out in my memory as one of the most refreshing moments of my life. We visited and shared some of our New Mexico adventures while not mentioning why I, a sailor, was assigned to the desert in the first place. With about three weeks of leave to make the transition to Clarksville Base, I planned for us to make it home to North Carolina by way of visiting Berea, Kentucky, then celebrate Mary's birthday at her family home before heading west again. My orders called for reporting to Clarksville Base on 11 August. With the location of the Base unknown to me, somewhere in the Clarksville, Tennessee area, I was somewhat apprehensive about my new assignment.

Back on the road before sunrise again the next morning with our North Carolina homes the objective before sunset, we had a long way to go. Crossing the Mississippi, this time just as the sky donned morning hues in pinks and blues, oranges and reds, with shafts of light piercing the clouds broadcasting the arrival of the new day, we drove toward the rising sun as it peeked over the horizon to slowly grow into a giant red ball brightening the day; morning on the river and my life-long admiration of Mark Twain's writings about riverboats and the Mississippi filled me with a sense of being witness to, and briefly a part of, the flow of time through America's heartland river. We were soon in the Commonwealth of Kentucky, the state of my birth and always a pleasant place for me to be.

Ever since that sunset seen from Sandia Peak and the association I made between the sun and H-bombs, these glorious daily beginnings and endings held additional connotations beyond simply moments of awe-inspiring beauty. I wondered about the physics of the sun's workings, fusion energy on a scale that made the combined yields of all the warheads in the nuclear arsenal I now knew well simply nothing, a mental scale that I have since maintained.

Along our route through Kentucky, little attracted our attention except stops for the necessaries until arriving in Berea, my mother's college town and my hometown. No prettier or more satisfying town could exist anywhere, and because it held so many fond memories for me, I gave Mary a tour. She was attentive, but all of the locations I pointed out were little more than too many new places for her to keep track of. Our Alpine rolled slowly down Elder Hill where friends and I had spent many rollicking hours sledding in winter snow to arrive at the house on the left at the bottom of hill that had once been the Dr. James Chester Gabbard home where I spent some of my early teen years. Diagonally across the street stood the house that I first came home to.

I stopped to reminisce, thinking of times long past, and spent a few quiet moments remembering how things were then, now with houses and streets closely surrounding the Dr. Gabbard house. Moving on, I followed my paper route from back then in reverse. Turning left onto Prospect, I slowly drove by the homes whose lawns I had once mowed. Across the bridge spanning the creek where my friends and I went summer splashing and the site of my discovery of a gold nugget that was traded for several *Classics Illustrated* comics, I turned off onto the gravel parking area of the old store that was the turn-around point of my paper route, where I rewarded myself with a cold and refreshing "Frostie Root Beer" on hot summer days. The store was boarded up, greyed, a silent witness to those lively days a decade and more earlier.

Turning around this time in my car rather than on my bicycle, we rolled back up Prospect Street hill toward Berea College's stately Boone Tavern where I had often been shooed out the back door. The Tavern and several adjacent businesses spanned the block, and the door mid-way along them and the staircase behind it led to my grandfather's dental office that once occupied the space above the pharmacy, the same pharmacy where I spent many afternoons reading comic books, occasionally buying a *Classics Illustrated.*

We drove slowly around the college where I had spent so much boyhood time wandering and wondering, and I continsouly described to Mary the places of my past. From there we drove on to the house on High Street that had been my family's late-1940s to early-1950s home, and I told of the stone marker in the back yard that commemorated the founding of Berea College in 1855. That marker stood where another home a century before had been, and in its parlor a group of men gathered to form the College.

Back on US 25, the main artery through town, I pointed out the Masonic Lodge Hall where my father spent so much time, then the nearby theater where a dime bought "Saturday Serials" before riding my bike to the municipal swimming pool for a refreshing afternoon dip. Across the street from the theater stood the town's Baptist church. Behind it was the parsonage for the minister and his family. Their home bordered our High Street back yard, our neighbors who always made me welcome in their home and at their table.

Further on in the center of Berea stood the city school where I finished the 8th grade, then Upton's Drug Store a few blocks further on where ten cents once bought the most flavorful lemon-lime soda there ever was. Upton's was also the source of many model car kits I bought, one a week when I saved my 25-cent lunch money by not eating lunch. Rolling on, I stopped at the bridge over the railroad tracks where I often sat on my bike watching the coal trains heading south. The tracks came from the far distant northern horizon and faded into the far distant southern horizon as straight as an arrow. Further along, a tour by the homes along US 25 from the bridge to the city limits brought us to where "the Stand" once stood.

"The Stand" was my grandfather's retirement endeavor begun in the early 1950s, the first drive-up soft ice cream and sandwich shop I had ever seen. It proved to be a good investment for the first few years when everything looked fresh and clean, and I spent many afternoons after school and into the night working the windows to make all sorts of delectable treats and tasty morsels that also swelled my girth proportionately. All the goodies I consumed produced my "hey fat kid" period, the cause of so much ridicule and consternation because I could not perform with any of the athletic prowess that I was accustomed to while a country boy on the farm in North Carolina.

It was at "the Stand" one night while watching the late news on TV that we learned of the fatality of Bradley Theodore Cox, hit by a car. "NO!" we exclaimed. "NOT OUR BRADLEY!" The child, to be four years old in a few days, was our Bradley. Those became the saddest of days when my oldest sister, my "Big Sis" and her husband, L. B., faced burying their only child and living with the tragedy of such great loss.

"The Stand" was gone, cleared away to make a parking lot for a church standing on the ground that had been the site of 1950s era fall-of-the-year carnivals sponsored by Berea city organizations. The giant trees were gone, too. So were the swings that gave some cooling air movement on hot summer days. The picnic tables under the trees were only a memory. I could no more than point to places and recall what had once existed, now among nothing more than my recollections from before the church and its grounds. We motored on.

With Berea behind us, little was of interest, and we wanted to finish our trip. The drive across the Appalachians to North Carolina settled in, and, after the long haul through the twisty bits along mountain roads from Barbourville to Boone and on to North Wilkesboro, we pulled to a stop in the driveway of Mary's childhood home in Wilkes County. I had completed a San Diego - Chicago - Albuquerque - Route 66 - H-bomb marathon filled with adventures that seemed to far exceed the ten months all of it had actually encompassed. Yet, we had lived it, wonderful adventures in wondrous places as a result of my steps further into the shadows of the Cold War. Some of those recollections we hoped to never encounter again, northern winters in particular, but now with many new experiences, Mary and I added to our picture albums the photographic memories that only the two of us could fully appreciate.

Unimagined adventures awaited us. We were headed for Clarksville, Tennessee by way of Nashville and two years of new wonders once again in all directions.

Chapter 15

Clarksville Base

Once again, Mary and I packed our belongings into our Alpine and headed west. After visiting with family and friends, we were back on familiar US 421 and its meandering way through the mountains. Nashville by way of Boone, NC and Johnson City, TN was our route, and because of Nashville's acclaim, we looked forward to seeing its sights since we would be living in nearby Clarksville. Nashville had long since become famous because of the Saturday night radio broadcasts of the Grand Ole Opry and the country music that originated from the city's Ryman Auditorium.

This new leg of travels spawned by my Cold War involvement was taking us to new places, including another drive across the Appalachians and through the mountainous rural life that we were a part of. Being young, we looked forward to new places to go, and our good handling Alpine made driving curvey highways loads of fun. Hugging the sides of abrupt inclines and snaking through narrow valleys by rivers and streams was worth the drive alone, but, once beyond the mountain range, we settled into the long trek to Clarksville.

After traversing Davy Crockett country in upper east Tennessee, our routing took us to Knoxville and junction with US 70. This transcontinental highway, coast-to-coast from North Carolina to Los Angeles, was like Route 66 in that it was a major US highway, but unlike Route 66, it had no acclaim. Route 70 was just another highway. Route 66 had many sights of interest to us for two reasons: one was the destinations shown on TV's *Route 66* that we had seen for ourselves during our New Mexico sojourns, and, secondly, Route 66 had a reputation of fascinating places that evoked anticipation. Route 70 proved monotonous.

This Tennessee trek was the first of several of our traversals of the long state in both directions during the following two years, and with Nashville in our sights, getting there seemed to take forever. Like our Route 66 ventures, US 70 was pre-Interstate 40, so we traveled mostly two-lane highways with occasional 4-lane stretches that passed under a few overpasses with other overpasses under construction, the beginnings of I-40. The two-lanes tended to back up traffic behind slow movers whether in or out of town, problems solved when the four lanes of the Interstate were completed later. First glimpses of Nashville were enough to whet our appetites for coming back later, but on this day, a road map was our guide to Clarksville northwest of Nashville by way of Route 41A. We junctioned with 41A somewhere north of Nashville as we kept to my objective of finding Clarksville Base before the end of the day.

The mild August afternoon was warm and sunny, near perfect for driving. Once in Clarksville, I was without a hint of where to find a nearby Top Secret H-bomb facility. Recalling my Albuquerque experience of simply asking, I pulled off the highway into the parking area of a soft-serve ice cream shop, a more modern equivalent of "the Stand" that I had spent so much time in while living with my Dad in Berea a decade or so earlier. My plan was for us to refresh with cool treats, then I would inquire. But there, to my utter surprise, sat a car with a Clarksville Base military sticker on its bumper. "What luck!" I thought.

When the young man, a Marine as it turned out, returned to his car carrying a tray of goodies for himself and his companion, I struck up a conversation and inquired about how to get to Clarksville Base. He wanted to know why, and when I told of being a just-arrived assignee that didn't know how to get there, he gave simple directions; keep going on 41A to the first Fort Campbell entrance and turn left. Keep going several miles until arriving at the gate of Clarksville Base.

His directions were easy enough, but I was certain that he was leading me completely astray; in all of my discussions with senior GMTs I had in preparation for my new assignment, not once was Fort Campbell mentioned, a US Army post. I concluded that I was, once again, involved with subterfuge, another product of Cold War secrecy. Still, I wondered. Maybe.

After slurping down our chocolate malts, Mary and I took off again and watched for signs that the Marine had described, and shortly, a gate to Fort Campbell appeared on our left. The traffic was light along the 3-lane stretch that I would soon come to know well, and my first turn into Fort Campbell recalled my first drive onto Sandia Base; the gate was open and no one was on duty for me to ask directions. I was confused; how could it be that this second Top Secret installation could be so open? Still, the Marine's directions had been accurate to that point, so I crept through the gate anticipating a cadre of gun-toting guards to suddenly leap out of hiding and challenge me. I had my package of orders in hand, but no one emerged for me to present them to. Slowly, we rolled on, then mile after slow mile went by as we looked over the terrain until I was certain that I had been duped. Then, just as I was about to turn around, off in the distance... What's that? Fences! Aha! High chain link fences! Secrecy was here.

We came to a junction where another road crossed our east-west direction at a point where the fences made a 90-degree turn south. The left branch of the cross-road paralleled the fences, and both the road and fences went out of sight down a steep grade. The 2-lane road we were on followed the undulating lay of the land and ran parallel to the fences with only mowed grass and a roadway between them. We encountered no other vehicles, giving me an increased sense of being in the wrong place.

My first impression was of the trees inside the fences. A forest stood inside three continuous chainlink fence lines that contained a single-lane hard-surfaced road built up about three feet from the underlying land. The outside fence with three strands of barbed wire along its top enclosed a similarly constructed inner fence, but this second fence was built with its metal uprights standing on large diameter, brown, pan-shaped ceramic electrical insulators. Nowhere did the fence or its supports touch the ground. I had not seen an electrified fence like this before, and I now knew that I had found Clarksville Base. The road ran between the electrified fence and a third non-electrified chain link fence running parallel just inside the contour of the road. I immediately knew that this was the perimeter fence line with its security road for guard vehicles. I remembered the Marine at the ice cream shop, and, having wondered what Marines would do on Clarksville Base, I now realized that he was a guard.

Tall light poles stood along inside the outer fence, and a section of lights blared brightly even though the late-afternoon sun shone brilliantly. I immediately wondered why the lights were on, not realizing until later that sections of the fence were wired so that when activated, the nearby run of lights came on, a means for guards to quickly determine which section alarmed as they raced to the scene along the road.

Slowly rolling along to absorb all I could on this initial encounter, the same route that I would take day after day for the next two years, I noted nothing in particular beyond a manicured military installation off to the right and lots of trees: Fort Campbell. Later, I learned that this location was a German POW internment camp during World War II just after Camp Campbell, as it was known then, was commissioned from absorbing a vast region of privately held farm land into the war effort. Soon, we arrived at the entrance of Clarksville Base with its robust, concrete block guard house between the "in" and "out" lanes, each with a sturdy, chain link rolling fence cordoning off the way. Signs boldly displaying large, blue lettering with anchors confirmed that I was in the right place. We had arrived without a hitch. When presenting my orders to the guard, I was given temporary passes for both Mary and me and a one-day parking permit for our Alpine, then given directions to the Admin Building. With the entrance gate withdrawn, I was motioned on to check in.

As we drove through the main gate, just inside was another gate-fence-building of much larger proportions off to our left as the road we were on angled off to the right. This second gate for both pedestrians and vehicles was another of the flat-roofed block buildings of the military style that I had seen before, painted white rather than the normal grey for Navy, but its wide windows revealed a group of guards inside. Turnstiles on both sides of the building allowed going-in and coming-out foot traffic to pass through, while all vehicles passed through a single gate similar to the main entrance gate that we had just passed through. More fences added to division of the Base into security zones, the Admin area and much more behind the fences. This second gatepost was the entrance to the exclusion area, the "Q" as I would soon come to know it. This building with its turnstiles, gates and guards was the focal point of each work day to come; badge check in and check out. Alpha-Alpha-Delta-4-7-5 was its radio dispatch "handle" that I would also come to know well because this building was the nerve center overseeing all traffic of any type going into and out of the "Q". For the next two years, this gate was my passage to and from the Cold War's arsenal of H-bombs maintained at Clarksville Base.

Rather than going directly to the Admin Building, we drove around to discover that Clarksville Base was clean, neat, attractively maintained, and small; all of it was contained within perimeter fences giving a feeling of compactness, nothing similar to the sense of wide open spaces I felt at Sandia Base that had no fences other than around particular buildings. Here, the entire complex was enclosed with fences, rows of them, that gave me a feeling of being tightly contained. I wondered if a "big door in the forest" was somewhere behind the entrance to the "Q." It would open, and in I would go. That's what happened, sort of.

Initial check-in began with handing my orders to the clerk who then directed me toward my sequence of getting this signature, that bit of information, a small map showing the Admin area buildings and roads outside the "Q" area, along with information about living within Clarksville Base and surroundings of nearby Clarksville and Hopkinsville, KY. I was introduced to key personnel along with "Welcome Aboard" handshakes typical of US Navy protocol, and somewhere along the way, I initiated a request for on-site housing, wondering where Mary and I would spend our first night. Each person efficiently completed his responsibilities, asked no questions other than the general information type, and sent me on my way to location after location until I had completed the check-in.

Now with official peel-and-stick Clarksville Base bumper stickers on our Alpine, our car was cleared, and with a new clip-on ID badge similar to the type issued at Sandia, color coded for secrecy, I was "onboard." Included diagonally along the reverse side of my Clarksville Base ID was a surprise: bold letters read "Authorized To Transport Explosives." I wondered if any of the people I talked with had any idea of what that phrase meant, or what explosives I would be transporting during the coming months.

Each person I was directed to performed his job within security's "compartmentalized" process to isolate knowledge within narrowly defined segments. Doing their jobs in support of GMT operations meant knowing little, if anything, about the next job and nothing of our work. I recognized the military "chain of command" concept in this structure while wondering how that process would apply to me and my fellow GMTs who had complete H-bombs to work on, actual, live H-bombs, complete in every way except for SEPs. Once I joined the existing cadre of weapons experts, I would delve elbow deep with them into warheads, but some portion of my clearance was not in place, so I was assigned barracks cleaning duties until the paperwork came through.

More immediate was the question of where Mary and I were to stay the night. Because no apartment would be available on base for some weeks, we were told to find a place to live in the surrounding communities. I was given a list of "recommended" quarters in Clarksville, along with directives not to wear my Navy uniforms off base except to and from on-base activities and that I should not stop along the way: better to look civilian rather than face questions. I thought that not having housing available for us was a failure of planning; the normally efficient Department of the Navy and Defense Atomic Support Agency knew I was coming to Clarksville Base, but no preparation had been made for living quarters other than barracks. No one had noted that I was married.

Not knowing the town at all and with only a "recommended" housing list, we were on our own. No Guest House was available as at Fort Sheridan, so we spent the afternoon looking for a place. Finally, arriving at 215A Cave Street, we found the only accommodations available, a small trailer behind a modest home. Having no recourse, we took it, and our first night was spent sleeping on the trailer's bare mattress because we had no bed linens, items on our shopping list for the next day. Fort Campbell, home of the 101st Airborne, was composed of thousands of soldiers who had Clarksville's civilian accommodations filled to capacity. Initially, the trailer looked to be suitable for the short term we would need it, and reasonably priced, but once we moved in, we found it bug-ridden and a nuisance requiring cleaning and re-cleaning, de-bugging and re-debugging, until the place was made reasonably livable.

Since we traveled light, nothing more than clothes and kitchenware, moving in was quick. Moving out a few weeks later was just as quick, and while Mary got acquainted with our new neighbors and Clarksville, soon getting a job at the Fort Campbell PX procurement office, I went to work each day as a janitor and waited to do what I had learned at Sandia: H-bombs. My four weeks of barracks duties proved to be an excellent introduction to all sorts of Base personnel and facilities permitting rapid integration into the functions of the Admin area, such as the auto shop and NCO club. A few weeks passed before I received notification that a townhouse at 8 S. O'Bannon Court was available to us. Another quick move, and we were set. The time was beginning fall-of-the-year 1967, and Mary and I were to remain there for two years.

During the next several months, we settled in to our new lives with neighbors of all persuasions in our apartment complex, Navy, Marines and Army, with adjoining officer housing in a separate circle of duplex and single units further along. While I became acquainted with Clarksville Base, its personnel and operations, Mary became acquainted with Fort Campbell. Her new job continued PX office work that she had learned at Fort Sheridan, and soon she was offered a promotion to keep the PX gas station records. She was one of two candidates interviewed and moved into her new job that soon generated dinnertime tales from her day's work. Included in a regular lineup of characters, enlisted, officer and civilian and their doings, her most fascinating tales were about the Bell Witch, a ghostly spirit that had resided with previous generations of her boss' family. The story remained an often-revisited topic, to the extent of talking with various people associated with the story and acquiring a copy of a book from her boss. Later, Mary decided to take advantage of Clarksville's Austin Peay State University and began taking classes.

Once all my clearances were in place, I was assigned depot work in the Base's shops, then custodial duties of maintaining technical and classified documents to current status that began my direct association with DASA. The following spring, 1968, I was sent back to Albuquerque for advanced warhead training. In a class of just two sailors, I lived on Sandia Base sharing a room with a Marine sergeant who partied like a wild man. I spent the month renewing my acquaintances with Albuquerque and enjoyed as much of another magnificent spring as my feet permited, bumming rides here and there, especially to attend functions on the University of New Mexico campus.

One outing was to the art gallery where I got into a discussion with the curator concerning what was art. Many of the student works were displayed in gallery fashion, some with bold colors in lines and stripes and geometric figures, and I noticed that a painter was applying the same sort of work to a newly completed wall, bold blue with a broad yellow strip. "NO!" proclaimed the curator, his work was NOT art; he was simply following directions. Art was applying to a surface what the mind was inspired to produce, creating the mind's vision by eye and hand. I thought the painter's work to a blank construction wall equal to much of the "art" on display and pondered the point: why were students of art doing "art" under the direction of instructors who taught them how to produce "art" in particular ways? If inspiration was really creativity, why were instructors needed at all? The curator dismissed me and my line of reasoning as not worthy of further discussion.

Having arrived back in Albuquerque during the annual University talent contest, I was not impressed with much of the "music" performed by one hippy group after another. Then came Carlos and Miguel, the last act, who tipped the scale into the sensational index. As they stepped onto the stage in their black, tightly fitting Spanish waist jackets and pants, shined boots, white shirts with red ribbon ties, and coal black hair swept back, each with an acoustic guitar and foot stool, the demeanor of the large and boisterous crowd did not change. They took seats in straight back chairs on stage, set the microphones to guitar level, propped up a foot to position their guitars, looked at each other and strummed a ferocious volley of rapid fire flamenco that stopped everyone in their tracks. The audience gasped, quietened and held their breaths in a collective display of awe for these Spanish guitar virtuosos. Carlos and Miguel blazed through a lengthy dual guitar piece, their fingers striking note and chord perfectly complementing each other, and completed their performance as far superior to anything preceding them. The crowd burst into a cheering ovation that brought them back for another performance, this one equally transfixing. Massive cheers and applause erupted and brought them back for a third ovation. I was equally in awe and was so impressed that I wanted to play the guitar just like them, never thinking that growing up playing their instruments made a big difference. Politely bowing to the cheering crowd, they declined a further encore, and accepted their well-earned positions as winners of the contest. They were so superior to everything before them that I have since wondered what happened to Carlos and Miguel, clearly young giants in the world of Spanish guitar. I never learned anything of them again.

During my first tenure in Albuquerque, I completed a Plane Trigonometry course conducted on Sandia Base as a University of New Mexico course taught by Dr. E. R. Harrington, described as the most formally educated man in America, and I felt a part of the University in a small way. So, simply walking the campus among the largely adobe architecture was more than a springtime treat. Without a car, I was pleasantly confined to Albuquerque and had every afternoon and weekend to see it again. This "TDY" assignment for training was too short for another course, but I discovered that I had privileges at the Sandia Labs library. Those evenings that I had nowhere to go, I spent reading book after book on scientific topics including magnetohydrodynamics, the workings of fusion, and learned more about the physics of what made H-bombs go boom and what powered the sun and stars.

Once back on Clarksville Base with my new training, I moved into the assembly shops again, one after the other, and learned the workings of both complexes: disassembling warheads, checking components for proper operation, replacing those not meeting specs, performing modifications and alterations of warheads and bomb assemblies, cataloging every detail, reassembling and ultimately certifying that completed weapons would work when given the correct signals in proper sequence.

Meanwhile, from August 1967 to May 1968, I progressed through various levels of on-site work doing various warhead functions, traveled among the above ground and underground bunkers, learned access codes and procedures, performed warhead inventories and their configurations delineated by assembly codes, verified inventory data, and gradually became knowledgeable of the entire arsenal's operations, its hundreds of H-bombs and their movement. During months of working in either of the two assembly buildings, I was also a member of the inspection team that made regular outings to the "Volcano," a facility no longer used but maintained in working order in the event that it should become needed. Just a few years earlier, it had been a Mason & Hangar facility for assembly of warheads from core out, and I imagined that some of the locals knew this building well, even having participated in assembly of H-bombs before the work was moved elsewhere.

The "Volcano" cone rising prominently above the building was actually a vast quantity of sand contained underneath by a rupture membrane designed to collapse if a detonation occurred in the assembly room under the cone. It was a circular room with a contoured ceiling containing the sand, walls painted a neutral tone of green with a continuous copper strip attached around its perimeter. Its concrete floor was waxed and polished, and the most prominent feature of the room was its single entry door, a massive bank vault-type stainless steel door about six feet square. It was constructed in stair-stepped layers, each layer about a foot thick mating to its jamb in the thick wall of the room. The total of layers made the door about four feet thick, a blast door fixed on hinges that were so smooth that the massively heavy door was easily opened or closed with one hand. I was amazed at how well balanced it was and marveled at its craftsmanship. Inside the room, imagining from my explosives training what would happen in the instant following a high explosive detonation and collapse of the "Volcano" inward, I sensed foreboding as in a burial tomb. This was a dangerous place to be, evidenced especially by the copper strip, an electrical ground strap that all personnel were attached to in order to drain any electrostatic spark to ground rather than risk igniting a high explosive charge, the sort of hazard that would light off certain doom followed by the crush of the volcano designed to contain such an event.

Although the "Volcano" and attached building were bare, both of the well-equipped warhead maintenance buildings were kept in the high military order required by our work. Everything had its place, and strict order was maintained to insure that every device, every tool, everything involved in our work was maintained in prime condition and accounted for. Those items needing repair were taken off line and went through rigorous checkout before being returned to work status. Everything including the floor, or "deck" as it's called in Navy lingo, was kept clean, waxed and polished, duties that we GMTs performed during slack time. Unlike my training in Albuquerque, personnel were not divided into permanent "hooks." We were proportioned out to whatever the jobs of the day happened to be, and several weapons were serviced at the same time in the spacious and open, rectangular assembly areas. One shop was a concrete block building, the other a large, earth covered "Quonset hut."

Orders specifying what work we were to do came each morning, whether the large, silver colored Air Force B-53 of nine megatons or the sleeker, white B-43 of a quarter of that yield, or the diminutive, cannistered Mk 45 multi-purpose warhead for missiles like the surface-to-air Terrier and surface-to-surface Little John. Another day might bring the Navy's Mk 44 ASRoc anti-submarine warhead or the Mk 55 SubRoc that made every submarine a nuclear missile launch platform. H-bombs came for service, then went back into active status while some were decommissioned, such as missile warheads like the old Mk 30 Talos that were retired and being removed from service.

I recalled the Nike Hercules missile standing on display at the entrance of Fort Sheridan and recognized that the Mk 31 and its cousin the Mk 45 Terrier were the packages that each missile could deliver, yields from one kiloton to 40 kT from the Mk 31. In highest yield, it was twice the blast of the Nagasaki bomb, and wasn't actually an H-bomb in the sense of the B-53 or B-43. It was a new design, much simpler, lighter and more compact than the older warheads and was deliverable by smaller missiles from ground and air launch platforms. The Mk 45 was, similarly, a selectable yield warhead with maximum yield of 15 kT launched from Terrier equipped ships. Two kilotons was the dialed-in yield for intercepting aircraft. The Mk 45 had the same potential as the Mk 1, "Little Boy" as dropped on Hiroshima, but was so small that it could be carried by hand. As we got further into advanced warheads, quips about the "nuclear hand grenade" and the strong-armed Marine who could hurl it upon a battlefield enemy became more than quips. The satchel charge Mk 54 Atomic Demolition Munition was of briefcase size and no heavier. Its yield of 200 tons, a "grenade" deployed for demolition, was for clandestine placement and timer fused for destroying large constructions such as dams, bridges, and buildings.

Our duties as H-bomb mechanics were whatever the orders called for without knowing where the orders came from or where our work went. As my responsibilities increased, I moved into maintaining the database for the entire arsenal at Clarksville Base. At that time, I learned where the orders came from: the Pentagon's War Office, DASA. Also at that point, I was issued a Top Secret-Q Crypto clearance; my job was to keep a running inventory of every warhead and every component in each assembly as a daily "state of the arsenal" summary. The data received from each day's work in the two active assembly shops where I initially worked was coded onto IBM punch cards in such a way that only someone knowledgeable could make sense of the data. Various keys were used to sort the cards to compile a stack of cards comprising the components in each warhead. Each day's data was then reported to in-house operations personnel who updated printouts for computerized records and to run new printouts overnight.

Two of us cleared to the appropriate level, and only two so far as I knew, conducted weekly inventories of stored hardware in the main storage vault. Just driving by this building revealed nothing more than a small flat-roofed house raised somewhat above ground and fitted with doors and windows just like a normal house. Few people had reason to examine it closer for it was off limits to everyone except those with need-to-know. It was, in fact, a house made entirely of reinforced concrete about twelve feet thick from roof down, fashioned in such a way as to look like an everyday rectangular house. The entrance to the vault was underneath. A narrow stairway led to what appeared to be a regular outside door as if going into the basement of the "house" but it was only a locked, solid steel door opening to an antechamber containing a thick vault type door and communication links. The two of us plugged headsets into the link to establish voice contact with a mysterious voice, a person I never met or knew where he was located, but always the same voice. Upon providing ID codes for ourselves and appropriate codes of the day, locks constructed into the walls and securing the door were released and we were granted access to the vault by simply opening the door.

Here, in cubbyhole after cubbyhole, lay the heart of America's answer to "We will bury you!" All of it was kept dry with de-humidifiers that we checked to insure proper functioning, along with floor alarm water sensors also checked for proper operation. In the event that water did collect on the floor, the alarms were to announce its presence long before potential problems could arise. All sorts of bomb components were housed here, including highly enriched uranium target rings for the Navy's Mk 23 "KT" 11-inch nuclear shell for the 16-inch projectile. Each cubbyhole was serialized, and information for each item in each one was coded onto heavy-duty cards tied by wire to the component. We verified inventory sheets to the data with each component, one of us reading the codes, the other checking the record, then reading the data back, a double-check.

After learning about critical mass and water moderation and other criticality aspects of weapons grade fuels, I took it upon myself to relocate components in each cubbyhole in more centralized locations, rather than pushed as far back in its metal cubicle as it could go where it was adjacent to the mating cubicle on the back side. I also moved components leaning against a wall or back corner of their cubbyholes to maximize the distance between similar material in the adjoining cubbyholes. Although I knew that, if criticality was possible, the whole place would have long since gone up in a nuclear fireball, it just seemed the right thing to do to space everything out evenly. I was probably the only person that handled the fuels with bare hands. Later, when Clarksville Base closed late in 1969, the vault was emptied when all these components were packaged for shipment. I knew exactly what was on the last train from Clarksville.

During this time, my job entailed hand-carrying stacks of punch cards comprising each day's activities to the Fort Campbell communications center for transmission to the Pentagon. My drive back to the base often made my arrival late enough to have missed rides with other GMTs from the base to our housing, and Mary would have to come and get me unless I found another ride. Occasionally, I was able to get a ride with the base chaplain, an association that developed into becoming active in the non-denominational church on Clarksville Base.

It was also during this time that I began delving into philosophy books seeking answers to questions about my life in a world with enormously divergent and incompatible directions. I had come from a country church where everything said was simple and uncomplicated: either this or that, no grey areas. The world I now lived in was not black or white, as I came to realize when the Chaplain spoke of the "Prince of Peace" to a young man who was highly skilled and prepared to deliver massive destruction on a gargantuan scale. He spoke of the goodness of heavenly virtues that placed my skills in stark contrast. Talk about Heaven for the virtuous and Hell for the damned, otherworldly destinations after death, focused the very thing I could deliver in massive proportions, hell on earth. Truth and honesty were not where I lived; secrecy was my domain, and silence did not permit telling the truth or being honest. We were required to remain quietly in the shadows. I was one of the silent "good guys" on our side who kept the nasty "bad guys" on the Soviet Union side in check, but we knew, both American and Soviet, that each of us wrestled with the same issues, viewed only from opposite directions. This "guess what I've got in store for you" contrast, each believing himself to be the "good guy," kept me on a even keel as I remembered "We will bury you!" It was the reason I had become who I was, the product of decisions made by others, people who I never knew. I wondered if the Chaplain had even come close to this real world that I lived in. His world was confined to religious simplicity about how people ought to get along rather than how they actually do get along.

My arsenal of more explosive power than unleashed during the entirety of man's existence told me that we got along best by recognizing how badly the other guy could maul us if we started a fight: the essence of the Cold War. "Don't start a fight" was its mantra, because the first H-bomb lit off would bring an exchange sending the world into disastrous destruction. I recognized that certainty; my job was to insure that our H-bombs would work, and I had long since come to the conclusion that any scenario for igniting any of them was hopelessly naive because hell would also come our way in what had become known as "Mutually Assured Destruction," MAD. I was its operative.

As I read and pondered many issues, such as the Chaplain's use of the words "righteous" and "salvation," I came to a succession of incongruities. Where did righteousness fit into this real world stand-off that engulfed me, the knowing, and the unknowing? Were righteousness and salvation no more than imagined, simplistic, wishful thinking by idealists who were not attached to reality? How could righteousness sanctify nuclear war in any way? How did salvation fit farm boys and city boys who were molded into operatives "Authorized To Transport Explosives" and put them out on the fringes of international politics as pawns on the last line of offense at the precipice of mankind's destruction? Were we "good guys" if we hurled H-bombs onto the world's unsuspecting masses who had no chance of surviving them or their aftermath? How could a farm boy or a city boy entertain salvation once becoming a GMT? The real world posed tough questions and offered few answers.

As I read more and more philosophy, I found myself looking at my hands from time to time. They gently caressed my beautiful wife, moved chess pieces in an innocuous game of intellectual skill with an opponent, and assembled weapons of massive destruction as well. These were real hands like many others that had produced civilization's best works. Yet mine were also hands of destruction, the worst of civilization. I soon came to the realization that I was a product of the real world and that the world I lived in clearly stated the requirements of getting along without war's destruction. I resolved that just as the hopelessly naive quickly lost to a competent chess player, civilization could just as quickly lose to incompetent government that resorted to H-bombs for any reason. I came to the conviction that only the hopelessly naive could justify their use and would do so only on the basis of simplistic logic based on lack of knowledge and megalomania, the product of no foresight, and unleash the hell of nuclear war while proclaiming moral sanctity. I became convinced that no rational mind could arrive at such a decision.

Mary and me, 8 S. O'Bannon Court, 1968, and my favorite painting, *The Glory That Was*. Little did I know that within two years, I wouild be walking among and photographing the glory that was the ancient world that inspired the painting.

Chapter 16

8 S. O'Bannon Court

Not only was our apartment at 8 S. O'Bannon home for Mary and me, it became the frequent gathering place for friends and youth fellowships when we became "adult" coordinators of the young teen group of the Base's non-denominational church. Among friends were those with the uncanny ability to arrive just as another of Mary's cakes or pies was coming from the oven.

During my first few days onboard Clarksville Base, I noticed the North Carolina license plate on a new and beautiful Pontiac GTO, white with black racing stripes. Sometime later, I happened upon the car just as its driver was walking away. After getting his attention and introducing myself as a fellow North Carolinian, we began a life-long friendship. Sandy was from coastal North Carolina and spoke with a "down east" accent while my mountain drawl told of a different background. He was a career Navy Seabee living in base barracks and was always welcome in our home, his home away from home. Sandy was among the cadre of transporters assigned to Clarksville Base. His crew handled the heavy equipment, tractors and trailers and such, when moving the weapons and equipment from place to place, except when bombs were transported to Fort Campbell's air field. That was the job of GMTs who drove the high framed undercarriers similar to those used in lumber yards, slow but reliable.

Mary made new friends, too. Among them was Jill, a natural beauty from the Clarksville area who helped make Mary's transition into unknown surroundings and exclusion from my work more acceptable. Jill was a frequent visitor whose laughter and jovial demeanor added to the youthful, exuberant nature of our place. She became more attached to Clarksville Base when she met a Marine who looked like he stepped out of a Hollywood movie poster. Tom was trim and handsome with flowing hair and had a captivating smile, but being a young Viet Nam returnee, he was another of the soldiers whose life-shaping exploits living on the edge in jungle warfare came back with him.

Clarksville Base was a "decompression" installation that served as a quiet, cooling off sort of low-key assignment to help Army and Marine Viet Nam returnees re-adjust to non-combat life back home in the USA. The stories about Tom and his night patrols were legion, but being stories, who knew if they were fact or fiction? A whirlwind romance brought Jill and Tom to matrimony, and soon afterward, she learned that his exploits in Nam were continually replayed in his head, such as stealthy reconnaissance through nighttime jungle with only piano wire attached to palm-size handles. A loop over the unwary and another enemy lost his head with a single snap of the wire. He was said to carry only his wire and a sharp knife as he moved quietly and alone through the jungle. Being a "nightstalker" enabled bringing closely observed intelligence of Cong activities to commanders who commended his efforts, but shaping a young man's mind in such a way insured deep-rooted problems in civilian life, difficulties that Jill found too much to live with and parted ways.

John was another of us boomers, of the age to be heavy into cars, and had recently re-enlisted for another four years. His Variable Re-enlistment Bonus (VRB) of several thousand dollars was put into a sensational 1964 Chevrolet Impala hot rod built at the Base auto shop. John, like many young soldiers and sailors, spent his meager income largely on his car, a red on red Super Sport hardtop that was the wildest ride on Clarksville Base. With his VRB buying power, out went the perfectly good original engine in favor of a monster 427 cubic inch Chevrolet racing engine delivered in the crate from General Motors. Engine swaps were common hot rodding practice during the 1960s, so John and his fellow workers, including bit parts by me, put together a drag race car for the street, with four-inch square header caps exiting through the front fenders just behind the tires, big street slicks on the rear, and all sorts of suspension tricks. The car was jacked up a little, revealing massive traction bars underneath, and everyone knew when John was coming; the rumble of his Chevy was pure muscle car.

Our neighbors next door were career Navy about a decade older than Mary and me. They had arrived sometime before us from a California assignment in a location that had captured their oldest daughter's heart. Gary was in supply, but because of the differences in our ages and jobs, our social lives did not interlace. His wife, Dorothy, was a nurse at Fort Campbell's hospital who, later on, came to our rescue following Mary's near-fatal delivery of our first child in June, 1969. Mary and I have never been able to adequately express our appreciation for her help and devotion during Mary's critical post-hospital time at home. I had to work, leaving Mary alone with our new baby during a time when she was hardly able to get up and around during her extended recovery. Dorothy's attention and care became the bridge from Mary's struggle just tending to herself while staying alone most of the day, with a new baby, to being able to recover from such a difficult time. Our neighbor's continual checking on her and providing the care and attention that Mary and Squire needed has always stood out in our minds as a greatly appreciated gesture of enduring good will toward total strangers who became next door neighbors.

We were told that when the baby came home, we would have to get rid of our cat, Kit-Kit. But when Squire arrived in a wicker basket filled with cushions and wrapped in a baby blanket, he was greeted with feline curiosity. I placed the basket and baby on the floor and let

Kit-Kit investigate. The baby immediately became his possession and thereafter, he bristled and bowed his back and hissed aggressively when anyone but Mary or me or Dorothy came near the baby. He slept by the basket and stayed nearby all the time, so much so that we had to close him in another room when visitors arrived.

Kit-Kit lived with us from a kitten and grew into a much sought-after male, especially by the Siamese from across the parking area of our U-shaped apartment complex. This amorous female regularly came yowling around our windows, but Kit-Kit rebelled. He did not like the Siamese, and while on his leash on the rear patio, he took to licking his fur all over his body into armor, knotting it into dense matting that enabled him to fight the cat with little injury. His suitor's taunts just beyond the reach of his leash occasionally came close enough to produce a fierce duel of claws, teeth and screams. We kept Kit-Kit inside most of the time, but he was accustomed to letting us know when he needed out, and, during those daily episodes, the Siamese often came calling. During the day, her gravely yowling wasn't so bad, but during the night, especially when Mary needed sleep, it was very annoying and disruptive. Base regulations required all pets to be leashed, but this free-roamer was too much, and I reasoned that a stinging rebuke might solve the problem.

I borrowed a B-B air rifle and proceeded to shoot the Siamese as it sat under our windowsills singing to Kit-Kit. The impact of the B-Bs were summarily ignored, and I had to resort to chasing the cat away on late-night, skivvy clad charges through the parking lot in front of our apartment. I finally determined which apartment she returned to, a Marine and his young wife with their own new baby, and when I began phoning during the night to come get his cat, the late hour yowling episodes ended. When we moved from Clarksville Base upon closure of the base in late-1969 and my assignment to the USS Forrestal, Kit-Kit went to live with Jill and became the Big Daddy cat of the walk, enjoying lavished affection and more than ample meals.

How Sandy and John knew that Mary was taking another pie or cake from the oven became a topic of legend. Soon after the bakery fragrance filled our apartment, the door bell would ring and there would be Sandy or John or both, sometimes Jill, too, along with other friends just dropping by. Everyone was always welcome. They brought new dimensions into our lives, like the time that Sandy brought a bottle of champagne for New Year's Eve and proceeded to get Kit-Kit drunk. The cat liked the bubbly nose tickler, and lapped up dish after dish of it. Soon, his wobbly walk with flops to and fro among inebriated collisions with furniture legs produced rolls of laughter giving all of us a memorable evening.

Our furniture, supplied by the Base, was of sturdy quality and quite adequate, but with only single bed mattresses available, I arranged two of the small size crossways of a king size bed to make a giant bed where Mary and I slept and played. Squire soon out-grew his wicker basket and the dresser drawer he was elevated to. It was clear that we had to get a proper bed for him. A few weeks after delivery when Mary was feeling better and stronger, a visit by my mother and step-father, Jacob, resulted in their purchase of a real baby bed at Grandpa's Discount Barn. The basket that we had brought Squire home in became our laundry basket, and the chest began to house his belongings that collected along the way of his rapid growth.

Clarksville Base dated from 1947 when it was known as Site B, the second of thirteen nuclear weapons depots established throughout the United States following World War-II and rapid expansion of the nation's nuclear arsenal. It was established within the limits of the Army Air Force Base of Camp Campbell that was organized during 1941 for the war effort. Camp Campbell spanned the Kentucky-Tennessee state line into sizable segments of four counties, land that was previously private farms. During the 1950s, the Camp became Fort Campbell and home of the 101st Airborne. With a Defense Atomic Support Agency facility within its confines but outside its jurisdiction, a certain tension from the Fort's Army personnel existed toward Navy personnel. That situation was, no doubt, aggravated by all Army personnel having to halt, come to attention, face away from us and remain that way until our convoys to the airfield passed. Our Marine guards insured that no one saw anything, making us untouchables with our own authority presided over by armed patrols in front of and behind our formations. Since Army and Marine soldiers were assigned to Clarksville Base, also under the wing of Navy command rather than Fort Campbell, a strange mix of service personnel was the nature of the Base, and even though it had long since become integrated into the lore of the nearby cities of Clarksville and Hopkinsville, Clarksville Base remained distinct from Fort Campbell and wrapped in secrecy with its existence and its Navy personnel continually the topics of conjecture and myth.

Our housing, later to become Fort Campbell officer housing when the Base closed, was particularly good military housing of the time, and Mary and I acclimated well to the choice duty that assignment to Clarksville Base provided. Although all of us were there as transients, the nature of military duty everywhere, my two year assignment was longer than most, affording time for many excursions into our surroundings. One was clean-up day. The Base Captain designated a work day for personnel to scour the woods surrounding our apartment complexes to gather and remove debris, whatever sort it may be, including the rusted leftovers from the private farm days before Camp Campbell. Perhaps a hundred of us were divided into squads that were assigned portions of the woods, and we gathered up heaps of refuse, mostly rusted metal and decaying lumber, leaving the woods pristine, extending the area for the Base's children to romp and play.

Since many families had young children, Halloween saw an outpouring of little door-to-door goblins overseen by parents who had just as much fun as their children. One Halloween day, with goodies stocked to give away, the sky grew steadily more bleak with thickening overcast. Cold settled upon the landscape, and around mid-afternoon, before the evening parade began forming, snow began falling. Big, sticky flakes fell from the sky blanketing the ground, and by dusk a thick layer of snow stopped everything in its tracks. More kept falling in one of the prettiest snowfalls I have ever seen. The goblins mostly stayed in as all of us were fascinated with the freak but beautiful fall-of-the-year snowfall that accumulated to ten or more inches overnight. The next morning, it lay in the trees making a beautiful Christmas-like scene all around us, a memorable day requiring shovels to clear the snow from our walkways and from around our cars. A scraper from the Base cleared the main roads that were otherwise impassible, but getting to the main roads required moving lots of snow piled in our parking area. Most of our cars were not equipped for snow travel anyway, and such an early and heavy snowfall hastened speculation about the coming winter. Once out, though, the road from our quarters junctioned with Woodlawn Road, and a right turn on Woodlawn paralleled the eastern run of fences of the Base. That right turn led to descent off the hill down into the valley of the Little West Fork Creek and the hill up on the other side to make the left turn onto Mabry Road toward the main entrance of the Base. On this snow covered day, our regular drive of only a few minutes was not possible until later when the warming sun melted the snow on our roads as the day progressed.

The giant roll-up steel door at the bottom of the hill, the Little West Fork's eastern perimeter exit, was a source of further myth about Clarksville Base. It was manned at all times by a Marine guard who got there along the access road running between the surrounding fences and crossed the creek on a bridge from which the door was suspended. His post was the one-man shack on the south side of the bridge, similar to the post on the opposite end of the "Q". Guard duty at these locations seemed to be no more than being there because the door was rarely opened, unless the creek flooded. When heavy springtime rain caused the creek to overflow far above its banks, the reason for the large size door became evident. As the water rose, so did both the door and the myths about what was behind it. My favorite was the notion that the Navy caused the spring rains that swelled the creek so that submarines could glide into and out of the Base unseen. Such a notion accounted for a US Navy Base being there, however removed from a body of water the isolated Base might be. Another myth closer to the truth was the fear expressed to me one day that the high water might get into "the atomic bomb" kept inside the Base and cause it to go off, letting me know that the general populace had fairly accurate notions about what went on in spite of the high secrecy surrounding the complex. I wish I had written down all the myths and notions that swirled around Clarksville Base. They were legion.

For the most part, all of us were just people doing our jobs in the military, but doing so included required protocol such as duty. Like everyone else, I spent my late night duty time sitting at a desk with a phone that rarely rang. Across from the duty desk sat the desk of the duty officer who was there for anything that I could not handle. Since duty required staying awake, I used my duty time to read, study, play chess and talk with the various duty officers I served with to the extent that I learned a fair bit about who they were, where they came from, what they did. On one occasion, the duty officer was a Lieutenant Junior Grade (JG) who had become known as a stock market whiz. His duty time was largely spent on the phone making financial deals, and, being within hearing, I was able to learn about the stock market and investing by overhearing his conversations. He took time to explain to me the workings of the stock market to the extent that I gathered sufficient interest to begin investing imaginary dollars to study money-making. All the high finance was intriguing until I took a call for him late one night. A truck driver was looking for the Lieutenant, and the ensuing conversation was a revelation to both of us. The message was clear: what did the Lieutenant want to do with the truckload of eggs he had bought? He abruptly learned the risks of investing in commodities; he was financially burned by a truckload of eggs in California to dispose of. Tough lessons.

Playing chess involved much fewer variables, and as I played the game and studied it from various books, I learned strategies that led to wins from the first move. I learned offense and defense to the extent that I was tough to beat and rarely lost. When the Clarksville Base Chess Club was formed, I was chosen its first captain, and all of our members played regularly, during lunch breaks and duty hours, especially late night sessions. My skill became known to the extent that an officer invited me to his home to play on a new set that his wife had given him for Christmas. For an enlisted man to be in the home of an officer was against official protocol, but he was a gentleman chess player and his pretty wife a fine homemaker. When I remarked that I didn't want to outplay him on his brand new chess set, his wife cautioned that he was a very good player. He challenged that I should play my skill and humorously smirked that I should give him no quarter. I took him at his word, handily beating him in both games we played, and was never invited back.

During this time of fairly regular duty, I requested enrollment in an officer level course in nuclear physics. At first denied, I was later allowed to enroll, and upon receiving the US Navy course material, I spent many duty hours studying. Upon completion of each section, the necessary forms were completed and submitted with exams along the way, and I completed the course in far shorter time than allotted, receiving a score of 3.8 out of 4.0. At completion, having studied all sorts of nuclear applications including nuclear power, I recognized another piece in the puzzle of my future: I simply was not inclined to continue a career with weapons, but I did identify with nuclear powered ships. Under the glare of the duty desk lamp during the long quiet times of night watches, I learned the workings of nuclear reactors and power, recognizing that the principles enabling weapons to make such explosive energy was the same as ship-board reactors, although nuclear power plants were built in such a way that the energy of the atom was metered out slowly over long periods of time rather than in a blinding white flash. I decided that if the Navy permitted me to get into the nuclear powered surface fleet, I would re-enlist to become a career officer specializing in nuclear propulsion. I tucked that resolution into my memory for the appropriate time of decision.

A television ad of the time told about the "fast tomato," and since our Alpine was red, it was similarly dubbed "The Fast Tomato" by a salty old sailor who lived a rather singular life in the barracks. How he, a Second Class Boatswains Mate, came to Clarksville Base was an enigma because he seemed to have no particular expertise and mostly floated along each day as keeper of "E" barracks, the Navy barracks for senior NCOs to which I was first assigned. He had been a rather good boxer in his early years in the Navy, now a little punch drunk from too many hits to the noggin, and we were a little sad for him. The rumor mill told that he had been passed over for promotion so many times that he would be mustered out of the Navy if he didn't pass advancement in grade to First Class when exam time rolled around again. I wondered where someone like him would go in civilian life, but one day when he announced that he was getting married, we just grinned at more of his outlandish antics and privately guffawed behind his back. The laugh was on us when we discovered that he was right, and it turned out that she was right for him, a rather proper middle-aged woman who was willing to take on a man who needed direction. From the day he moved out of the barracks into her home, she put him on a routine of study to make the grade, a better diet resulting in loss of his pudginess, and a noticeable improvement in his appearance. Come examination time, "ol' punchy" passed, assuring his continuation in the Navy until retirement.

Another British sports car was on Clarksville Base, a new, cream colored Austin-Healey 3000 owned by a handsome, young officer, and its owner and I talked cars from time to time when our duty hours coincided. He was a motivated, well educated young officer on the way up and out of the Navy. We talked about what to do in civilian life, such as business opportunities, and although I did not know what his job was at Clarksville Base, he seemed to be quite good at everything with confidence expressed in his every move. His Healey and my Sunbeam, both with wire wheels, were the sorts of cars that any young, sporting man would take pleasure in driving, although we never socialized because he was single and living on base, an officer, and I was married and enlisted living off Base. He did, however, show particular interest in what GMTs did, so I chose my words carefully due to suspicions that he was with Navy Intelligence.

This officer was the sort that I wanted to be, the very model of a US Navy officer in my mind. Around this time, I was promoted to Second Class GMT just short of two years in the Navy. I had become convinced that I could make a career of the Navy and began investigating opportunities to advance in that direction. There were several, and I immediately set myself into the direction of finishing college and becoming an unlimited line officer in the regular Navy. Another route to wearing the braided uniform was through the GMT ranks, and, with my next promotion opportunity in just two years, to First Class, I could keep the grade toward becoming a Chief Petty Officer, or go either Warrant Officer with weapons specialty, or further specialize with H-bombs to become a limited line officer, a weapons officer whose progression was capped at Commander. Continued specializing in H-bombs with a cap of Commander was not the direction I wanted to go. A third direction appealed to me so strongly that I set my sights for the Navy Enlisted Science Education Program (NESEP). This program offered completion of four years of education at a university with an NROTC program, followed by OCS, as the beginning of a career as a Navy officer. The only catch was that each year of college required one and half years of sea duty, a long time to be away from Mary. However, I was assured that most of that time would be spent on those overseas shore sites with H-bombs where I would be a weapons officer. Although feeling as though I was rolling the dice of my future, I opted for NESEP and Warrant Officer and advancement to First Class GMT as back up, whichever was the most advancement at the fourth anniversary of signing on with the Navy, if I chose to stay in. I selected the NESEP program at the University of Colorado, to be followed by the Navy's Post-Graduate school in Monterey, California in the second four-year block of my Navy career, and waited for decision time at the end of my first enlistment.

Assignment to Clarksville Base was choice duty, and I came to admire the Navy life in almost every way, until I encountered another officer who was just the opposite of my model. After rising in responsibility to be handling the logistics of all the weapons and inventories at the site as a Top Secret-Q Crypto operative of the Cold War, I came under the direct command of another JG who made life difficult. He was a low achiever who had managed to complete an NROTC program and OCS and was less than perfect in wearing the uniform. His noticeably poor bodily hygiene and teeth with visible cavities, along with unruly hair that kept a sprinkling of dandruff on the shoulders of his officer's jacket, made my overseer visibly unkempt. He was also uninformed about H-bomb workings and my work other than the paperwork he had to sign. Ours was a personality conflict that taught me to interface with him as little as possible, and he seemed to look for a way to lower the boom on me. It came following a leave. When I returned to my files, I reported to him that they were in disarray with the wrong order of cards for weapons and components. Someone had attempted to do my work and did not understand the codes. As a result, a considerable snafu developed that had repercussions all the way to the Pentagon and required me to go through the entire inventory to properly organize all the data. On my next evaluation, I recognized words and phrases that he had used, but the evaluation was signed by the operations officer, not him. I knew immediately what had happened. Soon afterward he moved on, or perhaps out of the Navy, and my subsequent evaluations returned to statements of high quality performance, both knowledgeable and professional. As a top GMT throughout my tenure, his association was the only blemish on my record.

Burned by this encounter, I came to question my interest in a military career. Recognizing that a bad performance review could derail any and all prior performance and inhibit future advancements, I was less inclined to put my future in the hands of people like him. During my final months at Clarksville Base and subsequent year at sea on the Forrestal, I encountered no other officers like him, reassuring me that US Navy officers were both competent and professional in all but his case. Still, that six years of sea duty required for four years of college in the NESEP program stood out strongly in my mind. Was becoming an officer worth that commitment, not knowing if I would be assigned aboard ship or to a shore base? I thought about living on one of the many Navy Bases around the world, a grand adventure for a country boy, but if I was at sea all that time, I would miss Mary and the growth of our children. Separation would cause both my family and me to suffer, and the prospect of long absences did not sit well in my mind. Since my decision was not required until the end of my enlistment, I laid the foundations for advancement in several directions as mentioned and kept the option of getting out to that time.

When my mother and stepfather visited and purchased that much needed baby bed told about earlier, Jacob used his retired US Air Force privileges to tour Fort Campbell. They drove the family's '62 Studebaker Lark, the car that Mary and I had courted in and I drove to high school with my Mom who was the district music teacher. They pulled a tiny trailer that provided little more than the minimum accommodations for two, and that trailer caused some embarrassment because I had arranged for parking of their much larger Argosy trailer, rather like the rounded AirStream that was quite nice and livable accommodations. This little thing made my request into a laughable exaggeration. Because Mom and Jake could not get on Clarksville Base unescorted, with prior arrangements in place, I gave them the grand tour of the Admin area. Questions about the Base and what went on there were deflected, but the fences and guards were enough to draw conclusions that secrecy was the nature of work on Base.

It was during this visit that Mom told me about the FBI who had canvassed my home community of Little Richmond while doing my background investigation and how it had affected my grandmother. I wondered what the investigators had said to my grandmother for her to arrive at such a scathing conclusion of me, but Mom recognized that the investigation was just part of qualifying me for whatever I was doing on Clarksville Base. But the Navy in a land-locked Base in Tennessee still did not compute.

Chapter 17

Clarksville

Mary and I became acquainted with Clarksville for the same reasons as all the other military personnel: proximity to its attractions; shopping and dining mostly, about all that we had money for. Her job with the PX provided more income than mine from working on H-bombs, and with our on-Base housing no cost, our financial situation was the best it had been since we were married, although we still lived paycheck-to-paycheck. Throughout the remainder of 1967 and into '69, we were able to maintain a modest lifestyle of outings into Clarksville to Shoney's for drive-in burgers and shakes, pizza at Shakey's where we enjoyed the tavern atmosphere and sing-alongs, take-home bar-b-que at the small smokery across 41A from Grandpa's Discount Barn, and a few other family oriented restaurants around town. As we learned more about our new environs, I saw the city of Clarksville as trying to maintain its own identity while continually providing commercial interests catering to Fort Campbell's military presence that kept the area's cash flowing.

Grandpa's Discount Barn was a good example, an early-day Wal-Mart style discount store of local origin. Along with many other young military customers, Mary and I made it our primary shopping spot because of low prices and its wide range of merchandise.

Eateries were, however, more mundane than Albuquerque's excellent Spanish and Southwest cuisine amid slow-paced, old world charm. Clarksville's fare was overwhelmingly fast paced due to young military personnel who often ate on the go. A number of "all you can eat" spots around town were invitations to get stuffed, just what the hard-charging young men of the 101st Airborne liked to do. On one occasion, Mary and I planned to do our bit at a nearby restaurant offering a spaghetti special, only to arrive after the Austin Peay State University football squad had cleaned out the place. The restaurant's manager apologized, and we sampled a different choice.

I wanted to continue college, having tasted the elixir of learning, and Austin Peay's nearby campus was an immediate attraction to me, but with no time for classes I was constrained to studying on my own. By the fall semester of 1968, Mary and I had been married over three years and had thoroughly enjoyed our adventures together, but since we were without children by then, we wondered if one of us might be incapable. Regardless, we lived each day to the fullest and packed in whatever was within our means. For her, that summer was a turning point in her life because she enrolled at APSU as a freshman. She formed a lifelong attachment with the small but pretty campus, although her enrollment lasted just that semester. Within a couple of months of starting classes, she learned that our first child was on the way. Jill was one of her student friends who added new dimensions to our lives as mentioned earlier. Unfortunately, after leaving Clarksville, we lost contact with her and left Austin Peay behind as well, although noting from time to time when it reappeared in our lives for some reason, such as years later when a flamboyant basketball team made the small college a powerhouse.

Having lived in the area over a year by the time of her enrollment, we had become acquainted with further reaches, especially Nashville. Just an hour or so from Clarksville put us downtown, and our drives to various spots were memorable. One fulfilled an interest of mine; we drove through the Vanderbilt University campus, the first of several drives to come. The beautiful campus renewed my affection for the academic environment that I so thoroughly enjoyed while wandering the Berea College campus as a boy. I wanted to go to college with an intensity that remained unfulfilled even after more than a decade of college before and after my H-bomb years.

Another Nashville drive revealed a surprising and unexpected sight: sitting majestically on the green of a handsomely landscaped city park was a full size reproduction of the famous Parthenon of ancient Greek history. My immediate recognition of the structure recalled the photographs in various books I had studied with so much interest while in high school, and I immediately wanted to learn of this Parthenon's origin. Why Nashville, Tennessee? On that first visit, I was amazed to learn that the structure was a full-scale replica of the original, the best in the world, and was originally constructed as the centerpiece of Tennessee's Centennial Park, standing since that celebration in 1897, and I had never heard of it. Inside stood another full scale replica of Greek artistry, a statue 42-feet tall of the patron goddess of Athens, Athena. Both were recreations of originals dating back to 438 BC, right there in the middle of Nashville. Inside and outside the structure were wonders for me. Although interesting as the city's art museum, I saw little of the art for admiring the building. Never did I imagine that two years later I would be standing on the Acropolis in Athens admiring the original, fulfillment of high school dreams of wandering through the ancient world.

To walk in the steps of Pericles, to stand where the voices of Socrates and Plato were once heard extolling their great ideas that so shaped the Western frame of mind, to be in the ancient theaters where the great plays had been performed, to walk among the origins of the ideas that I continually learned more about in my reading, had become my aspirations. While admiring Nashville's Parthenon, I had no idea that my daydreams would come true courtesy of being an H-bomb mechanic, a far-into-the-future product of Aristotle's deductive reasoning that became the scientific method that spawned nuclear physics. As I encountered new ideas, I assimilated history, philosophy, art and politics by steadily connecting the dots of human existence, and this unexpected dot discovered in Nashville remained a lasting memory.

In contrast to historical artistry from the ancients, Nashville's country music scene centered on another famous building, the Ryman Auditorium. Built by a wealthy riverboat captain for a favorite minister, it was, by 1968, known worldwide as the home of the Grand Ole Opry, musical variety broadcast by then on both radio and TV. Up and down surrounding streets were the shops of singers blaring their recordings over loudspeakers to passersby who walked from tune to tune along every sidewalk. Merchandising a famous singer was the name of the game within each store, many being the personal sales outlet for the singer, and with the nearby Ryman the focus of country music, fans collected in the area. When Mary and I decided to go to the Opry one weekend to see a favorite singer, we learned just how avid fans were when we arrived early to find that the line of people had already wrapped around the building and the ticket office wasn't even open. We decided to watch TV and try again later.

That TV time had our attention when the first episode of *Hee-Haw* aired as a local summer filler. From then on, there was no need to combat the Ryman's crowds; *Hee-Haw* gave us front row seats to the best in country music entertainment. While living in Clarksville, we did, however, tour the Ryman and walked where the great singers past and present performed. That tour gave us a sense of awe for the hallowed halls of this once-upon-a-time church turned entertainment capital. The acoustics of the building were amazing; normal voices on stage could be heard almost everywhere in the seating. As we strolled through the building, it displayed the tattered appearance of a fine, old matron clinging to past glories. As a well seasoned structure of wood, the Ryman looked like a fire trap to me, one that would go up in smoke with the slightest spark and take high loss of life with it. The number of people regularly packed inside along with the building's limited egress through only two doorways looked like an enormous tragedy just waiting to happen. Some years later, the Opry moved to a new location, and the Ryman closed its doors to settle into steady decline. It sat on choice downtown real estate, and speculation told that the site was to become a high rise hotel, or maybe a parking lot. Fortunately, this great hall of country music was spared and revived when far-sighted investors restored the Ryman and returned it to service in its time honored venue. Even though a far bigger country music complex rose on the eastern edge of Nashville, the Ryman and nearby Printer's Alley were saved to become enduring downtown attractions.

Downtown Nashville had other attractions important to me, John Tune Import Motors in particular. Unlike Albuquerque, Nashville had a Sunbeam dealership where I could get parts for our Alpine. During our two years at Clarksville Base, jaunts to visit John Tune's parts counter were only occasional, but one trip stands out as a muscle car duel. Sandy had loaned me his GTO for a morning run to get another part, and just out of Clarksville I came to the last stoplight on a flat section of 41A four lane. I pulled to a stop to await the green light. Seemingly scripted for the moment, a new American Motors AMX pulled to a stop beside me; a legendary GTO and an upstart AMX side by side. I noticed its engine badge, 390 cubic inches, and recognized that this smaller, lighter car than the GTO had all the credentials to be a superior boulevard rocket, but I wasn't about to let the driver get away easy. Sandy's GTO engine was of 400 cubic inches fed by triple carburetors that he always kept in top running condition. In the moments before the green light, I set my attack: I revved the engine to launch under power, held the four speed transmission in first gear in preparation for power shifts to higher gears, checked the tach red line as the shift point, and was ready. The open road ahead and no cars behind, just the two of us on this sunny morning, seemed like a setup, but there we were when the green flashed. Unleashed, the GTO's HO (High Output) power roared off the line and steadily built a lead over the AMX. By the time I was in third gear and several car lengths ahead, the battle was over. The GTO won hands down. After that initial blast, we set the same pace for Nashville, and on the outskirts, the AMX veered off in another direction. I went on to get the needed part, and once back on Base, I bragged about Sandy's GTO, a proven muscle car at a time well before the term "Muscle Car" was invented as a nostalgic recall of the great cars of the 1960s. His GTO was one of the era's best.

Our Alpine was only a weakling compared to the GTO, but it was enough to meet our transportation needs: Mary to work at the Fort Campbell PX and to-and-from Austin Peay while I caught rides with fellow GMTs. Our "Fast Tomato" also took us on weekend outings of progressively greater distances, such as to Mammoth Cave with our Youth Fellowship group. Our cash that day amounted to a twenty dollar bill, more than sufficient for the outing, but when another adult director asked to borrow ten dollars, we suddenly had no cash when he, smiling, told me that he had decided to buy photographic film with the other ten dollars and hoped I didn't mind. He would pay me back on payday, which he did, but at that moment, Mary and I were financially stranded. I spoke with the Chaplain who offered a loan of twenty dollars until payday, and all of us went on our outing.

While in the Cave with its many fascinations, I learned that during the Civil War, deposits of saltpeter had been mined from it to make black powder and recognized another historical point in the progression of munitions. Black powder was the firepower behind America's bloodiest war, and I stood amid the cave's old saltpeter works thinking that just one H-bomb exceeded every ounce of black powder ever expended in all the death and destruction it had accumulated. My H-bombs condensed the expanse of mankind's existence into a blinding white flash of evaporating magnitude; everything explosive before them was little more than dust in a whirlwind, yet the bloody Civil War and continual wars since then continued the trail of humans made targets of firepower, all based on explosives that evolved unimaginably far into the destruction index with H-bombs.

For that day, though, living paycheck-to-paycheck was a lesson that became the basis for building some savings from our meager income. But when I did so with a local Clarksville bank only to be burned by a bookkeeping snafu on their part, I resolved that we should keep a nest egg ourselves. Mary was good at squirreling away cash, and I started putting Silver Certificate bills away in an envelope stashed in a drawer. Later, those one dollar and two dollar notes, a few fives and tens, even fewer twenties, helped us through some tough times. Then, a decade or so later, when Silver Certificates were long since out of circulation, a letter from the bank came in the mail one day with a check for the disputed savings. An audit of bank records exposed the error, and they had tracked me down to put the small sum of money back in my hands, about twenty-two dollars.

Clarksville Base site of graves of World War-II German POWs Eugen Ulrich (Dec. 3, 1944), Kurt Franke (Dec. 12, 1945), Herbert Lindner (Jan. 11, 1945), Josef Reidinger (Jan. 22, 1945), Guenter Cassens (Sept. 15, 1945). Death date after V-E Day indicate that repatriation of POWs was a slow process that kept some of them detained well after the war in Europe had ended.

Chapter 18

Five White Stones

One winter day early in 1968, I was driving from 8 S. O'Bannon to the Base when something in the underbrush caught my eye. Just inside the corner of the fences near the junction of Woodlawn and Mabry Roads stood... What? I made a mental note to look closer when passing this location again.

The next time, I was sure I saw the tip of something man-made, something visible just above the underbrush. I estimated that it had to be about six feet tall to be visible above the undergrowth, and with each passing I slowed to see more. In a day or two, I could make out what appeared to be a tall obelisk shaped like the Washington Monument in miniature. The brush laid bare by the season allowed only patchy visibility through to the area under the broad spreading limbs of the giant oak tree that had long held that spot. Under it appeared to be an obelisk in stone with its pointed tip just barely visible.

More sightings followed on subsequent mornings and afternoons as I drove slowly by until I was sure that a graveyard existed under the oak tree that spread majestically, covering hallowed ground underneath. This was an intriguing discovery: Could it be a graveyard for a family who lived nearby before the War and Camp Campbell, I wondered? I wanted to get a closer look, but dared not to approach the fences.

Then, a few days later, I made another even more startling discovery. At just the right place, I could see another gravestone, this one of military style: a small, white marble slab rounded on top. A military graveyard immediately posed all sorts of intriguing questions, and I presumed that Civil War graves lay quietly on the knoll.

What battle had been fought here, I wondered? Who were these soldiers? Many more questions fired my curiosity. I had no idea what I was onto.

Mary and I had walked the ramparts of the Civil War era Fort Donelson near the town of Dover just west of Clarksville where I learned more about the Confederate defeat that I just could not understand.

Years earlier as a boy with little to do on cold winter days, I had read several books on the Civil War and studied many battles to learn about all the leading commanders, the major campaigns, and the progression of the war in some detail. I had learned that Fort Donelson was a well fortified Confederate location on stone bluffs overlooking the Cumberland River from the south bank.

Union river traffic heading for Nashville faced massive assault from Fort Donelson's big guns, as Flag Officer Foote discovered when he opened fire on the Fort from his gunboats during mid-February, 1862. The Confederate gunners returned fire, their "Iron Valentines" smashing the Union fleet, and great cheers went up for beating off the assault.

The Confederate ranks, a large contingent of some 16,000 men, grew in number a few days earlier when troops abandoned Fort Henry, a much less formidable guardian on the Tennessee River located further west from Donelson. Union forces handily defeated Fort Henry, and they were jubilant in anticipation of another easy victory at Fort Donelson. Southern gunners thoroughly beating off their river assault appeared to be a turning of the tide of battle indicating a much tougher assault.

General Ulysses S. Grant's battle plan was unfolding first as river battles in the region, the western campaigns of the Civil War that began when his forces quickly took the small, river level Fort Henry that easily fell to Foote's gunboats. Withdrawal of Southern troops then supplemented Fort Donelson's ranks in both numbers and supplies. Taking Donelson would likely prove to be a long and bloody campaign.

Fort Donelson was a far superior fortification but was led by an incompetent commander, a political appointee rather than a military man. He turned and ran. Massing against him was a Union army under Grant, an unknown commander at the time who was to make his fame at Fort Donelson in the next three days. Behind Fort Donelson stood the Confederacy that could bring up reinforcements along the road from Nashville whenever needed, making well-defended Fort Donelson both strategically important to Southern defenses and well supported.

The second in command, another political appointee with some military experience but little will, turned and ran, too. Third in command was a battle-hardened military man, General Simon Buckner, but he had been kept isolated from command information by his superiors who did not include him in pre-battle intelligence. Upon assuming command of Fort Donelson, Buckner had little to go on to support his new position, including an officer staff thoroughly confused by the turn-coat departures of their two senior commanders just as the battle began to unfold. Many of them wanted to evacuate their troops as well. Some did, further weakening Fort Donelson's defenses.

The road to Nashville, however, remained defended and open to movement of troops and supplies. Lines of communications were maintained with more Confederate forces under General Albert Johnston further to the east of Donelson that could have been brought in to defend the road and the Fort's outer perimeter that ran along ridges, terrain that made assault an uphill advance against entrenched foes.

Grant's advance on Fort Henry and slow overland movement toward Donelson provided ample opportunities to assess Union strengths while providing time for movement of additional Southern troops into effective defense positions, if the Confederate command had stood firm. The time between the fall of Fort Henry and contact with Donelson's defenders offered short lived opportunities for Donelson's command to further develop defenses and make troop placements for battle. Instead, they turned tail.

Three miles was well within the turn in the Cumberland River that brought the Union gunboats in range of Donelson's guns long before the Yankee gunners got close enough for their guns to be effective. Formidable exchanges of fire, however, did not result in the quick defeat of Fort Donelson. Rather than fall to Union guns, Foote's seige of Donelson landed a single round inside the fortifications, exploding with no effect. In return, the Southern sharpshooters trained their heavy guns, accurate for three miles, on Foote's fleet and reduced it to wreckage.

Defenders of Fort Donelson knew that their position was important to the South because it controlled river access to Nashville, the transportation capital of the western Confederacy. The Fort's charter was to guard and defend the Cumberland River approach to Nashville, the lifeline of commerce and wealth brought by the constant flow of riverboat traffic before the war. If Confederate forces failed to hold, the South was open to Union invasion from the west, the military objective of divide and conquer.

Control of the Mississippi River, the lifeline of Southern commerce in the West, was the primary aim of the Union divide and conquer assault on the South. That objective was to cleave the Confederacy from supporters in states further west, and river campaigns produced hard-fought Union victories that sent Grant's fame skyrocketing, beginning at Fort Henry and furthered at Donelson where he became known as "Unconditional Surrender" Grant.

His victory came at a time when Union victories were few and progress of the war grim. News of his taking of Forts Henry and Donelson sent waves of jubilation throughout the North, and President Lincoln found that he finally had a capable commander with the will to win in the heat of battle. Keeping the Northern and Southern states together as a nation was highly uncertain at the time of Grant's assault on Fort Donelson, and his overwhelming victory breathed a measure of hope for a rapid close of conflict and re-unification of the States. It was not to be. Three more years of war were yet to be waged with Grant rising to become the field commander of the Union forces who accepted Southern surrender at Appomattox Court House in 1865, ending the bloodiest war ever fought on American soil.

Fort Donelson fell in 1862, yielded by capitulation to Northern forces whose approach got no further than the outer earthen works, never reaching the walls of the well defended Fort itself. With its fall, the fate of the Confederacy was sealed, beginning with the taking of Nashville and culminating with General Sherman's devastating march to the sea that split the South in the final year of the war.

The Union was saved but at enormous cost in lives and destruction. As Mary and I walked Fort Donelson, a National Military Park established in 1928, the only reason I could determine for the fall of such a well equipped and strategically located fort was incompetence. Had it held, though, the Civil War would have been protracted into a longer and bloodier fight. While there, I learned that one of the Union commanders who had strode Donelson's grounds was General Lew Wallace whose recollections of the campaign I had read, the same Lew Wallace of *Ben Hur* fame whom I had learned about in Santa Fe.

I was certain that some skirmish of the Fort Donelson-Nashville campaign had taken place on what later became Fort Campbell, and I itched to learn more about the white stone I had seen. Were there more that I could not see? I mentioned their location to Sandy one day, and he knew about them.

Their small patch of ground under the giant oak tree was part of the Base's groundskeeping, and he offered to take me there. During lunch one day, we piled into a pickup and rocked our way up a narrow, rutted mudwash from the railhead, a climb through the woods that was not kept as a road. Stopping at the edge of the site, the flat plot was maintained from overgrowth with modest ground cover of grass that grew sparsely in the shade of the massive oak tree that gave the knoll a cathedral quality. Six graves were in view.

The obelisk I had seen stood about seven feet tall to the left of the southern reaches of the tree, a lone grave that I immediately concluded was the resting place of a past resident who had favored this spot. The row of five white stones to the right of the tree were so low to the ground and mostly masked from view by the surrounding underbrush that I would never have seen them without the obelisk having first caught my attention. I bent over the first stone expecting to read the name of a Union or Confederate dead, and my mouth dropped open. The name was Eugen Ulrich, a German soldier who died December 1944. I quickly checked the other four, also German soldiers, all with death dates during 1945. POWs Kurt Franke, Herbert Lindnep, Josef Reidinger and Guenter Cassens lay there with Ulrich.

I was astounded. German soldiers! Not Civil War. I had no inkling that POWs were a part of Clarksville Base history, and no one I talked to afterward knew anything about them. There were no books in the Base library or the Fort Campbell library or the Clarksville city library that even mentioned POWs had been in the area. I found no mention anywhere, but I knew that, if POWs had been here some twenty-two years earlier, these five dying for some reason, local people ought to know about them. I found no one who professed to know anything, and the young librarian I talked to at the Clarksville city library gave me the impression that she thought I was perpetrating a hoax. After all, Clarksville Base was a mysterious, secret place, and I professed to be one of its operatives who had actually been inside the place. My existence in front of her was, itself, mysterious, and she wanted to know more about me and what I did on Clarksville Base than talk about World War-II German POWs that she knew nothing about.

Thirty years later, a quarter-century after Clarksville Base closed and the fences isolating the graves from the world were removed, the existence of those five white stones became sufficiently known to the general public that Clarksville's historical society and library began searching old newspapers, resulting in compilation of a chronology of articles about the camp and its internees, but not a complete enough history to suit me.

I read through the newspapers to learn that about three thousand POWs had been interned at Camp Campbell in three barracks, the first five hundred arriving July 24, 1943. When I began attaching names to the dates on the five white stones, I was able to associate a soldier or two with cause of death. One was Josef Reidinger. While on a work detail, he was shot and killed January 22, 1945 while attempting escape at the Clarksville train station.

Where did Josef Reidinger think he would escape to? Did he realize that he was in a huge country with an all-pervasive anti-German sentiment? Where did he think he would go? Where would he hide? Even if he got away, how would he survive? I wondered what might have been his reason for attempting escape by suddenly bolting to place a moving train between himself and his armed Military Police guard? Even if the maneuver worked, what would he do next? Did he even think that trying to escape might end with a bullet in his back? Did he even consider the risk of death, never to return to his homeland? Why did he not choose to wait out the war like the other, mostly, Afrika Korps POWs confined at Camp Campbell, then disappear into post-war obscurity with them?

Instead, this young German Corporal attempted to flee from his captors and died for a moment's impulse. Although his life and those of his eternal comrades remain obscure, his end and theirs had lain maintained within military boundaries removed from public knowledge in this location that I first saw that day, although originally in another graveyard within Camp Campbell, then relocated to what later became Clarksville Base.

Then I was struck by another question. Who built Clarksville Base? The POWs, I wondered? After inquiries to the National Archives about records concerning the Base and its construction resulted in notification that no such records exist in their files, I associated the POWs and construction of nearby Armed Forces Special Weapons Project Site B, later to become Clarksville Base, with post-war newspaper statements by some of the POWS who spoke of working in a rock quarry. Could it be that they hewed the rock along the southern bank of the Little West Fork Creek to make the complex of tunnels that became one of this nation's prime nuclear weapons sites?

Further clues came when I learned that construction of Site B was underway prior to 1947 and that all the POWs were not repatriated for as much as two years after the war. The overlap of time was sufficient to support the notion that close proximity of the POWs to Site B, and that some had worked in a quarry, posed the reasonable probability that German manpower had carved the original complex that became a nuclear weapons depot after their departure.

These questions and more swirled through my thoughts as my imagination prompted me to look for any clues to the POW internment camp that surely once lay somewhere along Fort Campbell's Mabry Road. I had managed to discern the gravestones through the underbrush, but, try as I did, not another thing, not the slightest clue, was found to indicate anything more than a 1960s era US Army reservation.

That quarter-century mentioned saw the secrecy surrounding Clarksville Base fade while interest among area historians grew regarding the mystery of the Base and its five white stones. Questions far outnumber answers and the whole story may never be known completely. Along the way, the obelisk that had stood so long to mark the first of the graves under the giant oak tree was removed, reducing to further obscurity the life that had once walked the knoll and so admired its cathedral qualities to be buried there, and whose monument first caught my attention.

Me and Mary with our Sunbeam Alpine, "The Fast Tomato."

Chapter 19

The Fast Tomato

Later on that Spring I was sent TDY to Albuquerque for advanced warhead training and gathered more adventures in the southwest as told earlier. Mary was left to hold 8 S. O'Bannon with friends and visitors dropping in as she felt comfortable. Sandy agreed to check on her from time to time, and, in preparation for the occasion in which she might need defense, Mary and I bought an old west style revolver, belt and holster from a local dealer. Sandy and I undertook to provide some measure of training and chose a suitable spot on Fort Campbell's vast reaches of woodland to set up a target for sharpening Mary's skill with the handgun. She quietly accepted all the "training" and waited her turn to shoot at the target. Then, suitably "trained," she took the pistol in hand, sighted down the barrel, pulled the trigger, and scored a bullseye on the first shot. Sandy and I were speechless. Mary commented that she had been raised on a farm and that her father had taught her how to shoot a gun when she was a little girl. "Training" was over; she was a better shot than either of us.

I returned from TDY a month or so later, on a beautiful afternoon of fluffy whites gracing a rich blue sky, and Mary greeted my return with hugs and kisses. I arrived to find her visiting with Sandy and Ethel, a friend from our dating days in North Carolina. Our reunion was even more enjoyable with the laughter that Sandy and friends always brought with them. I was thankful for such good friends who had taken their time to look in on Mary and help her through lonesome times, and the four of us spent the remainder of the day telling stories of whatever the moment conjured up, including those surrounding some small gifts that I brought from Albuquerque: a fasionable Spanish frontier type outfit for Mary, complete with a black felt flat hat and ribbon. I told of the Spanish southwest, Carlos and Miguel and their phenomenal guitar skills, saying that I wanted to play a guitar like them. We exchanged all sorts of stories, but not one from my training, just two of us GMTs learning the intricacies of advanced warheads.

Mary wanted to know more about the strange phone call that she had received from John, who was also at Sandia at the time I was on TDY but in a different capacity. Young men and pretty women; what more can be said? There was, however, more to the story, and we instantly had the attention of both Sandy and Ethel. I told that I had gone to the Sandia Base NCO Club that evening to call Mary and was hailed by John. I was not aware that he was also at Sandia, and we renewed the car stories of olde. Did he still have his hot rod '64 Chevy? No. John sat me down, put a tall drink in my hand, and proceeded to tell a sorrowful tale of misfortune.

A few months earlier, a wintertime fire had raced through his parent's home, and he had spent the last of his VRB putting them up in a motel. Waiting to the last possible minute to leave for Albuquerque, he carefully negotiated worsening weather until circumstances in Ohio conspired to destroy his car. While traveling slowly due to a slippery highway, the driver of the car in front of him abruptly stopped before crossing a bridge that looked icy. John stopped, too, but the truck behind him could not. It crashed into his shiny Chevy and sandwiched it between the back end of the car in front destroying his pride and joy from bumper to bumper. With orders to report for duty in Albuquerque in the next few days, he had little time and no money to negotiate for another car or to salvage his wreck. He had to leave his crumpled car and all the goodies in it to the junk yard scavengers while he took other transportation to his assignment.

John was a likable guy whose bad luck worsened when his insurance company refused to pay for the car other than replacement value for a '64 Chevrolet Impala. He had all the receipts for the fortune that he had put into the car, but his insurance balked, and he refused to accept their settlement which was well below the worth of the car. Meanwhile, he had no transportation, and, being confined mostly to Sandia Base, he had become a frequent patron of the Club. When he asked what I was doing living in the barracks, he perked up at the thought that Mary and I had split and that she might be available, indicating his deep affection for her. No, I reassured him. I had come to the Club to call Mary as I frequently did. He seized the moment, wanting to talk to her.

Well, this situation posed a touchy set of circumstances that were further amplified when I declined. He offered to pay for the phone call. Again I declined. He upped the offer and bought another drink for me, with the first still in my hand unconsumed. "John," I said. "Mary is my wife. It just wouldn't be proper for you to talk to her or for me to take money to do so." My southern upbringing of what was proper and what wasn't guided me. Still, he persisted. He WAS, after all, a friend who had been in our Clarksville Base apartment many times. He had ALWAYS liked Mary, especially her cakes and pies, and he JUST wanted to tell her how MUCH he enjoyed them. He JUST wanted to talk to her, to say hello again. What could he DO over the phone or say to her two thousand miles away?

Hmmm. I thought about it. Yes, John WAS a friend from Clarksville, but talking to another man's wife was.... Well, he HAD been in our lives previously, and he HAD talked with Mary many times before. It wasn't as if he was a total stranger, and since I had nothing more than my sense of propriety, he knew he had me, then clinched the moment by offering to pay for the call and give me five dollars for the privilege.

"Well, OK," I said. I stuffed his five dollars in my pocket; he took the phone, and I stepped away. While Sandy and Ethel stared in disbelief, Mary told of the revelation that John was a secret admirer, a surprise, then dispelled the notion as just another aspect of his outgoing personality.

After that TDY I lost track of John, never to hear from him again. But our time during 1967 and early '68 hot rodding on Clarksville Base, building his car and those fantastic burnouts on that section of pavement that I helped campaign for, to get it officially designated for such things, remain enduring recollections of fast cars and youthful exuberance during our days on Clarksville Base away from the H-bombs stowed behind massive doors nearby in the "Q".

A crusty Chief Petty Officer, a highly skilled mechanic, ran the auto shop and did so with an iron fist and a firm rule: everything had its place; use it, clean it, and put it back where you got it. He knew everything anyone needed to know about any car and was a major aid in my sorting out the Prince of Darkness that still plagued our Alpine. Shop time was scheduled during the day when he was on duty, and in his absence after hours, work time often extended into the night if he thought the guys working on their cars would leave the shop in the pristine condition he expected. On each departure, he placed responsibility for keeping order in the shop to the ranking sailor who knew, as we all did, that we had better follow the rules. If we didn't, the scorching of hell awaited us the next time we walked into his shop. In time, though, everyone using the shop adapted to his rules and received the benefit of his help and knowledge as well, along with the machinery that he kept in top working order.

When our "Fast Tomato" suddenly began running rough one day and responded to nothing I did, he diagnosed the problem as a burned valve. That was a major problem that would normally require a significant outlay of cash to repair, and I began wondering where I would get the money and how I would get the car to John Tune Import Motors in Nashville, the Sunbeam experts. Not so in his shop; this job was just another opportunity for him to teach us plebes how to properly work on an automobile. He directed me to every tool I needed for removing the carburetors and the head from the engine. Sure enough, there was a valve with its edge burned so that it no longer sealed the combustion chamber. Next came stripping the head followed by step after step performed under his watchful eye until the head was bare and all components laid out in order on his work bench. Then came cleaning and grinding each valve, then grinding the valve seats in the head, then polishing the surfaces, then cleaning the head and components of all debris. Before reassembly, he asked me if I had checked the flatness of the head. It was a cast aluminum piece, and aluminum was known to warp. "No," I said sheepishly.

"If you don't make sure the damn head is flat, you'll blow a head gasket, and all this work will have to be done over. Did you ever think of that, sailor?" He was giving me another lesson, and went a step further saying that if the head was milled properly, it would raise the compression ratio and give the car more power. I was all for that, and he proceeded to guide me through the process of setting up the emptied head on a Bridgeport mill, a machine that I knew how to use from my machinist training before the Navy. He guided me through the whole process step by step, and, with his help, I reassembled the modified head and reinstalled it the next day, mounted the carburetors, adjusted everything as a complete tune-up, then stuck the key in the ignition. The engine fired the first time and purred like a kitten. The Chief simply turned and walked back to his office. This masterful job had cost me no more than a rebuild gasket set and was a valuable lesson from a master mechanic to boot. I felt awkward and wanted to pay him, but with nothing more than pocket change, I could only offer my thanks, to which he scowled, "What the hell do you think all this is here for?"

"Yes, sir."

Our "Fast Tomato" ran smoothly from then on, and for the duration of my assignment to Clarksville Base, I did all the work on the car at the Base shop until I knew nearly everything about the mechanics of a Sunbeam Alpine.

Chapter 20

The Last Train From Clarksville

The last train from Clarksville pulled out from the Base rail-head loaded with H-bombs. Decisions had been implemented to consolidate the nation's nuclear arsenal and Clarksville Base, Site B, the second of thirteen warhead and weapon depots, was phased out. The specially built ATMX cars were rolled in place at the railhead, their tops removed, the only way into them, and each car became a beehive of activity. The H-bombs were transported to the railhead by truck, and the Seabees used a crane to lift each stack in their roll-around cradles up, over and into the cars where they were positioned. Their wheels were then set and locked. Robust tie-downs at each corner of their strong, custom machined cradle-carriages were hooked and chained in place to equally robust tie-downs in the floor of each railcar. Sandy and his crew made trip after trip emptying the magazines as fall-of-the-year 1969 and base closure approached. With each departure, I noted the reduction of inventory in my records and reported the state of the inventory each day to the Pentagon. Each railcar was loaded with as many bombs as would fit, two in the case of the massive B-53, a dozen or more when only B-61s or B-57s were loaded, the latter stacked two-high.

Back in the maintenance buildings, crews went through stripping out everything that was useful, leaving empty structures. Except for those shipments that went by air, every tool, every bomb component, every piece of test equipment, everything was inventoried, wrapped for protection, crated securely, and sent to the railhead. Because of my authorization, I drove one of the undercarriers from the base to Fort Campbell's airfield, arriving on one occasion to be confronted by a plane captain who was concerned that he was being overloaded. He was a senior pilot, an Air Force Major who counted the number of crates and cradled bombs to fret that we were loading too much stuff. He approached our duty officer with his complaint and wanted to know what was being loaded. The duty officer did not know the details. Since I was the on-site expert who knew the codes, I was detailed to reassure the Major that we were within both flight and nuclear load-out regulations for his plane. He was not convinced and pointed to the manifest wanting to know what each item was. I easily went down the list pointing to this set of cradled H-bombs and that crate with its warhead components until I came to an item label RESC. I was momentarily stumped, and he didn't like the situation one bit. I was supposed to be an expert on this stuff, but I couldn't tell him what an RESC was?

In the chill of the night with a flashlight exposing the codes listed on the manifest, I stood before him mentally checking off the warheads and components in the load but could not recall what an RESC was. "It is not a bomb," I told him. I knew that from the codes, but he declared that he wasn't going to accept the load until he knew exactly what everything was, including this RESC thing.

Tension between this Air Force Major and my Navy Duty Officer tightened with me in the middle. The magenta and red lights around us flashed; the engines of the aircraft hummed, kept warm for imminent take off; the lights of our vehicles pierced the cool night air; the engines of our tractors and carriers throbbed; I was on the hot seat. Both looked at me for explanations, and a moment of strained impatience permeated the airstrip. Then it occurred to me. "Oh! This is a B-28 tail fin section."

"A what?" the Major asked. "Is it nuclear?"

That was the reason I did not, at first, recognize the code. It wasn't a nuclear component, it was an air-drop stabilizer, the aerodynamic rear section for one configuration of the Mk 28 warhead, an old configuration that I had not worked on since training. None of the B-28s in my inventory were built into its configuration, but the components were still in the arsenal like a lot of other optional equipment. It did, however, contain high explosives.

"High explosives?" the Major questioned, his voice with some aggravation. "Damn! How much?"

I explained the B-28 air drop scenario to the point that a small charge in the fin section is ignited to blow off the fairing with the warhead continuing in freefall just prior to ignition. I assured him that the charge was small, about the size of a 20-gauge shotgun shell, and that satisfied him. All the hardware was loaded on his plane, secured in place, and he took off.

Load-outs continued regularly for days, mostly from the railhead, and as building after building in the "Q" was closed, personnel numbers decreased. In the operations center where I worked, assignments to empty bunker after bunker gradually depleted the work performed by two civilian employees until they no longer had jobs and departed. One was a retired E-9 Marine who became so disgruntled with losing his job that he re-enlisted as an E-8 and volunteered for Viet Nam, actions that I simply could not understand. Anything was better than Nam.

By late 1969 that jungle affair was still being called a policing action in most official quarters, while the word "war" was taking on wider use among increasingly outspoken critics. The nightly news brought the scenes of battle into every home at dinner time, and a growing distaste for body bags and battlefield gore was maturing into openly expressed attacks against the political decision-makers who perpetuated the affair. A growing segment of the population came to question US involvement halfway around the globe and increasingly found no good reason for our troops to be there. Thousands of young Americans had been killed by then, and many more thousands had received life-changing wounds as the result of orders to take this or that hill in Korean War infantry and artillery fashion, only to give up the ground taken when ordered to pull back. Viet Nam was increasingly seen as a political quagmire with no clear purpose, intense jungle warfare without meaning, and its enormous costs in lives and tax dollars was increasingly questioned. Ultimately, more than fifty-six thousand young Americans were killed in that conflict that ended with the US pulling out in the early '70s, all of them lost for nothing, each one a tragic loss to family, friends and loved-ones, each one a life of hopes and dreams and desires ended by penny bullets and cheap explosives manufactured by the ton for no other reason than to inflict death and destruction upon fellow human beings.

On the USS Forrestal later, I often stood reading the names of the sailors listed on the huge bronze plaque mounted in the hangar bay for all the crew to see. They had died because of the horrendous Tonkin Gulf explosions and fire in 1967. I sensed knowing each one, each young man like me filled with optimism for adventures yet to be lived, but with their lives cut tragically short by the combination of equipment malfunction, the decision to expend old bombs packed with munitions far more sensitive to shock and heat than modern high explosives, and rapidly unfolding sequences of events brought on by decisions made by planners who were not on the front line or were held responsible. Explosions ripped open the deck, and through the twisted steel came fiery death, burning jet fuel that rained upon off-duty crewmen below. I wondered if their names were included among the Viet Nam dead.

The nature of Clarksville Base was low key and quiet. Handling H-bombs was slow and deliberate with oversight by skilled operatives along with continuous scrutiny amid high level security. No one was in any hurry, and on the rather regular occasions when work was slack, building and grounds maintenance were the order of the day. One such bout of maintenance came with the order to strip the concrete floor of our shop of its overburden of layered sealant and wax. Keeping everything ship-shape was Navy routine, but I wondered if the crew on hands and knees with steel scrapers flaking up years of buildup was simply make-work. In any case, we were issued sharp edged scrapers and assigned sections of the floor, but scraping the huge bay floor became a bigger job than expected when our steel scrapers quickly dulled. Progress slowed to less than a crawl. Longer lasting tools had to be acquired, or the task would simply not get done regardless of the elbow grease expended. With my scraper in hand, I spoke with the Chief saying that it dulled so quickly that it was almost useless. Offering knowledge I had of engineering and metallurgy learned prior to the Navy, I could, however, harden the steel so that it would keep its working edge longer. With that suggestion, I was detailed to the shop next door and began a regular turn-over of dull tools heated to red hot, then doused in oil to quench harden them, their working edges then ground to a sharp edge and returned to the scraping crew. The pace of removing the long build-up of concrete sealant and turning it into dust quickened noticeably. Afterward, with application of a new layer of sealant, our shop took on a luster of newness. Paint was re-applied to stripe the floor as before, and then the walls, cages and work benches received sprucing up. Equipment was checked out for proper function, and after a couple of weeks our shop had never looked better.

The reason for the work became obvious one day soon afterward when we were told of a pending inspection by the Commanding General of the Defense Atomic Support Agency, a three-star Air Force General. I was on door duty the day he arrived at our shop, and, when the radio dispatch came through saying that the team was just outside our door and that entry was requested, I activated the electrical mechanisms that opened the door. In stepped the General followed by an Army General of one less star and our Base commander, a Navy Captain, and all the ranking officers of Clarksville Base. I yelled, "Attention on deck!" as the General walked through the door, to which he commanded, "At ease," and the inspection began.

All sorts of bombs and warheads in various stages of disassembly for maintenance were distributed up and down our work stations along our highly polished shop floor. With his at-ease command, each crewman returned to work performing whatever was specified for each weapon, large and small. Our facilities were spotless, highly organized, and every piece of equipment in use was in top working order. The inspection team strolled up and down our operations to the satisfaction of the General and his troupe, each man a high ranking officer who didn't have the foggiest idea of what, exactly, was being done or what each strange looking warhead component was. Questions and answers were exchanged, also to the satisfaction of the General and his staff, and they departed.

I thought it curious that every branch of the military was represented except Marines, and that our top command was Air Force, then Army, while we were Navy. All of us were, however, DASA. Clarksville Base was just one of many DASA sites under the General's command, and I imagined his inspection of each one to involve a great deal of travel from his War Office in the Pentagon.

Our shops were very well equipped with what seemed to be every tool known to man. Although much of the hardware was World War-II surplus and conventional hand tools, close attention to performance meant that everything used regularly was scrutinized and maintained for top performance with backups ready.

Since the "Q" was heavily wooded with only narrow roads winding through hills and valleys with occasional open grassy areas and undergrowth, it was also home to all sorts of wildlife. Animal sightings were everyday occurrences, everything from deer to turkey had the run of the place with no predators for so long that they did not fear our presence.

Speeds along the roadways were held low to avoid collisions with deer, which happened occasionally anyway. One encounter was strange: While the Seabees unloaded a delivery from a parked tractor and flatbed trailer at the entrance of the building where I was working, a deer bounded from the woods and attempted to run under the trailer. Misjudged clearance resulted in slamming into the understructure breaking the deer's back. It struggled under the trailer trying to get to its feet, but only its front legs worked. Finally, exhausted, it lay panting on the asphalt, and what to do wasn't so clear. Word spread quickly and authorization to put the deer out of its misery was given to the Marine guards, the only personnel on Base authorized to carry firearms. Then the chief cook took custody of the carcass, and venison was on the menu a few evening meals later. Prepared as steak, it was, however, tough and chewy in texture and gamey in taste.

The Clarksville Base mess always served good food prepared well, an aspect of Navy life I found at every installation I was on. In contrast, every Army post I was on served lousy food. Why such a difference existed was beyond me since both were military and presumably drew from the same supplies, but Navy chow was universally better.

Overall, Mary and I found Navy life rewarding, and our two year assignment to the Base were good years. Our 8 S. O'Bannon Court residence had been a lively spot for friends and neighbors, but when the last train rolled out, the end of the Base's twenty-two year run neared, and our apartment complex became a ghost town. Number 8 was the last in our block to be vacated of Navy personnel. Once all personnel were reassigned, the Base closed as a DASA facility and was handed over to Fort Campbell.

REPORT OF ENLISTED PERFORMANCE ●UATION
NAVPERS 792 (Rev. 6-65)
0105-402-3001

● OF REPORT 16 OCT 68 To 16 NOV 68

NAME (*Last, First, Middle*)
GABBARD, William A.

SERVICE NO. **B32 36 62** RATE ABB. **GMT2**
PRESENT SHIP OR STATION **NAU, CLARKSVILLE BASE, TENN.**

INSTRUCTIONS

1. For each trait, evaluate the man on his actual observed performance. If performance was not observed, check the "Not Observed" box.
2. Compare him with others of the same rate.
3. If the major portion of his work has been outside his rate or pay grade

during this reporting period, evaluate him on what he did. Describe what he did in the "Comments" section.
4. Pick the phrase which best fits the man in each trait and check left or right box under it. (Left box is more favorable.)

1. PROFESSIONAL PERFORMANCE: His skill and efficiency in performing assigned duties (except SUPERVISORY)

NOT OBSERVED	Extremely effective and reliable. Works well on his own.	Highly effective and reliable. Needs only limited supervision.	Effective and reliable. Needs occasional supervision.	Adequate, but needs routine supervision.	Inadequate. Needs constant supervision.
	* X			*	*

2. MILITARY BEHAVIOR: How well he accepts authority and conforms to standards of military behavior.

NOT OBSERVED	Always acts in the highest traditions of the Navy.	Willingly follows commands and regulations.	Conforms to Navy standards.	Usually obeys commands and regulations. Occasionally lax.	Dislikes and flouts authority. Unseamanlike.
	* X			*	*

3. LEADERSHIP AND SUPERVISORY ABILITY: His ability to plan and assign work to others and effectively direct their activities.

NOT OBSERVED	Gets the most out of his men.	Handles men very effectively.	Gets good results from his men.	Usually gets adequate results.	Poor supervisor.
	*	X		*	*

4. MILITARY APPEARANCE: His military appearance and neatness in person and dress.

NOT OBSERVED	Impressive. Wears Naval uniform with great pride.	Smart. Neat and correct in appearance.	Conforms to Navy standards of appearance.	Passable. Sometimes careless in appearance.	No credit to the Naval Service.
	* X			*	*

5. ADAPTABILITY: How well he gets along and works with others.

NOT OBSERVED	Gets along exceptionally well. Promotes good morale.	Gets along very well with others. Contributes to good morale.	A good shipmate. Helps morale.	Gets along adequately with others.	A misfit.
	*	X		*	*

6. DESCRIPTION OF ASSIGNED TASKS
Maintains stockpile record cards/work order cards for all classified weapons on the base. Conducts weekly reconciliation of Base Records with Field Command's.

7. EVALUATION OF PERFORMANCE (E-5 and above include comment on ability in self expression and command, orally and in writing, of the English language)
Gabbard continues to perform his professional duties in a highly competent and conscientious manner. Gabbard has displayed additional enthusiasm for his work since his promotion to second class on 16 Oct 1968. Gabbard is willing and capable of assuming all the additional duties and responsibilities of a second class petty officer. Being a completely loyal military man, Gabbard strives to perform his tasks to the complete satisfaction of his superiors. Gabbard's command of the English language, both oral and written, is superior to most second class petty officers and a definite asset to himself in the performance of his duties.

* 8. THESE ITEMS MUST BE JUSTIFIED BY COMMENTS IN ADDITION TO THOSE IN ITEM 7 ABOVE
1. Gabbard performs all his assigned duties in a most accurate and timely manner. Attention to detail renders his work very reliable.
2. His military behavior is outstanding. He complies with all orders given by his superiors to the utmost.
Continued.

| X SEMI-ANNUAL | TRANSFER | OTHER ___ | 10. DATE | 11. SIGNATURE ... SUPERIOR |

E. A. DUFF, OPERATIONS OFFICER

Chapter 21

The "Q"

After all the accountable material had been sent to other installations, the vaults emptied, the above and below ground bunkers cleared behind massive doors that were closed and locked, all documentation and records boxed and forwarded to prescribed recipients, the network of communications silenced, and all operations buildings left as hollow as the "Volcano," a large heap of stuff remained. All this non-nuclear, unaccountable hardware was leftovers from earlier H-bomb operations, hardware that was designed for obsolete bombs and warheads or no longer used yet kept stored, such as canvas shrouds and metal frames that had once enclosed the bombs to keep them from view. Disposing of everything left some hardware with no place to go. The decision to bury all of it resulted in a crew of Seabees showing up one day with a bulldozer. A deep trench was cut along the gentle slope behind the building where I worked. All the collected stuff from throughout the Base that had no other place to go went into the trench, and after several days the large mass was covered, the ground over it smoothed, and grass seed sown.

At that point, nuclear operations in the "Q" of Clarksville Base was officially finished, and personnel rapidly dispersed to other assignments. The gate to the "Q" was abandoned; the guard posts at the giant doors over Little West Fork Creek were no longer manned, the contingent of Marines reassigned. The electrified fence and its exploding snakes; the high intensity lighting surrounding the perimeter; everything was shut down. The entire Base was now open without the security net that had previously existed. Only the Admin area remained to be shut down.

Since I had been a frequent visitor to the library, I had gotten to know the civilian librarian well. Her last day was tearful as she carried her potted plants to her car, said her goodbyes, and drove away to begin another phase of her life somewhere else. The library, however, remained intact, and word came to me that I was the new librarian charged with the responsibility of cataloging and packaging its inventory for distribution to the fleet. Various addresses were supplied for shipment of books, but magazines were to be disposed of. I inquired about the fate of the extensive collection of *National Geographic* magazines and was told to do with them as I saw fit. After boxing them, I had them shipped to my mother in North Carolina and ultimately to me. Working alone, I completed the task of emptying the library, stepped out of its door when the job was done, locked it and walked away.

That walk was enigmatic; the Marines were gone, the Army as well. No Seabees were to be seen, their equipment moved elsewhere. The Motor Pool was empty. The gym where I had played basketball for the Clarksville Base Navy team and scored the winning shot in a game was now dark and silent. The NCO Club where Mary and I had attended one function after another, dances, seasonal celebrations, Navy related parties, or just a quiet meal served on white tablecloth and US Navy issue dinnerware, was now closed, its doors locked. The swimming pool that had been a favorite warm weather location for splashing and playing, always impeccably maintained, was now drained and collecting wind-borne leaves. The chow hall was the last to close.

The base was taking on an unkempt appearance of unmowed grass, leaves adrift in the wind, debris blowing across empty parking areas and collecting in the lee of buildings. Few cars were parked around, and I saw no one on my final walk. I was among the last of the Navy personnel to leave, the last GMT to walk Clarksville Base, having been part of its operations at the height of the Cold War, operations that were transferred elsewhere. With orders for reassignment in a few days, I walked from building to building that I knew well and was increasingly saddened to see them vacant, devoid of all the activity that had made them so alive for the previous two years of my life. One Navy grey pickup truck with an amber light on top remained and I used it to transport boxes to Fort Campbell for shipping. When driving around, I looked at the black marks made by John's hot rod Chevy and other cars on the asphalt of the burn-out strip, then drove up to the auto shop where I had worked on our Alpine. Its doors were down, empty inside, and the grounds vacant of all the vehicles that some among us were always working on. On my last drive through the "Q", I drove past the rows of bunker doors in the rock cliff along the Little West Fork that I had opened and closed, my locks still in place. I stopped in the paved staging area in front of each building where I had worked, then visited the "Volcano" one last time, then did the same at the vault. I sat there thinking about all the "stuff" it had contained during two decades of nuclear weapons work at Site B. The vault was the heart of the base in terms of its purpose of securely storing the weapons material that made nuclear explosions possible. I imagined the progression over the years of intense "Q" operations surrounding it, from Top Secret to empty, from that time on to remain a mysterious building of solid concrete and steel designed to survive unscathed a direct hit of massive proportions, a structure that would cause everyone to wonder what it was for.

I drove to the railhead, stopped and recalled all the activity that had taken place there just a few weeks before when hundreds of H-bombs were loaded into special railcars that were sealed, then rolled out of Clarksville Base. I sat on the empty and silent concrete dock by the tracks looking around at the open area that had been maintained continuously for years, now showing grass and weeds taking over. On the rocky ascent up the remnants of a road through the woods, I visited the graves under the giant oak tree one last time, wondering what would become of them. I knew that, in time, the secrecy that had so thoroughly enveloped Clarksville Base would cloud its very existence and these last vestiges of lives that were returned to the earth here, far from home, would likely be overwhelmed by brush. Only those of us who knew of them could remember, and I was a late-comer. I was certain that others knew much more than me, but who they were had already been lost in the flow of time. Grass on the burial plot before me had not been mowed for some time and was taking on an overgrown appearance. Who would know of these graves in years to come, I wondered? Would these final resting places of young German soldiers simply be forgotten as the underbrush reclaimed the ground and hid the five white stones that were their sole remaining vestments? Would anyone remember the man in the lone grave, the man whose final recognition was the tall granite obelisk that had once caught my attention?

My final drive through the "Q" was free of the multiple layers of security that I had become accustomed to, a strange twist from other eyes always watching, other ears always listening, codes and buddies required for everything, to no one at all. This part of the Base was completely empty of its past life, no Seabees transporting H-bombs and equipment, no GMTs going to this or that bunker with documentation in hand to verify which bomb or warhead was to be transported to the shops or to the Fort Campbell airfield or the railhead; no Marine guards on patrol; no one closing massive doors to conduct secret operations behind them. Everything was empty and locked and silent.

I had participated in the security of the doors and noted that the massive six tumbler Yale locks I knew well still hung in place. My assignment to the annual lock change during my first year involved checking each lock with its keys, locks with hardened bails and bodies designed to take massive abuse and not open. When I completed their records, I reported that several locks were duplicates, to which an immediate re-order went out to Yale for replacements that were not duplicates. Once a complete set of locks and keys with no duplicates were on hand, they were distributed to replace all locks throughout the "Q". The pair of keys per lock were separated with the operations center keeping one as spare while the other was controlled for access to the specific set of doors in the "Q" on a sign-out, sign-in basis.

Now, with everything displaying a ghost town aura, my slow drive through the "Q" gave time to reflect on events and times now in the past. Change was dispersing all of us and everything that had once been so secret, so important, was now gone. Clarksville Base was reduced to no more than recollections that I thought about while slowly driving the little winding road of memories ahead of me. Everything that had been was now my past.

When the USS Forrestal was launched on December 11, 1954, she was the largest warship ever built and the first of America's "supercarriers," a new class of aircraft carrier grown from the smaller "straight deck" ships of World War-II. The ship's new angled deck design enabled launch and landing of aircraft at the same time. Even though displacing 59,900 tons and 1,046 feet long, she was fast at 33 knots, thus the designation CVA, the Navy's designation of Fast Attack Carrier. With four aircraft elevators, three on the starboard side, one on the port side, she could quickly handle movement of planes and large quantities of equipment and cargo to and from the flight deck to the hangar bay immediately below. She was built by the Newport News Shipbuilding and Drydock Company and home ported in Norfolk, VA. For most of her life as an active warship, the Forrestal was assigned either to the Second Fleet operating in the Atlantic or the Sixth Fleet in the Mediterranean. She was decommissioned September 11, 1993 and rests today awaiting an honored berth in retirement as one of the most significant ships in US Naval history.

Chapter 22

USS Forrestal

Once again, Mary and I loaded our Alpine and pulled out of the driveway of her childhood home in Wilkes County, North Carolina. But this time we headed north and east, this time with our new baby in a car seat in the area behind our seats. After a short leave following the closing of Clarksville Base, we were on the road again for my next assignment, the USS Forrestal ported in Norfolk, Virginia. After two years of shore duty, sea duty was required, and I requested a big ship going to the Mediterranean. That assignment was most satisfying because my older brother, Johnny, had been a Forrestal sailor a few years earlier when attached to an A4E Skyhawk wing as an aircraft structural mechanic. The assignment also fulfilled my desire to visit the part of the world that I admired most, and I looked forward to liberty in as many ports as possible.

Our fall-of-the-year trek went north on US 21 into the Appalachians to junction with Route 58 running east-west across southern Virginia to Norfolk and the Chesapeake Bay. We had traveled Route 66, US 70, US 421, US 25, US 21 and many other highways in our Alpine, and now added US 58, the J. E. B. Stuart Highway, to our growing list of memorable drives. Route 58 was a spectacular two-lane snaking through mountain curves, an ideal drive in a sports car. Our "Fast Tomato" handled the turns and light traffic beautifully as we sailed effortlessly along, only to emerge from the western Virginia hills onto flatlands with boringly straight highway ahead for miles and miles, through the Dismal Swamp, then Norfolk. The three of us made the day's drive without a hitch, and the hum of our Alpine's engine must have been music to Squire's ears for he slept contentedly nearly all the way.

Upon arrival at the Norfolk Naval Station main gate, the temporary pass given us permitted driving around the installation to see the sights, including my ship in the distance, a giant that rested beside another aircraft carrier of similar proportions. When I handed my package of orders to the duty yeoman, the checking-in process began. Although assigned to the Forrestal, the ship was still being refitted and supplied. Reconstruction following the horrific explosions and fire that had killed so many crewmen in 1967 while on Yankee Station in the

Tonkin Gulf had been completed prior to the Forrestal's Med cruise the year before, and a second fire of lesser magnitude while in the Yards delayed readying for my departure. Refitting would not be complete for some weeks, and during the interim I was assigned more school to learn the nuances of H-bombs onboard ships, specifically an attack class aircraft carrier. The course was taught at Norfolk's Nuclear Weapons Training Group-Atlantic. With Mary and our baby with me, and without married personnel quarters available on Base, we were assigned to civilian quarters right on Virginia Beach. Our apartment was a short, sandy walk to the Bay, and with all the other married sailors quartered there, the following weeks turned into a continual beach party. The nearby Bay, the pool, slack duty, fine weather, and an apartment complex filled with young and vivacious Navy families combined to have something going on all the time, one clam bake after another in the evenings, or just quiet time by the pool.

We learned that the Bay's sandy bottom contained a vast quantity of hand size clams that we could feel with our feet, so two or three guys could gather a basket full of clams in about thirty minutes. A pot of boiling water on a stove in someone's apartment was all it took to have another beach party. Occasionally, we'd gather crabs for a feast, using lines with hooks and pieces of fat or bacon tossed in among the crabs that accumulated along jetties and docks. Beach music, dancing, and eating the area's abundant seafood was the plan of the day every day that combined to make an extended vacation for us. Neither Mary nor I associated her lack of interest in seafood with anything unusual; she simply did not like it and didn't eat it. Years later we learned that she was deathly allergic to all things from salt water, a condition that turned near fatal at one point. But during our youthful exuberance on the beach, we knew of no such conditions and partied on with her taste buds guiding her through the minefield of what to eat and what not to.

Those weeks were the beginning of a significant change in our lives: separation. I was going to sea, and Mary was moving back home. While we partied on the beach we also made plans for the coming year by talking over our options with her father, who offered to help set up a mobile home for her and Squire in the garden plot next door to his house. A cousin of Mary's just happened to be selling a nice mobile home located just up the road, and moving it to the new location with a farm tractor would be no problem. All things worked out, and we purchased the mobile home with a bank loan. During a few days' leave, our first purchased home was relocated and set up for new occupants.

The next time I headed for Norfolk I did so with my thumb held out. Leaving the Alpine for Mary, I hitch-hiked to take a berth on the Forrestal. Check-in proved to be a succession of interesting encounters, and, like multitudes of sailors who had walked up gangplanks of ships from times lost in pre-history, I stood on the pier looking up at the gigantic aircraft carrier with a young man's anticipation for adventure. I was ship's company for a Med cruise to locations that proved to be more than this farm boy could have hoped for. In dress blues with my duffle bag over my shoulder, I stepped up the gangplank to the

Duty Officer, came to attention in his presence, saluted, and said the time honored Navy phrase, "Request permission to come aboard, sir."

His "Permission granted" brought my first step onboard the USS Forrestal and my first salute to the flag that I was to perform every time I stepped on or off the ship. The Duty Officer looked at my orders and told me where to go to report in, and that set in motion a memorable sequence of events beginning with confusion. The duty yeoman knew exactly what to do, beginning with the first block on the checklist. He led me to a berthing compartment filled with sailors that did not look right to me. I reasoned that there could not be so many GMTs onboard and asked what division we were in. It was not W-Division, and he took a closer look at my orders; W-Division. He did not know where W-Division was located, and we went back through the ship, stepping through one oval bulkhead doorframe after another to his desk where he asked senior yeomen where W-Division was berthed. With new directions, he headed off in the opposite direction toward the bow of the ship with me in tow. Arriving at a small, empty and quiet compartment, he checked the bulkhead number, my home for the duration of the cruise.

I was among the first assignees to this compartment. With no other personnel around, I was unsure which rack and locker to take. The layout was two rows of three racks on either side of a stack of three lockers. Canvas bottoms of each rack were laced to smoothly bent rectangular frames of tubular aluminum with each frame hinged and strapped up to the overhead at sharp angles to maximize deck space. I chose the bottom-most rack because a fresh air outlet exhausted to the deck right beside it, then unstrapped my chosen rack to sleeping position. I would recline here each night about five inches above the deck for the coming months, discovering once at sea that my berth was at the waterline. The constant pulsating smash of the bow wave against the hull on the other side of the steel structure where I slept was the music of the sea that sent me off to sleep every night.

My first night brought an unwelcome discovery: the sagging nature of the canvas bottom gave me a painful back the next day. I needed something to make my rack and its three-inch thick mattress flat and discovered just what I needed in sections of plywood of the right dimensions. All sorts of crates were being brought onboard and broken down when empty. The hangar deck had piles of plywood, and I absconded with what I needed for restful sleeping without an aching back the next day, a flat, hard rack.

The stack of lockers, each one an aluminum cube about two feet on each edge, was similar to the stack that stood at the foot of the racks across from my new berth, all in an area of about seven by nine feet for six men. This area was cordoned off by cloth drapes from a similar set of berths further inboard. Further forward, similar accommodations provided room for about twenty-four men, but some berths remained unoccupied throughout the cruise. By selecting the bottom locker next to my rack, the duty yeoman noted that I had been assigned a berthing space, but everything else on the check-in list was still blank. He didn't know anything about the remainder of the list. I

realized that I was on my own once more and took the list saying that I
would follow through with it, knowing that he did not have the slightest
idea that I was a Top Secret-Q, Crypto cleared H-bomb expert and would
work in spaces that he didn't know existed.

As with my first arrivals at previous installations, I would find
my way again and did so when another GMT happened along while I
was loading my locker. Introduction to this young, dark-haired sailor
with a heavy New York accent and effervescent personality began my
real check-in. His name was Jajinski, but with a spelling not even similar to the pronunciation. He knew the ship well, his second cruise, and
off we went to the W-Division office where Jajinski introduced me to the
duty Chief Petty Officer who had been one of my instructors at Sandia.
Chief Presseau and I renewed acquaintances, and he introduced me to
the Weapons Officer, a well seasoned, no-nonsense Commander near
the end of a long career.

Chief Presseau assigned me to SASS-Forward, at which point I
learned that the Forrestal had four H-bomb magazines, two located in
SASS-Forward, two more in SASS-AFT. I was soon in one after the
other as Jajinski took me around, providing introductions and sorting
through the various check-ins internal to our operations. Winding our
way back and forth throughout the huge ship left me thoroughly confused, but quicker than I thought possible, I learned my way to the
important locations; my berth, the head and shower, the mess deck,
and to SASS-Forward, my duty location.

Portals to both SASS-Forward and SASS-Aft were in almost
hidden, inconspicuous, narrow, recesses along infrequently traveled
passageways. We slid our ID cards into a small slot in each steel door,
and once approved by the Marine guard always on duty on the other
side, he unlocked the door for entry. Jajinski led the way, and my first
steps into SASS-Forward went close by the smartly uniformed Marine
who had a small, bulkhead-mounted lamp and a platform for his log-
book, a handgun at his hip, and no other equipment, not even a chair
or stool to sit on. Every hour of duty at this post was spent standing in
a space the size of a small closet surrounded by nothing but steel bulk-
heads painted Navy grey. He was not permitted to even look down the
ladder leading from the water tight hatch that we descended. The hatch
was in the raised position so that we made our way to the next deck
below, down the ladder, with Jajinski making it in two quick steps. I
was certain that I would fall down the sharply angled, narrow steps if I
wasn't careful, and I slowly made my way down the ladder to join him
on the next landing, entrance level to the office area of SASS-Forward.

In time, I would learn the quick method for negotiating ladders
throughout the ship, but this first time required care. I noticed another
hatch identical to the one that we had just come through, also raised
on its hinges underneath the ladder we had just descended. Its opening revealed another ladder, this one to the next lower deck and magazine, more SASS-Forward spaces.

The SASS-Forward offices were laid out in what had once been
two separate spaces, now with the adjoining bulkhead removed to cre-
ate a larger space. The doors into each area had been removed, leaving

narrow, one man size openings side by side into each area. Built-in steel architecture of shelves, drawers, and desks spanned the forward bulkhead to comprise the official office area. An adjoining area was walled off from the office by a row of lockers and offered upright aluminum chairs around a table along with a couple of overstuffed chairs for lounging and watching television. This was the commons area, and the TV mounted at the overhead above the table on the inboard bulkhead was the focal point for all eyes. The aft bulkhead was sectioned off by rows of lockers similar to those in the berthing compartment, and when assigned one my space onboard doubled. This locker soon became my goodie bin for care packages sent by Mary and members of my family after I groused about the lack of consumable liquids once we were out to sea for a while.

Jajinski continued his tour to the magazine a deck below the offices, and there, sitting side-by-side on the starboard side in a brilliantly lit space painted white were familiar H-bombs in cradles stacked two high, B-43s, B-57s, and B-61s. They sat with wheels locked in place in two rows facing each other on a raised false deck that had a tough non-skid, deep red surface. An overhead crane along the high ceiling over them and a ramp to the elevator amidship was equipment provided for quickly moving the weapons to the aircraft above by way of the elevator. Its hatch opened directly into the hangar deck between the huge forward aircraft elevator doors on either side of the ship.

Along the port side of this H-bomb magazine were the shops with built-in stainless steel benches and latched drawers below. Familiar equipment and tools, both mechanical and electronic, were stowed in them and in various racks and clamps in each of three work bays. Additional hardware for the weapons, such as aerodynamic fairings for changing the configuration of a weapon, was contained in large lockers along the aft bulkhead. This magazine was the "Q" of Clarksville Base in miniature and tightly compacted into a warship.

After rounds here, Jajinski led a deck lower into the second SASS-Forward magazine that was similar to the one above but more for storage of weapons than working on them. This over-under layout connected by an elevator was similar to SASS-AFT, although the latter was larger and had more personnel. SASS-Forward proved to be rather quiet duty throughout the cruise, and, as a Second Class, I was among the senior GMTs. As I got to know all of the group, about a dozen, we came to know more and more about each other, where we were from and the like, while adjusting to the close proximity of our confines, the nature of shipboard life. As the cruise progressed, our duty proved to be mostly baby-sitting the bombs rather than working on them.

Being an early riser, each morning began with a shower and dressing before most of my shipmates. That put me in the Aft Mess before the rush for the Navy's excellent breakfast to order, prepared on grills by cooks who had developed their ability to grab two eggs in each hand, crack them, twist the shells just right to deposit their contents on hot grills, then repeat the same technique in a few eyeblinks, quickly building a layout of eggs sizzling to perfection. Always tasty bacon, hash browns and cinnamon pastry with milk was too much to eat, but

I followed breakfast with a walkabout to explore the ship, often ending with me standing on the fantail or sitting on the spud sponson or standing along the edge of the flight deck watching Norfolk and the Navy Base wake up. Then, checking in at SASS-Forward began the day's duty.

Although SASS meant Special Aircraft Service Stores, another cryptic attempt to disguise the nature of the spaces, all of us knew that "Special" was equivalent to "Nuclear" but less revealing to whoever chose the description. Each of us GMTs tried our hand at one time or another at concocting other meanings, such as Special Atomic Security Spaces or Special Atomic Secret Service. Each of our ID cards with "Unrestricted Access" boldly emblazoned across them gave us authority that we were yet to explore, and with our spaces off-limits to everyone except the Weapons Officer, Executive Officer, Captain and Admiral, we were assured that no one but GMTs could get in, guaranteed by an armed Marine guard and rigorous security protocol.

After the tours, Jajinski and I got better acquainted with exchanged details about who we were, and I learned that his previous Med cruise had taken him to many ports that piqued my curiosity. On this cruise, he and I were to spend a lot of foot time exploring the ports-of-call as the Forrestal steamed the Mediterranean.

Having arrived from Clarksville Base, the only GMT among the group from the Tennessee location, I had a number of conversations with my fellow crewmen regarding the differences between shipboard work with H-bombs and depot work with bombs and warheads in a much broader array. Those conversations told me that shipboard assignees did not have the range of warhead training and experience that I had, and no one else had my clearance level, although all of us were Q-cleared.

As the following months unfolded, little actual work was done on the bombs and no warhead work was performed, so our time was spent checking and certifying equipment and record keeping. That was fine with me. I liked my shipmates, each of us from different backgrounds but similar in the eyes of the Navy, and each of us had his own adjustments to make for living onboard the ship. Our advantage was that our magazine and shop spaces provided places to go to avoid the crowded office area, places that permitted workouts on mats or just quiet, climate controlled reading space. We were to spend the coming months living and working closely, and among my guys were some with bold ideas about how to improve the conditions of our cruise toward making the months ahead more enjoyable.

The time was late 1969, and the Forrestal was scheduled to depart Norfolk in mid-December. With lots of time on our hands before getting underway, these entrepreneurs concocted plans to improve our quality of life while at sea. We assembled one day in SASS-Forward to hear the plan: each of us was offered the option of participating by buying one seven dollar share in the slush fund that would be used to buy a variety of goods that we wanted. In came the money, and our first dispatch was to acquire cases of canned soft drinks that were stowed in the bottom of our elevator shaft, space that was unused even when the elevator was in its lowest position. Next came acquisitions from the Naval Base mess supply, such as sealed containers of dry soup mix, coffee, cocoa mix, cooking oil, salt and all sorts of other long-lasting goodies, anything that anyone thought was needed, such as a supply of popcorn. All of it came onboard under our coats and hidden in duffle bags. As inventory built up, distribution rules were established. All of us agreed to only one soft drink a day with each one logged out to keep track of inventory. Any additional cans were sold at one dollar each, a sum that provided further investment potential by the slush fund. An electric soup maker, an electric frying pan, an electric popcorn popper, an electric coffee pot and various other utensils came onto the ship, each unauthorized contraband certain to cause a lot of grief if discovered. But since everything went into our spaces that were off limits to everyone but the command officers, once onboard, everything was simply SASS-Forward equipment. Who knew where it came from? Everything was stowed away for our pleasure in the SASS-Forward "kitchen" adjoining our office space. The "kitchen" was a narrow, stainless steel counter with a sink on the aft bulkhead end. With running hot and cold water, we were set for cooking and cleaning, and under the counter onto shelves went our contraband cookware, hidden behind drapes.

One day someone knitted his brow and asked how we were going to keep the soft drinks cold. We huddled again and hatched a plan that only we could pull off. Success was not guaranteed, but if it worked we would have all the comforts of a home kitchen: we needed a refrigerator. The leader of our entrepreneurial gang took it upon himself to ramrod the acquisition, but all of us had to go along, and we had to keep it to ourselves because, if discovered, we would be in serious violation of regulations against contraband and misuse of government property. After scanning the Norfolk newspaper for refrigerators for sale, he settled on a good deal offered by a lady selling one from her home. He and an accomplice went to the Naval Base Motor Pool and requisitioned a truck, then drove through Norfolk suburbs to the home, made the purchase, and loaded the refrigerator. But getting a refrigerator onboard the ship was more complicated than smaller items that we could easily hide, so our plan was to be completely open: we would bring onboard a classified official transfer to the USS Forrestal.

In our magazine shop below, a bag of appropriate size was made of hermetically sealed canvas with all the appropriate and official codes and tags attached to impart to the viewer that the enclosed item, to which no one had access but us, was official and destined for SASS-Forward. We reasoned that among the quantity of material coming onboard in preparation for getting underway, another transfer would just be more of the same, but we also knew that transfers to W-Division involved a lot of people far beyond simply onloading everything else. Our plan had to work smoothly and officially and began when the truck arrived on the pier. Our point man walked up the gangplank, saluted the Duty Officer and the flag, then handed him the package of orders. The Duty Officer knew exactly what to do; he had the ship's communications signal Chop Sticks operations, our code.

The blare of, "All hands man your Chop Sticks stations," was our cue. Our communications man logged onto the network and confirmed with operations that W-Division was prepared to receive transfer of... no one knew but us. Armed Marine guards in quickstep cordoned off a perimeter in the hangar near the forward aircraft elevator door on the starboard side; fire crews in fire fighting gear hustled out to their stations, attached their hoses and charged them, with additional gear close at hand. A crane operator took his position at the controls to haul onboard the... whatever it was. Chop Sticks communication links were established with all parties, and once cleared, the Forrestal was ready to receive the transfer. Several of us GMTs took our stations as W-Division contacts and watched the proceedings as qualified receivers.

The crane hook was lowered and attached to strapping on the transfer that was easily lifted up to elevator level. The transfer slowly rose to just above the elevator, to the point where lifting stopped and lateral movement began, and the crane operator gave too quick a movement causing the transfer to swing precariously to and fro. In unison as if choreographed, each of us GMTs drew our breaths in a wild-eyed "OH SHIT!" maneuver that instantly got everyone's attention and racheted up the tension of the moment. The Duty Officer leaped into play recognizing that he was about to witness a Broken Arrow on his watch, a nuke dropped into the bay, and he screamed orders to settle the crane. Each of us GMTs visualized our wholesale courtmartial and cells in Leavenworth once the Navy extracted the "Broken Arrow" from the bottom of the bay only to discover it to be a refrigerator.

All eyes were on the transfer and hearts pumped fast for very different reasons, but once it was in position above the ship's elevator surface, we GMTs swung to and had our transfer lowered onto a wheeled cradle for movement into our spaces. Our man on communications told the deck coordinator that we were ready to pop the hatch. Alarm bells rang and the Marines made certain that no one but us got near their line or our operations. Hydraulic motors activated the thick door pushing it up from hangar deck level, then slid the massive piece back on ways embedded in the deck.

A crew of GMTs rode up with the elevator, and the transfer was made to them. The elevator then withdrew into our spaces, the hatch was relocated to sealed position, and appropriate codes were communicated saying W-Division now had responsibility for the transfer. When ship's communications blared, "Secure from Chop Sticks stations," all of us breathed sighs of relief. We had pulled it off, and once in place and working, our new acquisition proved to be a worthy purchase that contributed significantly to our cruise.

The next day, Chief Presseau was in SASS-Forward and saw the refrigerator. He did a little head scratching, wondering if he had somehow missed an item that must have been in place a long time, and said nothing. And neither did we.

I was of the opinion that "All's well that ends well," and I was prepared to defend its acquisition as Chop Sticks training. As an observer of the entire operation, I could say with authority that all parties performed their duties as required, all equipment checked out, and we did not have to put an actual H-bomb at risk doing so. We were not scheduled to have a Chop Sticks drill but we had accomplished the purpose of a drill on our own with means that produced a high level of camaraderie among us. That refrigerator proved to be our most valued acquisition and the focus of some tense moments to come.

Chapter 23

Underway

One new addition to the ship was the library, the rebuilt space previously having been berthing compartments of the sailors killed in the fuel fires that poured down upon them once the deck had been blown open in the Tonkin Gulf explosions. No vestiges of that horror remained; commemorating the dead was the huge bronze plaque on the interior surface of the starboard side forward aircraft elevator door. From time to time I stood before it reading the names of the victims, and walking the passageways where many of them died, now the quiet library and chapel next door, gave me a sense of hallowed space, a sailor's respect for those who had gone to sea and met their fate.

The day of departure, cool and sunny, was filled with fanfare; the Forrestal was returning to the fleet. Along the pier a huge throng had assembled, families of departing crewmen waving and calling out well wishes and last minute details of their lives. I walked the flight deck observing this Navy tradition, knowing that Mary and our baby were not in the crowd, no one for me to wave back to. Mary was back home, I was heading out to sea, and while the band played upbeat music, various calls came over the ship's communications for getting underway, a such-and-such party to do this, another party to do that, everyone now under the Captain's command.

Tugs churned the water below as they slowly nudged the giant ship away from the pier and turned it toward the Atlantic Ocean. Once clear of the pier and under its own power, the ship eased through the waterways of the Chesapeake Bay, and I watched the pier, then the docks, then Norfolk fade into the distance beyond the horizon where sea met sky. I had never been to sea before, and while standing on the flight deck surrounded by ocean to the horizon, I had a sense of being a tiny speck in a vast new world.

The roar of jets coming onboard became another new adventure, and I watched until well after dark. The tail hooks of plane after plane grabbed an arresting cable that brought them to sudden stops accompanied by the intense screeching of the hydraulic system that absorbed their energy of motion, stopping each plane in a few hundred feet. Following each landing, the choreographed work of handlers, each man in a jersy colored to denote his job, steadily filled the hanger bay with Skyhawks and Phantoms, helicopters and prop planes, and all the aircraft assigned for this cruise. Darkness brought on ship lights in their various colors denoting features of the ship that pilots had to rely on during their landing approaches. When jets touched down, each pilot immediately went to full afterburner for maximum thrust to have the power to get back up if an arresting cable was not caught. Blue, red and white flames roaring from their engines made a colorful and dramatic scene, all under the watchful eyes of Flight Ops and the Bridge. This was an aircraft carrier at work.

I watched from various points around the island and up and down the flight deck as I would many times during the months to come. I also thought of the ultimate challenge of each pilot and his plane, mere mosquitos delivering a sharp nosed H-bomb from my magazine toward some target, the pilot then banking his plane hard under full thrust to get away from the impending blast that would change the course of history.

Our week long crossing to the Pillars of Hercules was filled with near constant flight operations and training, training, training. Every department held exercises over and over to sharpen the skills of its personnel for quick and effective response for whatever the training was for. The ship's communications repeatedly rang its BONG, BONG, BONG notices, and when the first "All hands man your battle stations" rang out, every member of the crew sprang instantly into action, each one of us getting ourselves in order as quickly as possible wherever we were and making our way through the ship in accordance with instructions. "All hands proceed up and forward on the starboard side, down and aft on the port side. General quarters. General quarters. All hands man your battle stations."

To this day, recalling that command and the fervor it produced throughout the ship brings a shiver up the back of my neck. Streams of men hustling along passageways, racing up and down ladders, reporting in for check-offs to the man, closure of doors and hatches, spinning each one into water tight condition, each space reporting through ship's communications to be fully manned and secure. Then.... We waited.

Were we under attack, or was this just another drill? I thought about "We will bury you!" and wondered if that threat was beginning for real. A drill was more likely, but no one knew anything until communications let us know. Sealed within our compartmentalized cocoons throughout the ship, we were entirely dependent on the operations center where the efficiency of securing the ship for battle was assessed. In the months to come, regular drills were held for everything, and of the top four awards granted by the US Navy to the most efficient ship in the fleet, the Forrestal received three. One was for weapons. Each efficiency award was denoted by a giant white-over-black letter painted onto the sides of the island, prominently displayed for all to see.

Training included regular doses of fire control for fighting compartment fires, deck fires, aircraft fires, fuel fires and every other kind of fire. Films of the explosions and fire that sent massive black clouds billowing from the Forrestal during its Tonkin Gulf burn made effective visuals. The ship in the films was our ship, and although the USS Forrestal had since collected the moniker "the firestall," we sailors onboard her were committed to doing our part to keep the ship in proper running order so that fires were prevented. The films left no doubt in our minds about fuel and munitions fires; deadly serious business for a warship of any kind.

I spent quiet time off watch in the library or on the fantail or on the spud sponson reading more philosophy. My grand adventure, a farm boy's exposure to the world, culminated in a fourth year in the Navy at sea with lots of time to explore the intricacies of human existence. From the first science and philosophy books I had bought in downtown Chicago three years earlier, from those bought, borrowed and studied in Albuquerque and in Clarksville, then the ship's library and purchases in each port of the cruise itself, I read more than four hundred books, books on the great human adventure collectively called history, books that told the stories of each port-of-call I walked, books that spoke of the whys and wherefores of all existence and beyond.

While on watch or in the off duty lounge, Flight Ops as shown on closed circuit TV was a favorite. Occasionally, links were made to the cockpit of a plane, and we could listen to exchanges between the pilot and bridge in addition to following flight deck operations through the camera lenses. TV time was composed of a steady diet of reminders and instructions about shipboard life and needs along with Armed Forces television's sports programming and evening movies. Mail call was about every day, and each of us receiving letters from home sought quiet seclusion to catch up on the news.

Christmas at sea that year was as festive as could be made on a warship with personnel who barely knew each other, but each of us receiving gifts from home had items that gave personal touches and shared good cheer. My birthday a week following Christmas brought notice to get to the mail room on the double, a strange order, I thought. Upon arrival, I discovered why. Mary had sent a birthday cake, now a jumble of crumbs, and a can of chocolate icing that had been mashed open with the goo spread throughout the bag of mail. My charter was to clean the icing from the interior of the bag and all the letters and boxes in the mess. Succeeding in that endeavor, I wondered what other sailors thought when they got their mail smelling of chocolate and soiled with dark brown discolorations.

Late night entertainment from the ship's closed circuit TV crew had competition. Our enterprising slush fund leaders had endeavored to pursue the entrepreneurial potential offered by our off-limits and "Unrestricted Access" status. A reel-to-reel projector and selection of skin flicks had been purchased, and for just fifty cents a head, darkened recesses of spaces were packed night after night with sailors paying to watch. Such enterprise proved highly profitable, and our slush fund steadily grew.

Where were skin flicks purchased? I didn't know, but the first viewing revealed that a cleverly perpetrated bait-and-switch scenario had hoodwinked the purchasers. Somewhere in Norfolk was a joint selling the flicks, and after watching them and making selections, a distraction of some sort resulted in the selected films being replaced with cartoons. With high expectations among female starved crewmen, the jeers that the 'toons brought was a humorous lesson in how to insure acquisition of clandestine goods. With a return to the film vendors and a near-future porting in France, the home of explicit films from the country's notorious underground, new purchases were more closely observed to arrive onboard as the entrepreneurial fuel for our slush fund. There was no lack of paying customers, but after seeing the flicks ourselves, they became old hat, and we settled into our own individual worlds to pass the time.

Within a few months, the slush fund grew to such proportions that trouble simmered closer and closer to becoming a divisive issue. Chief Presseau saw to it that the fund was dissolved to prevent its existence becoming known outside of our group, and each shareholder received his due, well over ten times the seven dollars of each original share. That disbursement supplied the money for liberty and to buy mementos for family back home.

The Chief and I continued our chess playing begun in Albuquerque, and, although he won a few games, his tactics took on any proportion available to him beyond game strategy. In order not to smoke up the office area, smokers were restricted to the landing at the bottom of the ladder from the Marine guard's station. As we bent over the checkerboard for game after game, the Chief blew his smoke in my face. I was a non-smoker, and he knew such tactics were both distracting and annoying while he claimed to be concentrating so intently on the game that he was unaware of smoke blowing, yet he constantly employed that tactic.

As we played more games, I became increasingly determined to beat him, using such tactics as standing up, walking around the board to where his smoke didn't go, and even making moves from behind him over his shoulder, maneuvers that were particularly annoying to him.

Mary had given me a nicely carved and compact wooden chess set with a green felt bag sized to spread the folding checkerboard onto, and from Clarksville Base to all around the Mediterranean Sea, it was the focus of many hours of gaming, many of them with another book in hand for studying another strategy. How other crewmen learned that I played a rather good game I don't know, but one day I was talking with a couple of members of the band who presented me with a challenge. One of them WAS good at the game, the other not so, and by the time that we had played a number of games, we were about even in wins. I had, by then, developed the capacity to think out sequences of twelve or more moves ahead, and for most opponents I simply controlled the game to the extent that few would play me.

On one occasion, the skilled bandsman and I were deep into a hard-fought game monitored by another skilled player who recorded our moves for later study. I viewed middle game strategy as an extension of the opening and played to control position, first with sound openings, then with strategies for steadily gaining control of the board toward final victory. On this occasion, the game was into four hours at its conclusion, and the analyst remarked that I was fortunate to have won following a blunder during the middle game. We set up the board from his notes, and I revealed that my "blunder" was actually a key pawn move that cascaded into a dozen or more moves that had to go exactly as I planned, resulting in checkmate. My adversary and the analyst were amazed, especially that I had been awake from before reveille the previous day and had stood the Mid-watch, awake for almost twenty-four hours and still capable of playing an overwhelming game of chess.

One memorable late-watch was a revelation about Navy life on a big ship. My watch partner and I had gotten off duty from the First watch and had gone back to the aft mess deck for mid-rats (the fourth meal of the day, around midnight). Our cold cut sandwiches and pickles, potato chips, cake and glasses of milk were consumed at one of the built-in tables and stools on the mess deck with no indications of anything unusual. Our walk back up the hangar deck to our berthing compartment came to a sudden, chin-dropping surprise.

About mid-way up the hangar deck, a wave crashed through the open port side forward aircraft elevator door, rolled down the deck toward us, and soaked our feet above the ankles as we stood watching in complete awe. We knew that the elevator door was several stories above the water line, and for a wave of Atlantic surf to crash through it took a very tall wave. I eased over to the opening and looked out upon an angry sea. Poseidon was throwing one giant wave after another at the ship, and we had noticed none of them. The ship did not make the slightest pitch or roll, and so far as we knew we were steaming in dead calm seas. Not so. In the patchwork moonlight I could see massive waves caught in such intense wind that their tops were sheared off and blown sideways. The ocean roiled with wave after wave slamming into the ship, but the Forrestal's massive weight, flat bottom and length sufficient to span several wave crests hardly moved.

Later, while in my rack, I listened to the repeated smashing, crashing bow waves against the hull just beyond where I lay and drifted off to sleep. A few hours later, I was up and out to discover in the Plan of the Day that we had come through the edge of a hurricane. I marveled at how the ship had given no indications of stormy seas, and when I stepped onto the fantail and saw the enormity of the black clouds spanning the western horizon, the storm that we had steamed through the night before, I was further amazed.

With the wake of the ship spreading into a shallow angle V pattern behind and the Forrestal's four screws churning up the water beneath me, I watched our trailing destroyer negotiate the waves. The storm lay behind us, no wind blew, and the waves were only wavelets compared to those I had seen the night before. As I stood there in my dungarees, I watched our Destroyer tail pitch deep into the surf, then rock back to stern, its bow rising sharply out of the water and hurling massive spray back over the ship. A roll to port, then a roll to starboard, then another dig into the surf with another enormous wash over the deck, then another roll and a dive and another was an instant education. The Destroyer's unceasing motion, every dive into the drink, every pitch, roll and rock was repeated over and over while I stood with one foot propped on the fantail railing, my chin resting in my palm. I now knew why I selected a big ship.

"Old salts" of the Navy had told me that "real" sailors are Destroyer sailors, but that first display of the pounding that our Destroyer tail took solidly reinforced my conviction that an aircraft carrier of the Forrestal's size was the place to be, not on some dinky tub that bounced around with every wave, with the crew having to hold on to something or get tossed about while locked inside, with everything onboard tied down or risk flying missiles, with every door and hatch closed to Circle-W, water tight conditions. I liked my ship and had no interest in becoming a "real" sailor.

We eased through the Pillars of Hercules (Gibralter) during the night, and I saw nothing but lights. So began our Med cruise.

On those occasions in port when I found my way to the USO to telephone Mary, I often came upon soldiers and sailors playing chess, a huge waste of time, I thought, when the entire port was to be seen in the short time available. Following casual observation, I determined in most cases that the game was not challenging enough, but once when in Athens and watching a rather good British player use a host of opening tricks to vanquish player after player, I decided to challenge.

Since my game was mostly opening for position, I was not strong against opening attacks and lightning quick moves, tactics he used very effectively to his advantage. I kept telling myself to be careful not to fall into one his traps, although I had watched a number of his quick games and recognized what he was up to. I fended off each attack and placed my pieces to steadily build a stronger defense. Advantage slowly shifted to my middle game strengths, and by gaining a point here, a better position with a stronger piece there, I was, after an hour or so, in a position that I could do the lightning moves because I was many moves ahead of him. At the conclusion, we neither exchanged names nor shook hands. Hardly acknowledging each other, we parted company with no more than smiles and nods. I wanted to see more of Athens.

Somewhere off the coast of Spain, January, 1970.

Chapter 24

Mediterranean Sunrise

We had arrived during the night, and I wanted to see my first Mediterranean sunrise so much that even though I had been on the Mid-watch just a few hours earlier, I was up before dawn without needing a wake-up call. The ship was at its quietest so early in the morning, and I met no other crew as I eased out of my rack, dressed and left my berthing compartment to walk the steel passageways with their soft red glow of Lights Out, then climbed the ladders to the flight deck. The immense table-top airfield was also quiet, an unusual condition since I had become accustomed to the noise and bustle of flight operations about twenty hours every day. We were anchored and without a headwind, so all the planes except our air cover circulating high above had been stowed along the rear edges of the flight deck and in the hanger deck below. All the customary activity of running such a huge warship was absent; that absence made the drama of the morning all the more unusual.

I stood on the starboard side ahead of the island and looked into the Mediterranean darkness with anticipation. Then I noticed a tiny but intense light blinking off and on irregularly well out to sea. I immediately recognized it to be Morse Code, catching a letter or two that I recalled from my boyhood when I had learned a little of the code. We were relieving the USS America from her Med cruise with a similar show of force, another supercarrier, the USS Forrestal. "Big A" was heading back to the States while we would be on station for the next eight months or so, to be relieved afterwards in similar rotation.

The morning was cool with thin, low-lying fog engulfing this pair of mighty warships. Overhead I could see the faint glimmer of stars and satisfyingly predicted a beautiful day soon to arrive with the sun. As I watched through the fog, the outline of the America slowly took form, and I reckoned that sailors onboard her could see the similar form of my ship emerge with the coming light. With my trusty Kodak Instamatic in hand, I captured a photo of her dimmed hulk in the midst of a pin-point signal flash and wonder to this day how I did that. That image remains significant in my memory; my very first photograph in the Mediterranean Sea, one that I was certain no one else added to their collection because I was the only ship's company not on duty witnessing the arrival of the new day. Although I knew that the bridge was manned and signalmen were exchanging messages necessary for a change of command, they were working; I was admiring.

The only sounds were squawks of sea gulls and the beating of helicopter blades. The helo lifted off with diminishing beat as it faded into the distance, and in its absence I noted how silent the morning became, punctuated only by the bleats of gulls. They seemed so much a part of the scene developing in my consciousness that I breathed deeply, touched a bit by the convergence of having admired this part of the world from high school history books and now actually being in what seemed, back then, to be unattainable dreams.

This first day began a most satisfying Mediterranean cruise as a member of my rich uncle's yacht club. Being among some five thousand crewmen onboard this huge warship may have made me just another sailor, but like me, each of my shipmates was an individual from somewhere in America, who, by forces largely beyond our control, came to this place and this time as highly trained members of our country's uniformed fighting force at sea. Only a few onboard knew what my job was, the most senior officers and my fellow GMTs, but in the Navy's uniform, I was just another sailor.

Since my workday did not begin until 8 AM, I had the next couple of hours or so to wander around and capture the morning. My Mid-watch also gave me some latitude if I should arrive on station a little late, since we were not likely to be doing any warhead alterations or mods until orders came down, usually arriving later in the morning in the hands of the chiefs after they were dispatched from meetings with the Weapon's Officer. My leisure permitted me to stand in the bluish tint of first light filtering through the haze, and I surmised that a briefcase in the possession of one of the Admiral's staff officers arriving onboard contained orders for our arsenal of firepower surpassing all the expended munitions of the Second World War. The Admiral, ComCarDiv-4, (Commander Carrier Division-4) wielded enormous responsibility, along with the welfare of each of us under his command and a hold full of the most destructive weapons known to man.

Daylight slowly surrounded me, and I watched the large disk of the sun, first its perfectly round entrance peeking above what I imagined to be the distant horizon of the calm sea, then growing into a full circle of red, brighter at the top to dark red at the bottom, standing beyond the fog proclaiming the new day. I had never seen such a magnificent sunrise. The disk of the sun was uncommonly large and so richly red, seemingly pasted in the fog for long moments, and nothing like sunrises I had seen back home. I knew, however, that similar sunrises were common in this part of the world, seen by the Romans, the Greeks I so admired, Phoenician sailors, Minoans before them, the ancient Egyptians, all spanning time long before recorded history. But this one, because it was seen by me, was unique and still stands out in my memory: my first Mediterranean sunrise.

I stood watching the new day arrive like nothing I imagined, and I failed to take another picture. Moments passed from night into morning, and as the day brightened, I stood awed by the beauty surrounding me and simply did not think to take a picture.

With the rise of the sun the fog quickly evaporated, and all around lay the Mediterranean Sea in the richest blue water I had ever seen. The sky yielded to its own bright blue with only the occasional filament of white and lazy, ribbon-like clouds floating along overhead. Gulls sailing and darting around fueled my imagination of Poseidon rising sleepily from the sea somewhere, yawning and stretching in the warming sun and was pleased. I was.

Off to starboard lay the "Big A" silhouetted against the new sky, nestled in a large, hilly, crescent-shaped bay with low-lying points of Balearic Island shoreline east of her stern and west of her bow. We sat parallel with her a substantial distance away facing the opposite direction, two "battleship grey" warships with large black and white numbers on the sides of their islands, 66 for the "Big A" and 59 for us. A nearly invisible plume of exhaust from burning black oil filtered upward from her stack like that from our stack, both similarly diluted in the gentle breeze.

These fast attack aircraft carriers had enormous capability, with the Forrestal coming along prior to the nuclear powered surface fleet and the first of the class of supercarriers. The America was fitted with conventional power even though the Enterprise, CVA 65, before her had received nuclear powerplants. Being the first of the supercarriers, the Forrestal set the model for the giant ships that was refined further with the USS America and later carriers, forebears of the slightly larger N-types that came to ply the world's oceans on nuclear power while carrying a belly full of warheads that could use the same energy producing principles to obliterate any target within their range.

As I walked along the perimeter of the deck that morning, the view below was into water so clear that I could see straight to the bottom; shades of blue, lighter upon massive stones and sand to darker in crevices, patches of light that constantly moved interspersed with sundry, irregular forms of shadow made by sunlight filtering through surface action, all contributed to my immediate concern that we were grounded. Viewed from my elevation, perhaps a hundred feet above the waterline, the bay looked deceptively shallow and required careful noting of features to provide reassurance that its depth was more than sufficient to buoy my massive, flat bottomed ship.

When I noticed the "Big A" belching a puff of black smoke, I took it as a signal that transfer of command was complete and that she was building a head of steam to move toward home. We had just crossed the green Atlantic from Norfolk during the previous days, and I was primed to see all of the Mediterranean I could before we made a similar change of command and returned to the States. Our crossing was the beginning of long remembered exploits that a farm boy would never have had without joining the Navy, and while I was new to shipboard life, although a petty officer with three years' service by then, I found the ship accommodating and my time aboard her a new set of adventures.

Our crossing was uneventful, largely due to the immense size of the Forrestal. The revelation of slicing through a storm one night as described earlier reinforced the pride I felt in being a crewman on the aircraft carrier that was the first of its class. I didn't know where its number, 59, came from, but I wondered if it was associated in some way with the ship displacing 59,900 tons, far more when fully burdened for a cruise and loaded with several air wings. At about a fifth of mile long, the flight deck was an immense airfield at sea, the first one to have an angled flight deck. With two catapaults forward and the angled deck, both launches and recoveries could proceed simulateously, a feature that defined the modern attack carrier, the Forrestal class.

I never learned why ships were always referred to as "she" even if named for a man. The Forrestal was named for Secretary of Defense James V. Forrestal, deceased, and his wife had chrisened the ship with his name when launched during mid-December, 1954. Being ship's company fifteen years later gave me pause to consider the rapid changes in both aircraft and weaponry that the ship had carried. Now with a full complement of jet fighters and fighter-bombers that far exceeded the capabilities of propeller driven planes and first generation jets of the early 1950s, the Forrestal was still at the forefront of Naval power. Wondering what stories the flight deck could tell, I imagined that libraries of sea-going history had already been logged by the ship, and this steel behemoth showed no signs of being antiquated or incapable of handling its modern complement of planes and munitions.

She had been built by the Newport News Shipbuilding and Drydock Company, a firm that I had been hired to go to work for after college but didn't make it because of being drafted. With Norfolk her home port, the Forrestal had literally grown from the wharfs and docks a giant of the sea always to return to her port of origin, except in retirement.

Since she was so big and advanced when first launched, learning her many new features took more than a year before the first plane was hauled down on her deck by an arresting cable, and her flight operations thereafter provided extensive training for pilots prior to her first deployment in January, 1957. The mightiest ship of the US Navy was assigned to the Sixth Fleet and made its first cruise to the Mediterranean that year, a show-of-force ambassador that made many foreign ports with much fanfare.

The Forrestal repeatedly made history on the high seas, such as in late 1963 when an 85,000 pound Air Force C-130 Hercules touched down and was brought to a halt in less than three hundred feet, proving that such a massive plane had seagoing capability on a big aircraft carrier. The Forrestal further broadened her capabilities as a cargo transporter when the Navy designed a new cargo plane for her, the smaller C-2A Greyhound commissioned into the fleet during the mid-1960s. The plane was called the "Willie Fudd" for some reason, perhaps for being a dual engine prop plane among sleek jets.

The C-2A became the Carrier Strike Group main aircraft for transporting cargo, mail and passengers, then became the Navy's "eye in the sky" radar plane when a large diameter disk stuffed with surveillance equipment was fitted on the back of the plane, creating the E-2 Hawkeye. As an all-weather early warning and battle management plane, the E-2's five-man crew could remain circling some five miles in altitude watching everything below for hours on end, the equivalent of more than a thousand nautical miles at about three hundred miles per hour.

During my many flight deck excursions, I watched these planes come and go, their engines alone capable of launch without catapults, and wondered if the pilots of such mundane planes envied the jet jockeys. A-4E Skyhawks and F-4B Phantoms roared off the deck with regularity while the lumbering C-2A and E-2 plodded along.

The Atlantic extended to the horizon in every direction, and so did the Mediterranean. I took advantage of time off to sit on the spud sponson on the rear, port side, previously the platform for two 5-inch 54 gun mounts. From there I watched planes circle for landing approach and heard launch after launch as I soaked up life on the sea while reading philosophy in search of the meaning of it all. From my perch on stacks of crated onions and sacks of potatoes, thus the moniker "spud sponson," I could not put my finger on why the ocean was so appealing, so invigorating, so satisfying. Perhaps I had become enamored by adventure on the sea from books I read. Or, perhaps I had been a man of the sea in an earlier life and retained connections to past lives as only hints in the shadowy reaches of my mind. Perhaps, as described in the history books I enjoyed reading, I was simply filled with anticipation for places I hoped to see. Perhaps I was fascinated by the stories of Jason and the Argonauts, Homer's Iliad, Odysseus and his Odyssey, and the Greek islands I looked forward to exploring. Perhaps my interest lay in all of them, each bound by the sea and my imagination that had been piqued early in life by pirate stories, Long John Silver, and adventures of buccaneers on the Spanish Main.

I walked the length of the hanger deck every morning to stand on the fantail and observe the ways of the ocean, a very different world from my mountain boy days back home. Even when foul weather kept me from my spot on the extreme aft of the ship or my spot on top of potato sacks, I looked out through hatches upon stormy seas, knowing that following the wind and rain came another bright day. "Red sky in the morning, sailor take warning/Red sky at night, sailor's delight" became my mantra as I looked for sunsets, each one as fascinating as the preceding sunrise. I was beginning a lengthy cruise with this first magnificent sunrise on the calm, blue Mediterranean Sea and found it very satisfying.

Chapter 25

Barcelona

When word got around that I was going to Spain, a request came from a cousin. Their son had married a Barcelona girl, and not a single member of the family had met her family. Would I? Of course.

Arrival in Barcelona was anticipated with a young man's enthusiasm for adventure and with the goal of meeting relatives. Going to Spain evoked images of gunshot heelwork by fiery flamenco dancers, blazing guitar, and sweaty Gypsy barrios where love burned with Spanish passion. Because of growing up in a home filled with music, I had been introduced to Carlos Montoya and Andrés Segovia on 33-1/3 long playing albums, and now I was to visit their land. Catalonia Spain held many adventures for me.

Port-of-call dates were posted a few days prior to arrival, if not preceded by rumor, so I planned my exploits around getting as much time ashore as I could by trading watch with my fellow crewmen. Few of my buddies wanted to stand the Mid-watch, midnight to 4 AM, so I often doubled up my watch time at sea with their watches so that when we were in port, I had extended liberty while they stood my watches. I also learned that first day splurges usually exhausted their money and their interests in going ashore, so I was able to trade watch with buddies who chose to stay onboard the later days of liberty. My plan gave me day after day on the beach and proved the motto, "Join the Navy and see the world!" was true in my case. I accumulated liberty to do just that, see every port, and I took every opportunity to do so.

Liberty in Barcelona was for three days, Friday through Sunday, and I was in the first liberty launch that Friday morning. Crewmen on liberty rode the launches that taxied us to and from the ship throughout each day. About sixty sailors filled the launch that ran ship-to-shore from about three miles out, beating the choppy surf with rhythmic pounding, occasionally spraying mist back onto us. The Forrestal was much too large to make port, and being a warship, I suspected that international waters provided less controversy than having a giant aircraft carrier dominating the city's southern skyline had anchorage been closer to shore.

Barcelona was our first port-of-call, and most of the crew, young men who had been cooped up inside the ship, were primed to cut loose in the first bar they came to. Not being so inclined, I wanted to see Barcelona, and I had family to meet.

The warm Mediterranean sun made the January day a delight. In my dress blues and white "dixie cup" sailor's hat, I walked from the dock along routes noted in the ship's *Forerunner* newsletter distributed just prior to making port. It told me that Barcelona was one of Europe's oldest cities, founded by Hamicar Barco, father of Hannibal, and named Barcino. Being a Carthaginian colony, time would see it change hands to the Romans, the Visigoths, the Franks and the Saracens (Arabian soldiers on conquest). By the 12th century, the city was the capital of Aragon and Catalonia, then grew to rival Genoa and Venice in commerce. Columbus sailed from Barcelona, and Columbus Square where the king and queen gave him their charter remains a celebrated site. This port, rich in history, held unexpected events that kept me from seeing much of the city but produced memorable shore leave anyway. Once on the beach, I picked up a map to navigate by, and everywhere I looked I saw another inviting adventure.

While thinking of what I could send back home to Mary and our infant son, Squire, I wrestled with the idea of buying a real Spanish guitar for me. Remembering Carlos and Miguel, I imagined spending long, dull watch time learning to play their style of guitar and to arrive home an accomplished Flamenco guitarist. But, given the modest sum of money in my pocket, I knew I had to use my cash carefully to cover all the things I wanted to do. Taxi fare was out. Since I had a map, I walked.

The spacious street leading up from the docks was lined with unusually wide sidewalks with trees planted near the street curb, each providing shade at every pub, every eatery and shop along the way. As I neared the center of converging streets, I came upon a guitar shop and was drawn to it like a bee to a flower. This was it, my mental image of a family enterprise crafting fine Spanish guitars. The storefront window was filled with guitars, beautiful works in various sizes and colors of wood. Upon entering the shop, I was greeted by the line of guitars hanging in unison from the wall behind the counter, and I knew in an instant that one of them was to be mine.

A congenial, silver haired old man behind the glass counter running the length of the store, divided about mid-way for passage behind it, asked in his heavily accented English if I wanted to buy a guitar. Being a wise old man, he knew that sailors didn't come to his shop unless guitars were on their minds. My favorable response led to him reaching for an elegant example from the row overhead. He tuned it quickly, strummed a chord or two and handed it to me. It was then that I learned something important about my construction; short, fat fingered Al had a hard time placing finger tips on strings to prevent the incongruous "twang" from spilt-over fingertips onto adjacent strings. The pleasant old man recognized immediately that I was less than a novice, but a sale was a sale, however bungling the purchaser.

Through the doorway at the end of the display area was a workshop, and I wandered into it, fascinated by the cluttered work benches lining three of its walls. All sorts of odd wood-working and shaping tools hung on pegs on the wall behind the benches surrounding the room, also hanging from overhead. On top of the benches were several guitar components in various stages of construction. The room smelled strongly of wood and glue, and a wall of opened windows opposite the benches provided ample light along with refreshing breezes that flowed in with every puff of wind. Wide, thin shavings of near white wood lay piled on the floor along with those kicked under the benches, and in the middle of the room was a massive cutting board type island also of wood. Tucked into pockets around it were hand tools, files, rasps, shavers and such, and I recognized that the three craftsmen bent over their labors knew the tools well.

From a door leading out of the shop into what I presumed to be family living quarters came the very model of a young Spanish guitarist, tall, slender, and handsome. Thinking how much he looked like Carlos and Miguel, I later learned that he was the owner's son. With his modest English, he inquired if I wanted to buy a guitar. I told him that I didn't have much money and didn't know how to play the instrument, but I was thinking about buying one. At that, he reached up and took down a freshly completed model, propped his left leg on the center island, tuned each string and strummed the most vibrant chord I had ever heard.

This stunning Spaniard, mid-twenties I guessed, must have grown up with guitars because he was superb. What initially took me by surprise was his clothes. Propping his foot up on the center island revealed highly polished black boots with silver buckles. Tight fitting black pants to his slender waist were adorned with a wide, black leather belt with its own silver buckle. Over his white shirt with its blousy sleeves and wide cuffs, open at the neck revealing a silver chain with a cross, lay a black, short-waisted bolero-type vest with silver chains between buttons. His handsome features accentuated by a head full of shiny black hair combed back into a ducktail struck me as a costume for a performance. As warm-up to convince me to buy a guitar, he demonstrated fiery picking and strumming punctuated with thumps on the body of the instrument with his thumb and third finger. His finale reminded me of Carlos and Miguel, a succession of lightening strums up and down the strings that nearly left me breathless. He played impeccably and, just as I had been in the New Mexico sun, I was overwhelmed with desire be able to play a guitar like that.

While the workers simply turned back to their work, my rapt expression must have been humorous to him because he smiled wryly, probably thinking that I was certain to buy one of their fine guitars now and it would wind up unused in a dusty closet somewhere. He handed me the instrument, but it wasn't the same in my hands. I didn't know what to do to get it to sound the way he did, and my bungling fingers made a mockery of his virtuoso performance.

Then and there I decided to buy that guitar, and he took me back into the display area saying something in Spanish to the old man behind the counter. As the handsome virtuoso strode back through the shop and out the opposite door, the old man began telling me that I should buy a seasoned guitar, not one freshly made, because aging ensured that the instrument was properly set. I asked about costs, and as he told me a range to well over one hundred dollars, depending on the decorations and quality of wood I wanted. My enthusiasm quickly waned as prices rapidly exceeding my cash. Undaunted, I began contriving how I could borrow from my buddies to cover the cost, but when the old man laid a glistening five-string constructed of highly polished light and dark wood on the counter, then recommended that I also buy a case, I recognized unfulfilled desire. Opening a black case to reveal red crushed velvet told that fine instruments need proper protection, and when the sum of both the guitar and case were tallied, the total was double my cash. With desire turned to disappointment, I thanked the old man and left without a hand-crafted Spanish guitar.

Back on the Barcelona street, I had not gone more than a half-block when a strolling salesman approached me about a beautiful leather jacket for my lady. A hand tailored leather jacket? Hmmm. That was interesting. I tagged along to a doorway that led into a large, brightly lit leather factory, recognizable by its pungent odors of leather and dye. On display racks were fashions galore, and in the next room, also large, crafters bent over their labors. They were mostly older men and women whom I imagined to be skilled tailors with long years of working their trade. In the center of the room were two large band saws, one stacked with layered leather covered with a pattern of sheet metal used to guide the saw blade,

The other saw was about to receive a stack of leathers freshly smoothed by hand and laid up by a couple of men. Two workers at one saw slid their stack around using the pattern as a guide and produced leather cut to size, black and white cow hide that I recognized among smoothly tanned reds, browns and blacks that were then distributed layer by layer to sewing machine stations around the room. Heaps of leather lay on tables at each station, and when one seamstress completed her job, the assembly was passed to the next.

Their output of leatherwear was constant and told me that this enterprise had to have major outlets handling its sizable output because large boxes were being filled with folded and bagged products indicating that orders for many examples of their work were about to be shipped.

Young Spanish women, all of them trim and beautiful in varying sizes, tried on each jacket for fit and finish, and each jacket was examined on its model after it came off the line to insure quality construction. One of the girls modeled a beautiful oxblood colored zipped jacket for me. Dark eyes flashing, sultry lips in an inviting little smile, this girl was clearly too hot to handle. Even though a married guy, these beauties were titillating, and I thought how sharp Mary would look in a real hand-crafted leather jacket from Spain, something that no one else would have.

Back out in the sales area, the sales women were attentive to a potential sale and mentioned over and over how fashionable their jackets were. But, once again, prices separated me from their buyer list. The least expensive would consume over half my cash, and I still had family to meet. I resolved to conserve my money for the time being and decided to return to buy Mary a gift jacket on my last day of liberty. But when I returned to the factory, it was closed, Sunday, and later that day we steamed out into the Med and did not return to Barcelona on this cruise.

After the factory and a snack along the way, I was needing a pit stop and didn't know where to go. Not being aware of where to find the right facilities, I was stumped in bustling, downtown Barcelona. Then, up ahead, a familiar sign beckoned, Sears. Once in the huge department store, I approached a salesman and asked as best I could where the men's room was located. We did not communicate, and I was growing more desperate by the minute. Finally, his gesture of his hand cupped around his thumb held below his waist, and saying psss, psss, psss inquiringly, connected.

Once relieved, I asked the salesman if Sears had children's toreador outfits. Soon, I had a blue silken suit in miniature in my bag, its shining sequins, gold and red stitching was just the ticket for Squire, a beautiful outfit at a surprisingly low price.

My Friday liberty was to see the sights and to buy chosen mementos. Then, after some familiarity with the city and studying maps to find my way to family, Saturday liberty was a long walk through Barcelona. Since I had all day I didn't mind the walk because everything along the way was fascinating. Near my destination, I passed a bull fighting arena filled to capacity and boisterously echoing "OLE!" over and over. I had thought I might see a bull fight, but I didn't get around to it.

I stopped a passerby to ask directions, showing my letter with the address of my Spanish relatives, and was pleased to learn that I was nearly at the building. Inside, I wound my way to the third floor door displaying the appropriate number and knocked. Mama opened the door, surprised to see an American sailor at her door, no doubt concluding that I was in the wrong place.

Mama was short, modestly rotund in a simple cotton dress overlaid with an apron. Her greyish hair was pulled into a bun on the back of her head, and she beamed a most pleasant smile accented by sparkling eyes. I immediately determined that she was cooking, perhaps a noontime meal, because aromas of the most inviting kind reached me. Mama spoke no English, and my failed attempts to tell her who I was made no headway. Then, in a moment of inspiration, I showed her my letter that I suspected was addressed in her own hand because she took one look at it and burst into excitement exclaiming, Dobson! Dobson! Dobson!

Dobson, North Carolina was where her son-in-law was from, and my appearance at her door was a complete surprise. Mama's excitement lapsed from momentary hand waving gyrations into gestures for me to stay right there. She ran down the hall to another apartment, exclaiming with little hops all the way, and appealed at the door of a friend who could speak English. Mama hurriedly led her friend back to me, and the questions began. I got the impression that the interpreter, tall, middle aged and well educated, was seized by the irony of the moment, a uniformed American sailor in an uncommon location.

With our interpreter, all things were quickly set right. I was family from far away and was asked in. Mama motioned for us to be seated, and interpreter and I began getting acquainted while Mama made one phone call after another interspersed with passage into and out of the swinging doors to the kitchen. By the time she returned to learn more about me, Mama was nearly breathless. She sat on the edge of the couch, hands tucked in her lap, and expressed over and over how happy she was that I came to visit. We talked for an hour or so, and I told where I lived in America amplified by pointing to locations on world atlas maps.

I described Dobson, the seat of North Carolina's Surry County, as a small southern community surrounded by farms, highlighted by Salem Fork west of Dobson where my grandfather's family was from, and they thought it all to be wonderful. We delineated our family connections, most of which I was unable to absorb, although I learned a little about Mama's family. She showed me photos of her beautiful daughter, whom I had never met, and I immediately recognized how a southern farm boy could have become entranced by her.

Clearly exhausting topics to talk about for the moment, Mama, with a huge smile, asked through our interpreter if I could come back tomorrow for Sunday dinner. Surprised and delighted, especially having breathed such inviting aromas surrounding me, I agreed. Mama beamed with satisfaction. Not only would she have our interpreter there, she had invited kin from all around to come and meet their American relative.

Sunday began just as the previous two days, magnificent blue skies, warm sun and gentle breezes. My walks had given me some touristy insight into Barcelona, and unexpectedly, I became the focus of nearly overwhelming attention from my Spanish family.

In the previously open living room of the day before, Mama had set up a long table for about 20 people. Soon after I arrived, the food began pouring out of her kitchen. I was introduced to a couple of daughters who helped prepare and serve sumptuous food like I have never eaten since, and, along with the interpreter and a son, an accomplished architect who spoke considerable English, interchange between me and other guests made for a busy day. The people, the food and the atmosphere were delights for me, all laden with warm Spanish hospitality.

Papa was not there, and I learned from his son that as a colonel in Franco's army and not entirely aligned with US international affairs, my presence placed him in a troubling position. Rather than host an American serviceman, he chose to stay away in order to avoid conflicts of interest. I don't know the outcome for him, but from my perspective, Mama made their home friendly and inviting.

First came hor-d'oeuvres, sliced fresh vegetables and fruit, nuts and candies. Since everything brought from the kitchen came to me first, the guest of honor, I thought it appropriate to show my gratitude by sampling the goodies and complimenting the cooks. Observing how others handled dish after dish became my guide, and just the finger food soon became filling.

Around midday, after a round-robin of tasty morsels and conversation, Mama and her helpers began setting the table with steaming bowls and plates heaped with food. Delicious aromas filled my nostrils, all uncommon to me. When asked to take the head chair at the end of the table, I politely declined saying that was Mama's place. Giving her an arm-around hug with thanks for inviting me to dinner and pulling out the chair for her, everyone erupted in cheers and applause. Mama was pleasantly embarrassed and blushed.

I took a seat between my interpreter and the son, and thanked them for helping me converse with everyone else. We fielded lots of questions about America and where I was from and what life in America was like while everyone dug into dish after dish. When a plate of what looked to be deep fried onion rings came to me and everyone quietened, I suspected something unusual. Not knowing what to do, the son leaned over and whispered that it was octopus.

"Octopus?" I said. "That's interesting. I've never tried octopus before."

My first bite into the chewy, clam-like ring told everyone that I was an adventurer, and they cheered their approval, contributing to the festive atmosphere. Soon I was quite stuffed, but the bowls and plates kept coming my way. I tried everything, all of it savory and de-lectable, and I considered myself lucky to have the opportunity to ex-perience real Spanish home life. Soon, I was near to being unable to eat another bite.

Then, what I interpreted to be the satiated lull common follow-ing a hearty meal actually proved to be the interlude to the main course. Several of the girls began asking Mama to bring on the paella, pro-nounced pi-e-ya.

Paella was new to me, but I could tell from the complimentary gestures and rythmic clapping that everyone knew Mama's to be the best in all of Spain. When she got up from her chair, everyone burst into applause, and I imagined paella to be some sort of special desert. Was I ever surprised!

Mama came back through the swinging doors carrying the larg-est skillet I had ever seen. Hot, right from the oven, she majestically carried its handle in both hands with pot holders as though presenting a queen's treasure. Another roll of cheers and applause erupted for Mama, to which she blushed again, and the center of the table was quickly cleared to make room for the massive black skillet. Mama's smile of satisfaction told the whole story as she set her hot, steaming creation before us.

Well now, this most aromatic dish presented new problems to me: how was I going to eat another bite? After such accolades for Mama, I certainly could not allow her masterpiece to go unattended by the guest of honor, and one of the daughters saw to it that large spoonsful heaped on my plate began the performance. This most delectable dish of saffron flavored rice and vegetables, along with a chicken piece, a large shrimp in shell, and a slice of pork chop on my plate was a meal in itself. As everyone dished out servings onto their plates, it was ap-parent to me that family members worth their popping buttons had to partake of Mama's paella, and I was no exception.

Where everyone had put such a sumptuous meal completely eluded me. And here they were diving into paella with compliment after compliment to Mama. I resolved that I was in the embarrassing position of having to decline, I had simply eaten too much, but my first taste nearly stopped me in my tracks: Mama's paella was not just good, it was a once-in-a-lifetime taste that I have never duplicated since. One bite led to another, and before I knew it, I had packed in a meal's worth of paella.

Recollections of Mama's paella still makes my mouth water, and I'm sure that this Spanish family tells stories to this day of the American sailor who came to dinner with an appetite like nothing they had ever witnessed before or since.

After-meal chit-chat continued with me learning that everyone in Barcelona had the opportunity to learn English from daily newspaper lessons, and that was where the son had acquired his ability. I was his first opportunity to converse at length in native American English, and he asked many things to supplement his knowledge. When he asked about cars in America, I told of owning a Sunbeam Alpine sports car. He excitedly exclaimed that such a car was much too expensive for Spain, and I was forthwith elevated to their rich American relative.

By mid-afternoon and after cleaning up, various members of the family had shaken my hand with goodbyes and broken English statements of their pleasure from meeting me, and I noticed that Mama seemed tired. The son recommended a drive around the city to show me the sights, permitting Mama time for a nap while giving me direct service to fleet landing rather than the long walk back.

Once in the son's small Seata, a Spanish Fiat, he drove along pointing out buildings that he had designed, all impressive architecture, while telling of Barcelona sights along the way that, in my lethargic state from too much food, I was unable to absorb. Various stops at famous sites amplified by his descriptions made a most informative tour, such as the tall, strangely gothic spires of an unfinished cathedral under construction for hundreds of years. With the setting sun, we were on the old stone dock with my ship in the distance and the liberty launch bobbing in the surf awaiting enough crewmen to make another run out to her.

Such a superb day of friendship and hospitality stands out in my memory to this day, and as the son and I parted, his driving off back into the city left me wishing I had a lot more time to spend in Barcelona. It was not to be.

Chapter 26

The Blue Coast

We ported in Cannes to a world very different than what I had seen in Barcelona a month earlier. The Spanish city displayed an unpretentious kind of atmosphere of hard working people living with modest opportunity and marginal earnings. In contrast, Cannes was a playground of the rich who delighted in flaunting their wealth.

The narrow, coastal Côte d'Azur beginning around Cannes and stretching easterly to Italy is the famed French Riviera. Shielded from northern winds by the western extremities of the Alps, this region of France receives no wintry chill and basks in sunny warmth while the blue of the sea rolls at its shoreline, making a garden spot of the world.

My initial vantage point on the Forrestal about three miles out from Cannes showed that the city did not span much of the horizon. It appeared small and compact, but once onboard our launch and pounding the lightly choppy seas toward our landing, I began getting a much better impression of the wealth drawn to Cannes. Many expensive yachts lying idly at anchor in its harbor spoke of the means with which the wealthy maintained their lifestyles and leisure. Beautiful crafts sleek and well tended, mostly with white hulls, ranged in sizes from tall masted sailing yachts to multi-decked power cruisers. Smaller boats sat anchored and bobbing gently in the bay or were tied in row after row along docks. All of them, large and small, spoke of bundles of money set aside by carefree owners who came to Cannes for its wintertime warmth, elegant hotels, restaurants, casinos and women.

Once on shore, the riches of Cannes were immediately apparent. All along the spacious coastal road passing in front of elegant hotel after elegant hotel, each standing magnificently over the bay as if a bit better than its neighbor, rolled cars bearing the nameplates of Rolls-Royce, Bentley, Ferrari, Jaguar, Maserati.... More exotic marques than I had ever seen filled the street and sat parked as commonly as the unexotic, all in the relaxed atmosphere of elegance bathed in sunshine and swaying to gentle breezes. I saw that Cannes also displayed opulent architecture of refined style for the moneyed class who came to play among flowers and palms, just a few of its attractions that drew the wealthy from Europe and around the world.

Wondering how Cannes and Barcelona could be so different, I

later learned a bit of Cannes history to discover that it had blossomed in the 20th century, the seed having been planted a century earlier when rich patrons took notice of the mild French winter climate and brought their wealth in pursuit of glorifying beautiful women. A few splendid villas on surrounding high ground dated to a little before the mid-1800s. Prior to relatively recent expansion, the little fishing village that modern Cannes grew from had survived for centuries, from about 200 BC, and had been regularly destroyed by roving armies and pirates to become little more than a poor countryside town whose inhabitants lived simply on olives and onions, chickpeas and bread, fish and goat cheese, fruits and vegetables.

Local history placed the birth of modern Cannes in the year 1834. It seems that Lord Henry Brougham, Lord Chancellor of England, and his daughter, Eleonore Louise, were on their way to Italy on official business when they were stopped at a closed border checkpoint with notice that Italian authorities were attempting to contain a local cholera epidemic and temporarily banned entry. Returning along the French coast that night, they happened upon the small inn of the Pinchinat family in Cannes on today's Rue du Port. Intending to stay just the night, Lord Brougham was charmed and decided to stay for a while, then to build a vast villa, naming it Villa Eleonore, and within two years, all of London's high society began flocking to Cannes. Because of its arid grounds, Lord Brougham established a company for the purpose of building a waterway from inland to his villa and to the town, the Canal de la Siagne, that still waters the city. With water, Cannes began to flourish.

As more English visitors chose to stay and enjoy the Mediterranean coast, they built new villas with lawns and flower gardens that, in the next century, expanded into the town as the Promenade de la Croisette that quickly captured my admiration as I walked along. The Promenade grew from the previous trail along the coast, the "chemin de la petit croix" (trail of the little cross) to become a paradise of the exotic. The cream of European aristocracy came to enjoy Cannes and left their imprints among impressive construction while transplanting strange and exotic flowers and trees not common in the area. They spiced the air with citrus, palm, eucalyptus, and yucca among many varieties from around the world.

The Promenade grew additional hotels, each intended to outdo its predecessors, but none captured the French imagination as did the first of Cannes' large, multi-storied luxury hotels. This elegant edifice to a man's admiration of a woman, the Hotel Carlton, was designed in the early 20th century by Marcellin Mayère who is said to have so admired the breasts of the famous courtesan, Le Belle Otéro, that he adorned the top of the hotel with twin cupolas of perfect proportion. Ever since then the world's richest men have entered and withdrawn from the Carlton making it the most famous hotel in the world, many of them investing millions in Cannes as they vied for the charms of beautiful and fashionable high society women.

One was the Aga Kahn who became entranced with the newly elected Miss France, a girl from Cannes, and spent millions as her suitor. Among the aristocracy enamored with Cannes were the Baron and Baroness de Rothschild along with England's King Edward VIII, just the Duke of Windsor upon abdication of the throne, who came to live in Cannes.

The uniqueness and beauty of the area rose to such renown that artists came for inspiration, and film makers made Cannes Europe's "Capital of Cinema" by mid-century.

My arrival was no more than a sailor's liberty call that grew from the beach and its interests to the narrow back lanes of the working class. While my buddies favored the first pubs they came to, I strolled to see the sights for my two days of wondrously blue Mediterranean skies. I suspect that mine were days similar to those that so entranced Europe's aristocracy that they chose to escape frozen northern landscapes to spend their winters in this warm, coastal town.

Cannes was perfection, the prerogative of wealth, and majestically displayed itself in an array of color from whites brilliant in the sun to flowery petals in every color to the rich green of manicured lawns and gardens. Walkways through palms swaying in the breeze lined the beach with parks where Frenchman and tourist alike basked, reclining in fold-up, canvas bottom chairs for rent.

The beach angled up gently to the Promenade in places, particularly along "hotel row" opposite the high, stone seawall that provided protection against stormy seas. A wide walkway continued the promenade and paralleled the street, across which rose the hotels. The walkway and its handrail just above beach sand provided an elevated grandstand for beach watching, and while I walked along, I came upon a spectacle of girl watching unlike any this farm boy had ever seen.

Occasionally along the seawall were steps down to the beach, and while the day was sunny and warm, I noticed that no one was in the water. Unhurried sun worshipers lay lazily on beach towels soaking in the warmth while guys lounging along the handrailing above rated the view with whistles and cheers. I happened upon another of the parades taking place.

My first step upon French soil just a few hours before was with no awareness of French customs regarding exposure of the human form, but I was familiar with the notion presented in the popular song, "The Girl from Ipanema," a refrain about a bikini-clad girl of magnificent form slowly walking in beach sand as if unaware of the world around her, yet the focus of oohs and ahhs from admiring males watching every movement. That was the song's lasting impression, and on this Cannes beach, that very image was unfolding with its European twist.

I suspected that this impromptu beauty parade was a daily feature that began with the slow migration of statuesque Mediterranean beauties entering the arena as they stepped down onto the beach, then slowly walked to chosen spots of sand, all judged by the men watching every motion. Old men smiled; younger men whistled; shouts, cheers, and clapping told their stories.

Girls in pairs trickled onto the beach with unchoreographed entries, most often without regard to the admiring and complimentary catcalling. This was not a parade of the rich who had hotels, yachts and fine cars to fill their days. This was the real Cannes, locals attracted to the beach and its sun along with tourists who came to soak up some Cannes rays. The girls who noticed the guys with a smile and a wave, a purposeful wiggle or display designed to tempt, received the highest ratings measured in outbursts of cheers and whistles. The lone girl making the right moves left the guys breathless.

Bikinis were the fashion and, while the March breeze carried a cooling nip requiring modest leg and arm coverings, the beach of sun-warmed sand lay in the lee of the wind and invited sunbathing. Each girl carried a fish net handbag of necessities with a large towel or two, and as they walked to claim their spots the guys voiced approvals. A pair arrived at their spot, and, while one girl held a towel blocking the view, the other shed her clothes and donned her bikini amid sounds of disapproval from the peanut gallery who could only imagine the view from the sunny side. The two girls reversed places for the second to change, and, with the first girl holding the towel with outstretched arms, the mood of the gallery changed approvingly.

I had not been watching this parade for long when a particularly striking young woman, tall and slender with long, light brown hair, its curls cascading down her shoulders, temptingly flipping about in the breeze, stepped slowly down the seawall steps to the beach. I sensed from the quieted crowd that the sensuous movements of this girl made her the French soulmate of the girl from Ipanema. Every movement was perfection in motion without a single acknowledgment from the guys who were in stupified awe. Slowly walking down the beach, all eyes upon her and every mind thinking, "Oh My!" she picked her spot, took a large towel from her bag and spread it on the beach, then took a strange canvas item from the bag and placed it on the towel. Stepping into it, she pulled up the canvas bag to her neck and tied it to produce a convenient changing room. Although each motion of taking her clothes off and putting her bikini on was hidden from view, her performance in movement surpassed anything seen so far as judged by the increasing volume of cheers from the gallery. Once in her string bikini of cotton fish netting, she slid the canvas bag down and sent the boys into wholesale breathlessness. Then an ovation erupted. This long legged beauty among beauties returned their favor with a kiss blown to them and a smile, then she stretched lazily onto her towel warmed by the sand and out of the breeze. Cheers complimented this most magnificent of sun worshipers. I walked on shaking my head: why, of all days, had I forgotten to bring my camera?

My wanderings took me back into increasingly hilly and narrow streets of old Cannes, into a district of small shops of stone and stucco and the occasional sidewalk café. This area was far removed from the rich along the coast just a few blocks away and told of French life as it was lived by Frenchmen, the sort of life that drew an abundance of artists, judging from the oil paintings leaning against walls along the sidewalk. At a sidewalk café, tables hosted a sprinkling of couples talking as they sipped tea or wine. Lone patrons in white, scroll-backed iron chairs sat reading newspapers. Tables set with red and white table cloths and a flower in a tall, inexpensive glass vase or empty wine bottle made a classic outdoor setting. From inside, lively accordion music filtered out into the day, though never obtrusive, and gave the scene the ambiance of a Hollywood movie set awaiting arrival of the stars. This was the life I found all through Cannes back streets, all of it speaking of the city's abundance of romantic and picturesque settings.

Along the way I came upon a flower garden that drew my attention. Row upon row of chest-high rose bushes, resplendent with pink blossoms, grew from the soil of a small city lot, a strange location I thought. This plot was not a styled garden as along the Promenade and was completely surrounded by fences and dense shrubbery except for the low stone wall and shrubs along the sidewalk. My attention was drawn to two old women in working clothes of long sleeve aprons over ankle length dresses, their hair tied back in scarves. Both were carefully picking rose petals and placing them into deep, broad brimmed wicker baskets.

Picking rose petals? I could not ascertain a reason for picking off the outer petals since the entire rose flower was the object of praise in my experience. The women went from bush to bush, their baskets nearly full of pink petals. A gate from the sidewalk led into the garden, and when they came out through it with their baskets in hand, I wondered what they were doing. They crossed the street and went into a door of a well maintained and fashionable building a few doors down. Above the door I read "parfum" in the sign and realized that I had stumbled upon a perfume factory.

That gave me the idea of buying some real French perfume for Mary. Since I now knew something about its making, beginning with rose petals, I was curious to see the final product.

The arrival of an American sailor in uniform in their store must have been unusual because each of the three people present, whom I perceived to be a mother and two daughters, stopped what they were doing and looked at me when I entered the showroom. The matron of the store was a small woman dressed nicely in layered sweaters of grey, her middle-aged hair showing silver streaks swept back stylishly behind her ears. Her daughters were similarly presentable, each wearing a stylish sweater and skirt making a trio in up-scale fashion. The matron approached from behind a glass front display and asked if I was looking for perfume for my lady, never having to guess about the presence of a man in her store. I answered her rather good English that I would like to look around for a possible purchase. She smiled and bid me to my leisure.

The room, I deduced, had previously been the main room of a home that was converted into a showroom with high quality glass everywhere: shelves, cabinets, and display cases, each softly illuminated by overhead lighting that accented the room's pink and white decor. All around the room were bottled scents in various shapes and sizes, and fragrances of the feminine sort filled the air. Dividing the room from the next was a passageway with a drape drawn across the door sized opening behind the cash register. Since this was my first perfume shop, a family business at that, I was intrigued; but what selection among the hundreds of bottles on display could I afford?

I had learned about currency exchange from the ship's *Fore-runner* newsletter that gave the rate of one American dollar being worth a little over five French francs. Armed with that conversion rate, I quickly realized that the small card by each decanter displaying its price placed most of them well beyond my means. While slowly looking over the inventory I noticed a small decorative bottle, about fist size, sitting alone on a shelf behind the cash register. Its price card read 15 centimes, less than a franc. I could afford that, mere pocket change. While the matron and the eldest daughter talked quietly and left the room, the youngest daughter, about twelve I guessed, remained to handle the exchange of cash for goods when I made my purchase. I pointed to that small bottle and asked the girl if I could buy that item. She smiled and placed it on the glass counter top beside the register and began ringing up my purchase.

Then, something about the richness of the golden colored liquid inside, or perhaps the small price compared to other bottles, or perhaps the decanter's lone perch among the others... something caused her to reconsider. Graciously saying, "one moment, please" in French, a phrase I understood, she went behind the drape to ask a question.

A shriek broke the store's calm and the matron tore through the drape toward me with the decanter clutched in both hands at her bosom. Visibly shaken, she had to calm her high velocity French to explain to me that this item was not 15 centimes. This item was pure rose petal extract worth thousands of dollars and was not for sale. Each drop in the bottle was the product of a thousand petals.

How the price tag got located near it went unexplained and didn't need to be. After catching her breath and delivering the bottle to the eldest daughter who whisked it out of the display area, she graciously offered me a nicely prepared parcel of six tiny bottles of French perfume, one a round, flat bottle, black and shiny as obsidian bearing the name embossed in gold, JOY. Each of the bottles was pure French perfume at a sailor's price... what a deal! I paid for the gift for Mary that came with a fascinating story from Cannes, thanked the matron, and left the store certain that she needed time to recover from her near faint at almost losing a year's worth of rose oil extract.

Chapter 27

Pancakes

I took every opportunity to get out of our spaces and see what sights each day might offer on the deck above. The fantail was my first stop, and my perch on the spud sponson was favored, usually alone sitting as high as I could get on bags of potatoes and onions with my back to the steel hull. As the cruise progressed, my "mountain" gradually shrank down to the deck as we ate its contents, mostly as hash browns and fried spuds. When we left Norfolk, many crates of other long duration food stocks and equipment were also stacked where two mounts for 5-inch, 54 caliber guns once stood. During refitting, Naval architects deleted them, obsolete 1950's era armaments in the missile age. All eight gun mounts around the ship, two per sponson on each side, one sponson forward and one aft were two gun platforms. Each mount had been removed to open considerably more storage space both on the sponsons and in nearby magazines within the ship once used to store munitions and equipment for the guns. The starboard aft sponson was now a jet engine storage area with each engine housed in its sealed cocoon and secured to the deck. That sponson also contained a jet engine test stand that was frequently in use. Throughout the ship, men were busy every day all day long. Only after lights out did the ship become quiet, especially between midnight and four in the morning, the Mid-watch.

The Plan-of-the-Day one day called for on-board replenishment. We had been steaming for some weeks with the most notable loss to me being lack of milk. After our first week at sea, milk had either run out or soured. With replenishment, I looked forward to fresh milk again, a welcome respite from more "bug juice." Supplymen for the cruise must have included tons of that green, odd tasting powdered drink mix that became normal fare day after day and universally called "bug juice." Since I didn't drink coffee, the norm being a cup of it stuck onto the fingers of about every sailor, I was at a distinct disadvantage for refreshment beyond our stock of soft drinks. "Bug juice" was neither tasty nor refreshing and was barely on the consumable list, so I was confined mostly to water with meals. The Forrestal continuously distilled its own fresh water from sea water, and when a care package arrived from home, it was a banner day.

Mary always included a variety of powdered drink mixes that went into my goody bin locker in SASS-Forward. I tried to meter out my supply carefully to make it last until the next package arrived, but my plan never worked. Those small boxes contained trade-worthy goods, and I ended up trading or selling or otherwise disposing of the contents down our gullets. Our refrigerator became the repository for a container of Rootin' Tootin' Raspberry or Choo-Choo Cherry, or orange or grape flavored mixes that brought pleasant variety from more "bug juice," although her provisions of mixes never lasted long.

Within the first couple of weeks after leaving the States, our one-a-day soft drinks emerged as a royal treat. With each can signed out on the honor system as noted on a sheet of paper taped to the refrigerator door, each of us discovered ourselves longing for a cold, refreshing soda every time someone in our midst signed out his allotment. In time, our stash became known to our Marine guards who forked over the required one dollar as we did for each can beyond our allotment. They never revealed their sources, each can a rewarding respite for standing on guard duty for hours on end.

How replenishment at sea was conducted was of interest to me, and on this occasion I arrived at the starboard side forward aircraft elevator door just as the supply ship pulled along side. Connecting the ships with lines, high-lining began once both crews in life-vests and helmets had taken their stations on their respective ships. The supply ship fired a gun with its dumb round attached to a line that came sailing through the air into the hangar bay. Heavier lines were then attached and hauled over to include steel cables that permitted heavy loads and sizable fuel hoses to be winched over, each hung from rollers that rolled along the heavy cables and pulsed back and forth as the ships moved relative to each other.

The Forrestal was an oil burner, not a nuclear powered ship, and ran on black oil. Replenishment brought thousands of barrels of ship's fuel along with aviation gas and jet fuel that flowed through the lines as the pair of ships steamed along in concert keeping their separation uniform throughout the entire operation.

Additional lines came across, permitting pallets of food, equipment and supplies to be high-lined over in tandem to similar activities at each elevator platform on the starboard side. When each loaded wire basket from the supply ship came to rest on our ship, it was quickly unstrapped and contents parceled out, then sent back empty to the supply ship for another load. Once on our ship, quickly moving the supplies along was accomplished with warehouse style roller networks set up in the hangar bay. Hundreds of boxes of everything were sent over, frozen steaks, fresh eggs, fresh milk, and more. Crewmen were stationed along the rollerways to shove the boxes along, each rollerway ending where the supplies were chucked into the ship, tallied and stored.

My crew from SASS-Forward was assigned the freezer locker deep within the ship under the aft mess deck. The frigid conditions quickly showed that we were unprepared for this duty, so I went to the foul weather locker and checked out heavy overcoats, boots, hats and gloves, and for the next two hours or so, we packed cardboard boxes of frozen food into the giant lockers that were designed to contain long-term reserves to feed the crew of nearly five thousand. About mid-way through the on-loading and thoroughly cold, another crew arrived, and we were dispatched to wherever we were needed.

Upon emerging from the freezer lockers, I learned from scuttle-butt going around that a Soviet ship was trailing just astern off the starboard between us and the supply ship. My curiosity led me to the fantail where, sure enough, a Soviet warship was close astern with film crews on her bow filming our high-lining operations. Our guys on the fantail waved and smiled while swearing through their teeth at the Soviet crewmen who were, no doubt, doing the same to us. Curious about the Soviet presence, I inquired to learn that high-lining and at-sea replenishment were techniques that the Soviet Navy had not mastered. Each of its ships was outfitted in port and had to return to port to replenish. Our ships could stay on station indefinitely with replenishment. Filming our operations was, presumably, for teaching aids that the Soviets used to finally master the techniques some years later.

Unknown to me, a plan had been hatched by my crew. Some-one had noticed that hundreds of cases of steaks and eggs were flowing onto the ship, and we just happened to have a nearly empty refrigerator. One of our young seaman had endeavored to snatch a chef's hat from an officers' mess, and dressed in whites like officer's messcooks, he and a senior sailor made their way to the rollerway looking for a suitable suspect. When the Masters-At-Arms were not around, the senior sailor said in an authoritative voice, "Take that case below, sailor," and our young seaman hoisted a case of New York Strips in hand and walked it through the ship in front of the senior sailor to SASS-Forward, not the officers' mess as other sailors along the way presumed. Into our refrigerator it went, producing satisfied smiles on everyone's faces that the heist had been pulled off. Quickly concluding that steaks were not enough, back to the rollerway they went just as cases of eggs were rolling by. Again with no Master-At-Arms in sight, the same authoritative, "Take that case below, sailor," resulted in a second heist, also taking up residence in our refrigerator.

That sequence began an unfolding of events that had all of us well fed and bearing smirky grins but knowing that discovery held severe repercussions. Keeping secrets was not new to us, though; each man was a high level "Q" cleared operative with "Unrestricted Access."

We knew that our steaks and eggs would not last long, a couple of weeks at most, and each of us undertook to do our part to insure that nothing went to waste. Once again having to determine how to dispense with the goods in an equitable fashion, we agreed that one steak and two eggs per man per meal was fair. With our limited kitchen and cooking capacity, we had to work around each other or double up. Rather than the ship's mess, we were in business for ourselves, but still drew from the same supply, just a different selection.

On our first day of steak frying, we didn't realize their mouth watering aroma was wafting throughout that portion of the ship. Tastebuds were piqued only to be sorely disappointed when hungry sailors arrived at the forward mess deck to find that steak was not on the menu. One of our crew hurried into SASS-Forward saying that Master-At-Arms were sniffing around trying to find the source, and we realized that our ventilation system was not on.

Being a sealed magazine containing nuclear weapons, the ship's architects had designed off-board ventilation into and out of our spaces to prevent contamination of the ship in the event that a magazine was breached as in a fire. Controls were within our spaces, and activating the ventilation soon produced a negative pressure that drew air into our spaces and dumped it overboard, thus cleansing the aromatic evidence of our heists from the interior of the ship.

Meanwhile, we were fortunate to have the entrance to SASS-Forward both off-limits to all other personnel and guarded by an armed Marine, more so for being located just behind the forward mess deck. In an effort to defuse the investigation, a couple of us left our spaces and went sniffing around, too, saying the aroma seemed to be coming from the officer's mess. No such mess was nearby, but the forward mess was, and the idea that officers got steak while the crew got cold cuts fit nicely with the normal grumbling and grousing about differences in officer and crew meals.

That situation defused, we settled in to steak and eggs three or four meals a day, each of us cleaning the cooking equipment after use or turning it over to the next guy. Along with heists from my mountain of spuds, sailors had never eaten so well for the several days that our supplies lasted.

Then word came that the Admiral would be inspecting our spaces the next day, and we had to pack in steaks and eggs quickly, then do away with the packaging to remove any evidence. We kept the fryer going all day long. Egg shells, meat scraps and cut up packaging piled up, all of it sacked and clandestinely trafficked through the ship to disposal after lights out. We turned to cleaning everything to a lustrous shine, every pot, every pan, everything in our kitchen, and our refrigerator, too, inside and out. No evidence of anything was left in our spaces. Tins of coffee, sugar, salt, oil, popcorn... everything we knew to be contraband went back into the bottom of the elevator shaft, then the elevator was lowered to block view of our stash. We spent many manhours that night cleaning and polishing, then did more of the same the next morning.

By the time that the Commander of Carrier Division-4 stepped down the ladder into our spaces, a highly organized nuclear weapons operations center staffed with top flight personnel was standing for inspection. He and his staff, the Captain, Executive Officer and Weapons Officer, presented an impressive display of high command, each a perfect presentation of a senior US Navy officer. The Admiral in his white uniform and white gloves was the very model of the Navy's top commanders.

When he pulled up the curtain under our kitchen platform to reveal pots and pans, coffee pot, popcorn popper, all pristinely clean and neatly stowed, we held our breaths. He looked everything over carefully, and each of us was thinking that an overlooked spot of steak or dried egg or spilled coffee or Rootin' Tootin' Raspberry on his gloves would be disastrous.

Everything was spotless, though, as testified by his gloves remaining unsoiled, and we collectively breathed sighs of relief... until he stepped over to the refrigerator. It was also spotlessly clean, and if it caused him to wonder why it was there, any questions he might have had were dispelled by the large, yellow box of photographic film that sat prominently on the top shelf, cold and well protected from aging. Nothing else was in the sparkling clean refrigerator, and his closing its door with no comment produced more quietly exhaled sighs of relief among us.

Satisfied with our office and lounge area, the Admiral and his troupe wound their way below to the first magazine and shops, then the second. Always spotless and with everything in its place and secure, the magazines were brilliantly lit showing stack after stack of H-bombs. I suspected that his slow walk among them was his stroll in the war room of doom, a war room he hoped never to call into service. No one said a word, but not one of the entourage, each man a senior officer in the US Navy, could take his eyes off those weapons: smaller than imagined, sleeker than conventional bombs, each one either white or silver in exact presentation, each one of such firepower to be unimaginable, and so many of them. I imagined each man thinking, "How could such small bombs contain such enormous power?"

All of us knew that this man wearing two stars, and this man alone, held the authority to bring this firepower of the USS Forrestal into service upon the command of the President and transfer of the necessary codes from the Pentagon. If he gave the command, we would have the complete flight line under Chop Sticks operations in a matter of minutes, and woe be unto the world.

The Admiral's inspection was a quiet affair, and no questions were asked. He made his way back up the ladders with his staff in tow, and we then went back into our normal mode with spic-and-span spaces, the most pristine that they would be throughout the entire cruise. No further inspections were conducted, and when the "Weapons" efficiency award insignia was being painted onto the sides of the island indicating that the Forrestal was a stand-out ship, I wondered what role our magazines had played.

From time to time while steaming the Med, we encountered Soviet ships. One was a guided missile cruiser with a high, sharp bow that came from the southwest at an overtaking speed. Word spread fast, and I went up to the flight deck to see the ship, then observed a high stakes game of chicken on the high seas. The Forrestal was a giant by any measure and was steered on a heading that would, I was certain, bring the two ships into collision if one or the other did not change course or speed. Would either ship's captain back down, I wondered?

As I watched, neither ship changed its bearing, and I grew even more certain that I was about to witness an international incident, a collision of superpower warships. The course of the Soviet cruiser drew her steadily nearer and nearer until she crossed our bow only a few hundred yards away. That short distance within the vast extent of the

Mediterranean Sea was a near miss of colossal proportions, and I envisioned a slightly faster pace sending the Forrestal's bow easily cutting through the Soviet warship.

On another occasion when word of a nearby Soviet ship reached me, I grabbed my camera again and headed for the Signal Bridge to use the "big eyes." When I emerged through the door onto the catwalk high up the island, I was confronted by the seaman on duty who told me that I was not allowed to be there. Presenting my ID with its "Unrestricted Access" pointed out, he backed off and I walked straight to the giant binoculars, sighted through one eyepiece and snapped a sequence of photos with my Kodak Instamatic through the other lens. Afterward, I watched the frigate-size ship briefly and noted that its engine exhausts were ports along the waterline rather than a stack up in the wind, an odd design, I thought. As the ship slogged through the waves, its exhaust noise was successively muffled, then open, muffled gurgling through each wave, then loud and smoking when out of the water.

I was gone from the Signal Bridge in a matter of minutes, and, once back on the flight deck among many other sailors watching the ship, I wondered why warships of any type were allowed to get so close to the Forrestal. The sailors onboard her must have been in awe of the giant aircraft carrier slicing through the blue Mediterranean parallel to their ship, and I concluded that they were also confused by the lack of any visible armaments: not a single gun pointed at them. A quickly-launched salvo of torpedoes from her could not have missed and would have inflicted heavy damage, likely ripping open our below-the-waterline magazines and crippling an entire airfield at sea at the expense of a near-worthless hulk that could easily have been blown out of the water. Hostile actions onboard the ship must not have been seen by either of the helicopter crews hovering over her, and their presence and imminent firepower likely kept the encounter to no more than curiosity. Once my film was developed, the photos revealed a small, old ship in need of a lot of attention.

Other confrontations included aircraft cat and mouse encounters between US and Soviet flyers. On the occasions when Flight Ops was broadcast over the ship's closed circuit TV, and particularly when voice communications were included, ship's company got ringside seats to both the serious and humorous. The most memorable was an engagement with a Soviet Bear bomber and escorts over the northeastern Mediterranean one day. Phantoms from the Forrestal intercepted the aircraft far from the ship, and the voice exchange between Flights Ops and pilots brought a round of cheers and laughter. One of the pilots reported taking up a position just in front of the bomber such that the bomber's pilots looked into the exhausts of his jet engines. The pilot then requested permission to hit double AB. Double afterburner meant that the sudden and violent rush of greatly increased exhaust would likely blow the cockpit out of the bomber. A strong and commanding voice quickly returned a "Negative on double AB. Negative...."

Influences of an international incident on ship's company became clear when a political crisis in Egypt changed the Admiral's plans.

The Pentagon determined that a show of force was needed, and for twenty-seven days we steamed off the coast of that country. Those twenty-seven days began at a time when we were scheduled for replenishment. Canceled. The Forrestal went to readiness conditions requiring closure of some watertight doors and hatches, and the crew settled in for the duration. Not only did we not have fresh milk, my goodie bin was about empty, and so were the ship's food lockers. Our steak and eggs days were long past, and so were the cold cuts that caused so much grousing. Our messcooks turned to long term supplies, and we had pancakes four meals a day every day.

Those pancake days were the most creative flour dough escapades I've ever known. Breads and rolls and pastries were the main fare day in and day out. And pancakes. Pancakes hot off the grill with butter and syrup for breakfast; pecan pancakes with more butter and jellied fruit for mid-day; peanut pancakes with butter and honey for the evening meal along with really salty SOS; yeast pancakes and applesauce for mid-rats; whole wheat pancakes and jam; buckwheat pancakes, sourdough pancakes, pancakes in every variety imaginable. And they were good! Pancakes had never been high on my list, but I have since been more receptive.

Our Carrier Division participated in combined Naval exercises with other countries, and, on the occasion when the French Navy put a ship to sea as the target of a hunter-killer exercise, the Forrestal was included as the primary US force. The ship that found the target, an abandoned World War-II vintage Destroyer painted day-glow orange, earned the right to sink her. The ship was underway somewhere at slow speed. Our pilots located the ship, and the Captain brought the Forrestal within view to watch our jets attack. Crewmen lined the flight deck to watch plane after plane make low-level assaults, strafing, rocketing, and bombing the ship. The play-by-play was called over the ship's communications, and after what seemed to be extraordinary punishment, the target was still afloat. A battery of Shrike missiles on the starboard forward sponson was called into service, and a variety of warnings rang out as the battery moved into position to fire upon the ship about two miles away. Collected crew in the peanut gallery were relocated to avoid the missile's exhaust blast. Anticipating a great show of fireworks, we watched as the missile blasted off toward the target, then exploded about mid-course. A hearty laugh went up from the gallery, but the missile battery and technicians had some explaining to do. Their battery was supposed to be ready and reliable defense but could not perform in a turkey shoot.

The target came back under aircraft assault, and when the wing commander approached on what I sensed to be the coup-de-grace, the bomb he released followed a path to the ship's waterline just ahead of the forward gun turret. A huge plume of water rocketed skyward followed by an enormous thud from the explosion that brought resounding cheers from my shipmates. Then, when someone noticed that the ship's bow was down, a strange quiet spread among us. In the following minutes as the keel slowly rose above the surface, its prop still slowly beating, the bow slipping steadily under the waves, each of us had a lump in our throats and a knot in our stomachs.

Real sailors had once been on that ship, and it was once new and proud. We knew that she had survived every engagement to become old, unwanted and soon to be forgotten, but we respected her existence and watched as the fantail rose higher and higher, the ship sliding slowly and silently beneath the waves. Not a sound was uttered as each of us sailors identified with what we saw in various ways, each of us recognizing that all warships on the high seas, including our own, were just hulls between us and Davy Jones' Locker.

When the target slipped from sight, I envisioned the silent descent of that once-proud ship into the murky depths of the Mediterranean Sea, joining the host of ships from across time that lay on the bottom, coming to rest in a cloud of slowly settling mud, never to be seen again.

Chapter 28

Athens

The triangular peninsula known as Greece is old Attica. Its gnarled mountains and fringe plains swallowed by the Mediterranean Sea along a thin, jagged coastline seem inhospitable to civilization. How the ancients clung tenaciously to this region and survived on its limited fertility to produce a people of the most fertile mind is a remarkable achievement in the history of mankind. Attica is the Greek word for promontory, a fitting description of the rough terrain and its influence on the history of mankind.

First came the Pelasgians, then the Ionians from northern reaches, peoples who learned to make their livelihoods from the sea and arable land best described as sparse amid a rugged landscape of stone. Not only did they master the sea and the land, they fashioned their landscape into monuments that survived more than 2,500 years. With their constructions rose a classical panorama under warm skies of purest blue during a time when the modern world was young, a time when people molded living into ideas about life that became the engaging tapestry of magnificence we call ancient Greece.

Legends tell of King Erechtheus who brought several villages of Attica into political union and dedicated that achievement to the goddess Athena. Kings resided on the prominence known as the Acropolis and ruled with singular authority. There was Dracon and Solon, the latter initiating a constitution for his peaceful home and colonies that transformed the small rural town of Athens into a city that shaped the affairs of man for centuries. Democracy by a voting populace rose with enlightened leaders named Themistocles and Pericles who united the people into brilliant achievements born of intellectual curiosity. Philosophy, the contemplation of man's existence, rose into polished form with Socrates and his student Plato, who saw the world as the product of ideas. Plato's student, Aristotle, saw the world as the greatest teacher, requiring only study to understand natural law governing the world's workings. Poetry blossomed into the great dramas of Sophocles and Euripides while Aristophanes polished satire into comedy. Many great men of ideas strode the stone ways of Athens and produced great works in all areas of creative life that remain widely admired today.

The richness of Athens and the Greek people attracted would-be conquerors who faced an adept foe on both land and sea, a foe that preserved its cultural domination of the Mediterranean region with victories and losses of heroic proportions. Conflicts among semi-independent Greek city-states occasionally led to lengthy wars and exhaustion, after which they returned to art and culture captured in the legacies of their time that focused on attributes of quality in mankind. And when the Romans arrived, the conquered Greeks became the conquerors; the refined life of Athens became the spiritual capital of the Empire. Here, young Roman patricians were introduced to refinements of reason and thought, and young warriors-turned-thinkers polished their temperament of conquest into a new Rome that recognized the varied peoples within its dominion as citizens with rights granted by Roman law.

The Emperor Justinian snuffed out the flame of Greek creativity when he closed the philosophical schools in 529 A.D. Decline of Greek influence continued for 900 years and was sealed in 1456 with the Turkish conquest. The Greek war for independence in 1833 finally secured Attica as Greek homeland, but repeated sieges had reduced Athens to near destruction. Although impoverished, the town of a mere 6,000 was chosen as the capital of their new nation, and the Greeks set to the task of reviving Hellenism in the modern world. Today, what is left from time, wars, and scavengers speaks of monumental achievements still dazzling in their proportions. What magnificence would they have displayed in their glory? We can only imagine.

My arrival in Piraeus, the principle port of Greece now merged with Athens, was the fulfillment of dreams. Why I was fascinated with Athens and Hellenism remains unaccounted for; it all came from high school and college history books, encyclopedias and the writings of philosophers I had read along with stories of great deeds among the people who achieved them. Through those introductions came a sense of connection; my American lifestyle traced its democratic roots directly to these craggy shores and those thinkers who shaped such ideas among the ancient architecture I could see in the distance as the Forrestal lay anchored off the Pireaus. On the horizon stood the Parthenon. Seeing the real structure recalled my fascination with its copy in Nashville just a couple of years earlier.

As in olden times, the port teemed with vessels arriving from who knows where bringing trade and passengers, the modern version of the great emporiums of the Levant dating to the 5th century B.C. That was the time of Themistocles who led his Athenians to build the long walls from Athens to the Piraeus, connecting the center of Hellenistic culture with the Saronic Gulf. The two small, semi-circular bays of olde that opened to the south, where slipways of ancient battle triremes can still be seen, have given way to vast docks for giant ships and ship building, testimony to Greek maritime legacies expressed in ocean liners to fine yachts to multicolored sails and dingies in every configuration. Along the "sailor's walk" common to all ports are yacht clubs and open-air restaurants featuring the sea's bounty brought in on the colorful ciaques beached below.

Ancient and modern are not far apart in Athens. Remains of

Conon's walls of the 4th century that replaced those of Themistocles still crown the cliffs of Akti promontory adjoining the Theater of Zea by the sea where lively folk performances continue the traditions of old Athens. Nearby are museums featuring magnificent marble and bronze statues discovered in 1959 below construction of the new street. All this and more made the Piraeus alone a worthy destination, but Athens stood beckoning me, and I could not wait to walk its legendary ways.

Arriving from the sea gave me pause to consider the immense proportions of Athens that completely engulfed the visible shoreline along the Apollo Coast. This introduction left ideas of a slow, contemplative atmosphere among classical ruins in the wake of a bustling city teeming with commerce and traffic galore. This was modern Athens with trade conducted among the old and new that beckoned with adventures in every direction.

Not far away lay the ruins of Mycenaean temples and tombs that figured in the time of Homer's Iliad and Odyssey, seafaring tales that are both the first written record of Greek life and its most enduring written product. Along another trek lay the sickle-shaped bay of Marathon, hemmed in by mountains and reedy marshland, the setting for one of antiquity's greatest military victories when 10,000 Athenians defeated 30,000 Persians in 490 B.C. and gave to the world marathon races to commemorate the long distance runner who ran the distance back to Athens to announce the victory, then fell dead.

A high point is a good place to begin, and the Acropolis permits viewing ancient Hellenism close at hand with surrounding panoramic views of sprawling Athens. This flat-topped limestone rock rising 230 feet above the city center was the ancient citadel of kings. Erechtheus was the first to build a temple on it, but Peisistratus transformed the old royal fortress into the sacred rock of immortality by erecting smooth-faced stone ramparts of Cyclopean proportions all around, leaving just the approach from the west open for five gates and a grand portico for processions to "the citadel of the gods." The way is the Propylaea conceived by the architect Mnesicles, and, though never actually completed due to the outbreak of the Peloponnesian War, its grand prominence was a sensational discovery two millennia later. When cleared of collected rubble from many centuries of neglect, the processional way up the Propylaea led to the first construction I came to, the high platform of the temple of Athena Nike (Wingless Victory) built to commemorate defeat of the Persians.

The Parthenon (Virgin's Chamber), built between 447 and 432 B.C., still retains history's repeated description as the most perfect of buildings, the crowning achievement of the age of Pericles, the "golden age" of Athens. Even though wars and rapacious thievery have reduced its grandeur to little more than marble debris, what remains is still hailed as one of the great achievements of the ancient world. This windowless rectangle without a straight line, of hewn stone segments held in position by poured bronze spikes, is a marvel of genius in the Doric style. Ictinos the architect shaped the monument on a slightly convex base with swelling and tapering columns leaning slightly inward along lines of perspective that meet miles away, with fluted columns whose flutes diminish in width but not in depth and join oblique cornices and gables in what is still described as aesthetic perfection in architecture. The decorating statuary telling the history of the Greek people that once adorned east and west eaves is long gone, along with the carved tiles that surrounded the building above the columns, each one a depiction of Greek history carried off by looters, trophies of conquest, that now reside in museums around the world. I had seen their recreation in Nashville's Parthenon and now recognized what the ravages of war had done to the magnificence that once was Athens' Parthenon.

Adjacent to the Parthenon to the north stands the Erechtheion, completed in 406 B.C. Here are the oldest and most sacred relics of the ancient Greeks: the Mycenean palace, the tomb of Kekrops the founder of Athens; the marks of Poseidon's trident; and the sacred olive tree of Athena. The Erechtheion's three porticos tell different stories, with the southernmost the famously complemented structure known by the six caryatides, maidens of stone who carry the weight of the roof on their heads. Six delicate columns stand guard around the eastern entrance to Erechtheus' own chamber, said to be the burial spot of this great Athenean. A second chamber entered from the north was a sanctuary dedicated to Poseidon Erechtheus.

Looking off to the north of the Acropolis is the old market place, the Agora, now completely surrounded by modern Athens. The Ford Foundation open air museum of antiquities in the restored Stoa of Attalus invited a walk among identified works and those whose creators are lost to history, all on display while much of the area is strewn with artifacts as stacked debris awaiting identification and placement in the puzzle of what was once old Athens. Amid the rubble is the Theseum, or more correctly, the Hephaisteum since it was consecrated to the god Hephaistos. This Doric structure is thought to be older than the Parthenon and is the best preserved of all Greek temples.

Just beyond the north end of the Agora, I happened upon workers clearing out excavations along a rail line. What attracted me to the work was unusual excitement among a throng of observers. After standing around a bit, I learned that the excavation was thought to reveal the site of Socrates' last breath, having been condemned to death (by drinking hemlock) for corrupting the youth of Athens with his philosophical reasoning.

On the opposite side of the Acropolis and immediately below the southern edge lie two theaters and remains of the columned portico between them. My imagination went into tilt as I walked onto the patterned tiles of the Theater of Dionysus. Dating to perhaps the 6th century B.C., this theater was for many centuries the official Athenian meeting place. It was here that great orators spoke to thousands of citizens who packed the stone seats that rise from eye level upward at least 20 rows and span the west-to-east arch of seating carved into the hillside. It was here during festivals commemorating the god Dionysus that the works of Aescylus, Sophocles, Euripides, Aristophanes, and other classical playwrights were first performed. It was here that great rolls of laughter roared to comedies and satires, and where the quiet

Athenian presence was gripped when witnessing the stage death of a tragic hero. I stood where they performed. I walked up the steps and along the musician's stage. I walked around the performing arena, among the semicircle of stone seats. I sat in the primus seat, the best seat in the house reserved for the most prominent Athenian, carved of stone and engraved with their names from centuries past. If only these remains could tell us their stories. If only....

Walking westward from the Theater of Dionysus toward the second theater, the Odeon of Herodes Atticus, the remains of a two level portico are visible. This connecting stoa was the favored walking and arguing spot of young Athenian philosophers who learned from the masters and earned themselves history's acclaim for perfecting the stoic philosophy. I stopped to listen, a phantom from their time wafting through the perfect Greek day, with only my imagination playing their time. Grass grew where the stone way was once the gathering place of great minds, where only the ground level bases of columns that once supported the portico remain.

I walked slowly with them, separated by over two thousand years and came to the second theater, smaller than that dedicated to Dionysus and completed in 161 A.D. Herodes Atticus was a Roman patrician who so admired the Greeks that he financed construction of the most modern theater in the world at the time as a memorial to his wife, a theater covered with a wooden roof to shield some 5,000 spectators from the Mediterranean sun. Still being restored, this compact construction in stone from hundreds of years after the Theater of Dionysus is the site of the Athens Festival of Music and Drama held every summer, among innumerable performances that continue the legacy of performing arts so compellingly Greek.

I found Athens alive with ancient and modern, with legacies that invite the world. My walks through the city took me under the gaze of bigger-than-life statues of Socrates and Plato, personas who overshadow all of western thought today. The Plaka opened from the northeast corner of the Acropolis with narrow lanes of shops, bazaars, taverns... the center of Athenian markets and night life. Here I purchased a tea set for Mary, a requested item. Further on and all around were open-air restaurants of sizes from the quaint to the lavish, from a couple of tables covered with colorful oil cloth to classy bistros and boisterous clubs that invited day or night sampling of modern Athens.

On my first of three visits to Athens, comprising a total of 29 days of liberty, I was approached along my way from the dock by a small man inquiring if I wanted a guide. I wasn't sure I needed one, but as I walked along he came along, too, and became my "guide." After a morning of sightseeing, we stopped for lunch in one of the small sidewalk cafés. He introduced me to his "cousin" who ran a spot that was actually a narrow walled off alley between two buildings. Three small tables sat waiting for customers, with "cousin" being the sole operator. His café consisted of a glass front 4-rack rotisserie with several chickens basting in the heat of smoldering charcoal. Lying on the charcoal was an iron skillet containing potatoes in a baked-fried form. Nothing else presented itself for lunch, and I at first declined while thinking of a more inviting location. But with insistence from my "guide" and thinking that this lunch might be cheaper than paying for two at a more upscale place, I relented and became witness to a display of chef finesse.

My "guide" and his "cousin" chatted back and forth, with questions coming to me. What would I like to drink? 7-Up. "Ah," nodded "cousin." From under the rotisserie, also a refrigerator, came a cold bottle of refreshment along with another for my "guide." Which chicken? I pointed to one through the glass dripping on the inside with broth, and in one smooth motion as fluid as a polished dancer, "cousin" opened the back of the rotisserie, slipped the skewer out with a gloved hand, slid my selected lunch onto the cutting board platform to his side, removed the glove, withdrew a sword length knife from the side of the rotisserie, swung it from over his shoulder, and with a single "whack" cleaved the bird into two equal parts along the breastbone. He slipped the sword back into its slot and slid each golden portion onto a plate, all before I could blink an eye. I was amazed. Back into the rotisserie he went with tongs to remove hot slices of potatoes from the skillet, and in a flash he placed both plates on the table before us.

I breathed the mouth-watering aroma of sizzling baked chicken and was about to taste the first potato when a plate full of greens was set between us. Sliced carrots, small peeled green onions, quartered radishes, small cabbage wedges, chunked lettuce... fresh and inviting, a welcome and unanticipated surprise added to my impromptu lunch. And before I could taste the first strip of succulent chicken, large slices of toasted, buttered and garlicky Greek bread came out on another plate. I was more than amazed. This was my first eating experience in Athens, and it was a delight straight out of fiction, a quaint Athenian sidewalk café in the midst of passersby who had to be tempted.

Since I was the only customer at the establishment, I wondered if I had wandered into something that everyone else knew better to avoid, then reasoned that this location for "cousin" must have preceded my presence. So, he had to be known among those who frequented his location in downtown Athens. Then, right behind us, a couple of young men wandered over to the rotisserie and made selections and, once reassured, I could see that "cousin" was an established businessman on the street.

My "guide" and I consumed a tasty and filling lunch in the midst of modern Athens on the go, and I imagined that similar fare had been served more than two thousand years ago in similar fashion: tasty finger foods. Satisfied and now among full tables, my desire to see more sights prompted giving our table to more customers for "cousin."

How much was our lunch, I asked my "guide"? A quick exchange with "cousin" returned a sum of drachma totaling about 70 cents. I was further astounded: all that for two for less than a dollar! I fingered through the small waist pocket of my tight-fitting blues and counted out a little less than a dollar's worth of Greek change, then made the mistake of asking if American money was OK. I held a Kennedy half-dollar in my fingers, a coin that instantly drew closer examination by my "guide." He and "cousin" spoke excitedly back and forth, attracting the attention of other patrons, and a close examination between them seemed to be the sort that treasure hunters would exchange upon finding a golden doubloon. "Cousin" was visibly agitated, pleasantly so, and took the coin in both hands with many Greek "thank you" bowings for having put such a treasure in his hands.

Judging that two of the Kennedy half dollars were deemed more than enough to cover the lunch and tip for us, my "guide" and I were on our way again leaving "cousin" still clutching his treasured Kennedy half-dollars in both hands. Our walk led through monuments where I recognized that I knew more about the ancients than did my "guide." Further on into the bustling plaka where the bazaar of narrow walking streets was full of closely packed merchants, seemingly having as much of a social gathering as commerce, we ventured through a carnival atmosphere. Unmistakable strains of Greek music enlivened the colorful arena of small shops, some behind glass, others open, with all sorts of arts and crafts on display for the tourists, turning my wanderings into a memorable passage.

By late afternoon we had walked over much of the center of Athens, and my "guide" mentioned that he must be getting back to his family. It was then that I realized that I knew nothing of him, not even his name, and we had spent a day together. He wanted to know if I would be pleased to offer him some pay for his services. Although my funds were limited, I realized that he had provided insights that I would never have known about, but I had no idea what a guide's fare should be for the day. I offered a Greek bill of value that was not quite to his expectations. Another one like it and his very own Kennedy half-dollar was acceptable, and he was off, probably with less than the real value of his day, but with a free lunch and stories to tell about his treasure that was, I imagined, passed around for his admiring family to see that very evening.

We ported in Athens two more times during the cruise, and almost a month of liberty gave me ample opportunity to see new sights and to return to those places I wanted to see again. On my first visit, I selected Greek ceramics that I favored and shipped them home to Mary. She wrote back saying the package, however carefully I had wrapped the items, arrived with everything reduced to shards. During my last liberty in Athens, I chose the tea set mentioned earlier, packed it away rather than ship it, and arrived home with the set intact. I look at it from time to time and instantly recall the noisy plaka and the shop where I bought it, a true shop with glass windows floor to ceiling and a glass door among other merchants displaying their wares on rugs in the open. Shelves around the walls displayed items so that tourists could see from outside what was available.

I amagined that multitudes of tourists like me had passed this way, each of us eyeing and handling the crafts and debating what to buy. With our selections made, newly acquired memories went quietly onto shelves and into cabinets and drawers, more "stuff" of life, each memento an artifact of our exploits that we look back upon later to remind ourselves where we had been, revisiting the imagery of our adventures that mere mementos can never evoke in others.

One of the modern pleasures of Athens was a park I came upon and there encountered love in the air. Well designed to escape the city's bustle and beautifully maintained with flowers and shrubs along grassy expanses interlaced with winding walkways, the large park's tall trees gave shade to young men and women lounging on blankets with picnic baskets that included bottles of wine and long loaves of bread. Mothers strolled with their babies in carriages, children played, and young people all around enjoyed the magnificent day with all sorts of outdoor activities.

With my 7-Up in hand along with my selection of baklava, that afternoon was of the most satisfying of circumstances. Gentle breezes made the quiet walkways a delight, especially so when I settled onto a bench and roving minstrels came by. In particular was a group of three men in red, white and black native Greek attire pictured on postcards in every souvenir stand around. They picked and strummed their bousoukis of three tones produced from mandolin size to cello, each held in hand as they strolled along, stopping here and there to sing another ballad. Their stringed lutes were the Greek national instrument like none other in the world, and they incited *Zorba the Greek* sorts of improptu dances among passersby while attracting lone players who joined in.

I did note, however, that their harmonizing was with glances and exchanged grins between them, and I'm sure that they went away chuckling about singing a naughty tale to an American sailor who simply sat listening, understanding nothing, and smiling back at them.

Later when searching for more Greek music, I came upon Mikis Theodorakis who became noted internationally during the 1960s for scoring the acclaimed film *Z*. Along with *Zorba the Greek* in film, I was particularly pleased to recall much of the scenery and music from similar places I had been.

About the time I finished my baklava, a young Greek sailor in uniform walked purposely toward me. With a big grin, he stuck out his hand. After shaking hands and being properly introduced, he wanted to tell me that he, too, was a Gunner's Mate, and that he was making a career of the Greek Navy. He had noticed the crossed gun barrels on my uniform and pointed to the same on his, concluding that we were associates by profession. His broken English was sufficient to carry on conversation, my non-existent Greek being no hindrance, and he described himself as the turret captain on a Greek warship that had been, just a few years before, an active US Navy destroyer.

I had to extract some of my Gunner's Mate "cover" and struggled to recall just how the 3-inch 70 and 5-inch 54 worked, guns that he knew and wanted to talk about, telling me how many shells he could get off in a minute. Our conversation went along well until he asked what ship I was on. I showed my shoulder patch for the USS Forrestal, and he was immediately confused, having seen her up close to note that she had no guns. "What did a Gunner's Mate do on a ship without guns," he asked?

Suddenly confronted with the simplest of questions, I had no immediate answer and struggled to come up with something convincing. On the spur of the moment, I told of being a munitions handler for the stores of shells that the Forrestal carried for other ships in the fleet and, even though we had no guns, our stores required Gunner's Mates to do the handling. He wanted to know how we did that, and I told of high-lining, at-sea replenishment that he found extraordinary. Ships steaming along side-by-side could transfer stores between them on cables! The idea was completely new to him, a revelation, and he expressed both his wonder and admiration for the US Navy that could do such wondrous things. Concluding that my duties were much more advanced than his duties, he bade me both his welcome to Greece and his farewell. As he walked off I only smiled, thinking; "If you only knew."

Further along, I came upon what I thought to be a classic Greek scene: young lovers. Under a tree lay a beauty, her head propped in hand, long black hair draped to the blanket she lay on while listening to her beau strum a song on a tiny bousouki smaller than a violin. Its strings resounded with the fast-paced action of his fingers while his voice, filled with passion, rose and fell at a much slower pace. What he was singing about I could not tell, but his expression with closed eyes seemed to be one of singing the blues, of troubled times rather than a soft love song.

I made my rounds of Athens by myself that day and had discovered many new things about this most intriguing city and Greece as a country. This was the real Athens. I had so admired ancient Greek history in the books I read, then discovered a bit of the Greek world in Nashville, then arrived in Athens to discover modern and ancient interlaced with much wonder and found it all immensely satisfying. Athens was a vibrant city whose ancestry lay distant in time with remnants that have stood the ages, standing throughout modern growth as only hints of ancient lives in the modern world entwined with legacies long past.

Like all our other ports-of-call, my sense of Athens was similarly, so much to see, so little time.

Manaco by night

Chapter 29

Nice and Monaco

Origins of the city of Nice are considerably older than Cannes, to about 350 B.C. and to a people who chased elephants, now lost to history. They gave way to another tribe who established the seaport town named Nikaia, meaning "victorious." The town rose from a natural harbor up the pine-covered slopes to today's fortress Rocher du Chateau. A plea some two millennia past for Roman help to oppose enemies from Cannes resulted in a Roman response to help the peoples of Nice. The Romans came to stay and built a second town, Cemenelum, next to Nikaia. In time, the two merged and grew to perhaps 20,000 inhabitants. Then, with collapse of the Empire, the Roman town faded and modern Nice emerged with ruins from Imperial times as reminders of ages long past.

Despite continual wars for control of the coastline surrounding Nice, the town grew to become a commercial rival to the Greek port of what is today Marseilles and became a shipping hub of the Mediterranean. Its long coastline also became assembly points for armies bent on conquest of the Alpine people in the mountains to the northeast and the people of the northwestern plains that the Romans called Gaul, later to become the land of the Franks and modern-day France. The 813 Saracen (Arab) conquest of the city brought devastation and the establishment of the Moorish Coast, today's Riviera. An opposing force under the Count of Provence arrived 161 years later and drove the Saracens out making the area the eastern extent of Provence. It wasn't until 1176 that Nice was recognized as a city by charter, and by 1382 it was a strong fortress port held by the Counts of Savoy against the French and their allies. Its citizens repelled a Turkish fleet in 1543 and spent the next 317 years of political turbulence molding themselves into a definitive part of France by 1860. The beginning of modern Nice was marked by unprecedented growth toward building a tourist and commercial economy enjoyed by many generations since.

I rode the rails from Cannes to see the entire Côte d'Azur and spent a day wandering through Nice and Manaco. So much to see in so little time made my sightseeing more of a broad sweep than an in-depth tour because inviting adventures lay all around me, far more than could be done without living the Riviera life.

Larger than Cannes, the Nice segment of the Côte d'Azur is also longer as it winds its way around the craggy Bay of Angels. Like all the towns along the way, its beaches were paralleled by the Promenade of Angels, that wide avenue I first set foot upon in Cannes that extends all the way to Monaco and on to Italy. Beside it ran the rail line I rode. I concluded that such manicured beauty in such an intriguing natural setting made the Promenade's passage among rose bushes, palm trees, flowers, and greenways a magnificent drive along the coast. Travelers arriving in Nice were rewarded with palatial hotels and beautiful gardens everywhere. Like Cannes, spectacular views of the sea were also this city's flair, and while the view from my rail car window was upon the blue Mediterranean, my stop in Nice was inside a station where commuters poured into the city at regular intervals.

Along the way the train wound its way through town after town, once separate and distant, now merged into rather continuous human coastline habitat fed by rail and roadway. Just out of Cannes the rails passed through Juan-les-Pins where, on March the 1st, 1815, Napoleon stepped from exile on the Isle of Elba back onto French continental soil. The next day he began his march on Paris to renew his monarchy, doing so just prior to rising sentiment among the citizens of Nice for his demise. With their strong sense of identity and independence, they referred to Napoleon as the "Corsican Ogre" and held little regard for his schemes of European conquest.

That same sense of identity cultivated and perpetuated local traditions espressed in feast days and festive holidays of celebration enjoyed with enthusiasm, such as the winter Carnival with its parade and Battle of Flowers. The list of outdoor events spans year 'round; the arrival of Spring feast called Cougourdons, the children's festivals, then the summertime International Folk Festival of music and dance, food and wine when the citizenry dresses in traditional costumes and celebrate in their native language, Nissart, a dialect completely structured with a vocabulary, grammar and syntax independent of French. Fall of the year celebrations include the grape harvest and uncorking a new vintage wine. All of its festivals have earned Nice world renown that continues to draw visitors year after year.

Like Cannes, Nice has a long tradition of resident artists, writers and performers who find stirring inspiration in the area's beauty. For me, just passing through wasn't at all satisfying but all the time I had. When I stepped down from the train, snapping a photo of a station sign inscribed with NICE over the heads of the crowd, my entry into this new place was among a train load of people who helped mold the differences in the city's quest to remain unique.

Also like Cannes, the favored colors of Nice were red and white. Among stylishly dressed young women in tailored sweaters, light jackets and skirts, reminders of American girls back home, were those in more traditional wear I thought rather drab, mostly darker colors. Nice lacked the luxury and glamour of Cannes, probably because it was much bigger and absorbed tourist wealth in less conspicuous ways. As I walked from the station, Nice seemed to be a working city displaying more of actual French Mediterranean life than Cannes with its ostentatious glamour. Hundreds of hotels catered to tourists on lower budgets, and the city's location an hour or so from snowy Alpine peaks just to the north and east in the French and Italian Alps, along with its expansive beaches caressed by the blue Mediterranean, made Nice an ideal Riviera destination, especially for a low budget sailor.

My liberty was mostly walking and sightseeing and, to avoid having to buy meals, I left the ship well stuffed with breakfast and chose pastries and bottled drinks during the day. Knowing that an equally stuffable supper awaited me once back onboard that night, my plan to conserve my cash allowed sampling the enormous variety of highly artistic pastries I discovered in the windows of every bake shop I passed. I was completely awed by the handiwork of these artisans of icing: tray after tray of intricately decorated cupcakes, palm size blocks of cake iced with detailed scenes in great variety, fruit-filled delights, chocolate and creme filled fingerlings, croissants clothed in the most imaginative of decorations... the most mouth-watering banquet of pastries this farm boy had ever seen. They were everywhere along the streets of Nice, and they were cheap. A franc could buy two or three, more than could be eaten without discomfort, and half a franc, about 10 cents, got a most delicious loaf of freshly baked bread for lunch. Nibbling it with a bottle of 7-Up, a brand that seemed to be everywhere as well, made a satisfying between-pastry lunch for no more than one franc. I quickly learned how to sample the Nice life on pennies.

Further similarities between Cannes and Nice were the plush casinos where gamblers tossed away their money. Just the buildings and grounds around them told me that lots of dough had to flow through their doors for upkeep alone. Each casino seemed to say to me, "If you have to ask the price, you can't afford it." I couldn't afford it, so I ventured inside one only to get a glimpse of the gambler playboy life. A sailor in uniform offered the doorman little prospects of a high roller, or even a tip, and his expressionless welcome as I walked up the wide steps on red carpet into the casino was his skillful noting that I was just looking. Plush carpets and elegance greeted me and spoke James Bond, the sort of location for movie scenes of intrigue that put Mr. Bond at the top of spy genre films. Within a few minutes, I was back on the street.

Wandering Nice was not as easy as Cannes because Nice was much larger with long streets of commercial buildings that seemed to hide whatever quaint behind-the-scenes French Mediterranean life the city contained. Perhaps more time to explore its "old town" would have yielded such discoveries, but my impression was that, as a smooth running commercial city catering to tourism, it was the bed and meals hub for mountain and beach activities. Or, perhaps it was those magnificent pastries that kept me downtown and out of the back street barrios.

Monaco was nearby and spoke of wealth that had conquered towering terrain, judging by the villas and châteaux and their gardens rising along tiered levels hewn from Alpine slopes that rose abruptly from the bay. This backdrop of the principality, rugged mountains yielding only the narrowest of beachfronts now jammed with docks and high dollar boats, told that Monaco was Cannes compacted on less inviting and more abrupt, more rugged terrain. Yet Monaco was heralded the world over as an unparalleled destination.

My main interest in this fabulous port was to see the home of the Monte Carlo Rally and the Monaco Grand Prix. Although no vestiges of either auto race was visible, I did see the bay around which the Grand Prix ran, the path I walked. The course was composed of main traffic arteries steadily flowing with all sorts of cars from the majestic to the practical when the race was not staged. Although without the lazy air of Cannes, Monaco displayed similar, if not greater and more sophisticated elegance for the jet set wanting to winter over in warmth with little regard for cost. What citizens and tourists got included spectacular panoramas of the Mediterranean day after day, and just one look around Monaco made it clear that enough money could make living the French Riviera life very entertaining.

A short tour from the rail station to walk the route of the race was all the time I had, along with a cold bottle of 7-Up at an outdoor café where I sat imagining Stirling Moss, Juan Fangio, Roy Salvadori and other great Grand Prix drivers of the time roaring by. Back onboard the train and return to Cannes about sunset completed my Côte d'Azur walkabout.

Chapter 30

Salerno and Naples

I grabbed a copy of the *Forerunner Liberty Call Supplement* for Naples as soon as they were available. With the Forrestal anchored three miles out in the bay about midway between the islands of Ischia and Capri, we had a panoramic view from north to south that included the cone of Vesuvius dominating the horizon. Naples and surroundings spread as far as I could see along the coastline but didn't venture far up the slopes of the volcano. I was already steeped in Pompeii lore and, with an itch to see such a famous excavation, I signed up for the ship's tour that was arranged through one of the local agencies, an excellent choice for my interests.

The Salerno to Pompeii tour was one of many liberty day-trips offered the crew, and, unbeknownst to me, I was the most senior enlisted man to sign on. That resulted in a call to me offering Shore Patrol status for the tour and the complete tour at no cost. I took it. That turned out to be a good deal, largely because of the Shore Patrol shoulder band issued to me and worn prominently. That arm band got me into places normally off limits and, since no occasion arose in which I had to use my new authority, I actually was just another tourist out to see everything I could and got more to boot.

In addition to liberty, another reason for making port in Naples was to off-load one of the two RA-5C reconnaissance planes onboard. A few weeks earlier it had made a hard landing and broke its back. I happened to be on the flight deck watching flight ops at the time and, since I had built a plastic model of that type jet, better known as the "Vigilante," I was interested in seeing one in operation. Because I knew about the plane as both a model builder and an H-bomb mechanic on weapons it was designed to carry, I was particularly interested in learning why the plane, among the most sophisticated aircraft in the Navy, had the reputation for being temperamental. News of another one lost somewhere over Viet Nam had become a rather common occurrence, two, three, maybe four a year. I noticed two of the planes onboard when we left the States, and I wondered what such a large plane, designed as a strategic bomber turned reconnaissance, was doing on an aircraft carrier.

My plastic model illustrations showed the central weapons tube between the engines. When assembling the model, I learned how tube launch of a nuclear weapon worked, and as I stood on the flight deck watching the real plane in action, my connection was also real; my GMT training had taught the loading and launching characteristics of two B-28 or two B-43 H-bombs the plane was designed to carry. They were the plane's purpose: a fast Mach 2+ jet bomber capable of sustained flight ten miles high with a range of over two thousand miles, the platform for launching two bombs exceeding a megaton each from miles away. Flight and drop capabilities were designed to obliterate complete cities. The bombs were loaded from the rear, nose forward, in line and launched the same way by an explosive charge that expelled them tail first when the plane was in level flight or climbing. We had studied the flight patterns and launch modes from earlier versions of the RA-5C as high flying, long distance strategic nuclear attack bombers, but the need for such a strategic platform had shifted during the early and mid-1960s to Fleet Ballistic Missile submarines, and all Vigilantes were retrofitted for reconnaissance. Although the central tube was still available for our bombs, in their absence additional fuel tanks were slid into the tube to extend flight range.

Most of the planes onboard the Forrestal were A-4E Skyhawks and larger F-4B Phantoms that also had nuclear weapons capabilities dropped from conventional underwing positions, but both were dwarfed by the RA-5C. Other planes included "Willie Fudd" prop planes that ferried mail, personnel and whatever else to and from the ship that could, I presumed, also operate as anti-submarine aircraft, and presumably, with nuclear depth charge capabilities, our B-57s. The similar E-2 Hawkeye with its flat, large diameter dome on its back told its purpose to be high altitude radar surveillance, the fleet's eyes in the sky. These planes in the air around the clock spoke clearly that we were in the midst of the Cold War with the need to keep an eye on the Soviets. Just where the RA-5C fit in that scheme was not so clear, but fit it did in our show of force in the Med, a show of force consisting of much more than just an aircraft carrier. Carrier Division Four was an entire task force, and all of us GMTs knew that calling upon our services meant dire consequences unlike anything ever seen before.

As I watched that RA-5C approach the aft of the flight deck, it seemed too big to be landing on a carrier, and I thought its nose up attitude was too high. The arresting cables were designed to stop jets in a few hundred feet, even planes of its size, and each time I saw a Vigilante land, the heavy plane seemed to strain the arresting system to its limit. On this landing, when the tail hook grabbed a cable, the nose wheel slammed onto the deck and the back of the fuselage just in front of the swept wings developed a noticeable wrinkle that was not supposed to be there. The stronger than steel titanium fuselage structure had fractured from the sudden and severe shock, and word quickly got around that the plane was no longer airworthy. It sat in a corner of the hanger bay until we arrived in Naples where attempts were made to off-load the plane onto a barge using the ship's crane. I watched that exercise as well and thought success would be some trick because of the choppy seas.

The Forrestal was as steady as a rock, but the barge brought alongside lurched up and down with the waves and rocked back and forth. Each time the plane was lowered near the barge, one end of the barge after the other rose and fell, promising to damage both the nose and the tail of the plane, if not buck the jet off into the water. After several attempts, the decision was made to call off the operation, and the broken Vigilante was brought back onboard to return with us to the States.

Naples was as big a city as I had ever seen, over a million people as told in my *Forerunner*, and from the flight deck the expansive view beckoned adventures galore. The legendary Campania region, with Naples its largest city and one of the largest in Italy, was ancient even in Roman times, and sleeping Vesuvius rose to such an elevation that it stood out on the horizon seen from every direction. I wanted to see all of Naples and go to Pompeii and to Rome, too, and to Vinci and Florence in Tuscany, but our three-day liberty did not permit more than a day or two in the city and another day of touring.

Early the first morning, our tour group gathered by a sea door and each of us was checked off by name. Onboard our liberty launch, we rocked along on waves that had not calmed from the day before. Our launch rode the waves to dock at fleet landing, a broad concrete and stone staircase in a pier network that rose out of the sea. We climbed it to our waiting bus for a ride down the coast while the tour spokesman described in his broken English the sites we passed: Sorrento, Positano, Amalfi on the coast, then a turn inland to arrive in Salerno, our first stop. I had read about Salerno as the site of a ferocious World War-II battle, but nothing I saw even hinted of anything but a slow-paced Italian country town basking in the Mediterranean sun, a place to stretch, relax and enjoy the spectacular weather. After several months in the Med by then, I had grown quite fond of the region's climate, superb in every way, and Salerno was no different.

Off-loading the bus first, I took up my position as Shore Patrol, posting by the doors and counting to insure that everyone got off, then followed my compatriots into a shop specializing in art crafts and fine carvings including cameos. An enormous assortment of carved stone and sea shells was displayed on walls, on glass shelves, and inside glass display cases along each wall. I was fascinated with the carvers, especially the hands of an old man who had carved for so long that the palm of his right hand had massive raised calluses matching the bulbous wooden handles of his tools. His workbench was along a stretch of windows that gave light to benches of all the carvers, and as I watched he broke off a piece of conch shell and stuck it onto a wad of sticky goo on the end of a rod about twice as long as my index finger. He positioned the rod in a small vice and began carving the top layers away. I watched him shape the entire cameo, doing so more quickly than I thought possible. He positioned the tip of each sharp tool on the shell and worked it around using trigger movements of his last three fingers against the bulbous handles of his tools, shaping the pattern he saw in his mind. He rotated the work piece, tilted his chisel this way and that, chipping away bits of shell to produce a nice cameo about the size of my little finger nail. He finished the carving surprisingly fast, polished it and set it aside to make another one.

I was astonished. Clearly, this man was a master carver whose craft dated from two thousand years of similar works that were refined to perfection first by the Romans, perhaps his forebears, whose techniques had been passed down for many generations ever since. I inquired if the piece was for sale, at which he smiled broadly as if I must be a dummy to ask such a question. All around the place were museum quality carvings, and everything was for sale. He pointed to a display case of mounts, and I looked at what I thought was certain to be far more than I could afford: gold and silver in the finest craftsmanship in a huge variety of shapes and patterns. A woman who must have been a beauty when younger was very helpful in selecting a gold-silver filigree bow with a center for such a cameo. The ease with which she worked told me that she had done this before and, when the cameo was set into the bow and the capturing wireform enclosed it, she smiled saying in rather good English, "Very beautiful. She will like it."

"How much?" I asked, expecting the price to be far more than I had. Seven thousand, five hundred lire. I had to think a minute. A mere twelve dollars! Mary would like that, and I would enjoy telling of its making. Without hesitation I bought it to take home with me, another of my Italian treasures. When I took time to think that the huge prices in lire didn't amount to much in terms of dollars I wished I had more to spend, but the day in Pompeii was still ahead, and I wanted to save my cash for mementos of that excursion.

The next day, after Pompeii and Mt. Vesuvius, Jajinski and I headed for the beach and Naples itself. We wandered through the city looking at all sorts of sites and, when he recommended going to a restaurant that he had visited on a previous cruise, I was game. He flagged a taxi, one of the diminutive Fiat Topolinos that darted incessantly through the city, and we piled in for the ride of our lives. The small car provided precious little room, but we slid hip-to-hip from door-to-door as the driver took off in Indy 500 fashion, then rocketed through traffic in the most exhilarating, if not the scariest ride that I can remember. Alternating each hand on the wheel, jerkingly steering right, then left, then right, then left at the last possible instant to dart by another car, his free hand always a fist shaken brazenly at every driver he passed accompanied by verbiage that only Italian taxi drivers understand, all of them zigging and zagging in and out of lanes, darting around each other and every other car as if the sea of cars on Naples' streets was nothing more to him than an obstacle course run so often that it was no longer a challenge to get anywhere in the least possible time.

When we arrived at the restaurant, a last-second dart from traffic into a tiny opening at curbside, screeching to a halt, aligned us perfectly with the curb. I got out bleary-eyed. A thousand lire, about a dollar-sixty, had taken us through Naples on a trek that would make a Grand Prix ace proud. Paid with a single note of the appropriate denomination, he slammed his Fiat into gear, cigarette still dangling from his lips, screeched out into traffic and was gone in an eye-blink.

Jajinski and I looked at each other and breathed deeply; a carnival ride could not have been more entertaining or as thrilling. Now with reason to watch the taxies more closely, I realized that our ride was just the norm.

Our restaurant was upscale for two sailors in uniform, white table cloth and maitre d' in tuxedo, but we were treated with the highest regard and were served a spectacular meal of tasty breads, fresh salad greens and pasta. Although it should be a favored experience, after that taxi ride everything that followed was anti-climactic.

Afterward, we walked the afternoon away and enjoyed the arrival of dusk that brought an interesting change to the city. At night, a completely different character emerged. The change of chaotic traffic under the Mediterranean sun became a show of red and white lights playing to the interplay of near constant horn blasts of differing tones. The show in the streets was like an arcade running wild, but no one paid any attention. Beyond the cars, the pace of life slowed with fewer people on the sidewalks and more gathered in various small parks along the way. We made our way through the city back to fleet landing where our liberty launch sat almost empty. The time was not late enough for the mass exodus of drunken sailors who would predictably arrive just before midnight, so our ride back to the ship was in an almost empty launch.

Once back onboard, we walked the quiet hanger deck under its garish overhead lights back to our berthing compartment and turned in. I stretched out in my rack, listening to the rush of fresh air exiting the pipe near my left ear, and drifted off to sleep thinking about that wild taxi ride, knowing that our fist shaking, bellowing driver was an undiscovered Grand Prix ace.

Chapter 31

The Ball Game

While steaming day after day with little to do but babysit H-bombs, each of us GMTs went quietly about filling our time with whatever was the interest of the moment interlaced with incessant training. Not only were we required to attend training sessions, we were also assigned topics for presentation. From October 1969 through June 1970, at least sixty training sessions were conducted on a broad variety of topics including ordinance safety, weapons training and tritium safety, and, of course, V.D. I suppose the latter influenced my own prespective that avoidance was the best policy, and among sessions that I taught, character education, first aid, leadership and Uniform Code of Military Justice Article 86, I must have practiced what I preached.

Each day, day after day, was filled with whatever requirements came our way, after which we pursued our own interests. Cramped quarters did not permit much in the way of hobbies, so most of our after hours time involved being close at hand with shipmates. Prior to lights out at 10 PM, the office area cleared out as men headed out to berthing compartments and turned in. By the time of setting the First Watch, from 8 PM until midnight, then the Mid-watch through to 4 AM, spaces emptied and quiet hours permitted concentrating on individual projects.

Our magazines were not off limits if two or more of us chose to go their direction for such things as workouts and bigger projects, or just to read. Since their doors and hatches were always open, except when at General Quarters, we could expand our personal space and often did so.

I happened to be rummaging through one of our shop storage bins one day when I came upon a heavy bronze specification plate for some piece of equipment. It was about six inches square with cast-in specs on one side, the other smooth. I wondered what equipment it should be attached to and went through both of our magazines looking for its proper place, finding nothing. Resolving that this piece was surplus, I began shaping it with hand tools, cutting and filing until I had fashioned the smooth side into a crest, a shield like knights of olde. The upper right corner was indented imitating the resting place for lances that knights used in jousting, and uniformly around the edge of the shield I carved grooves to make a decorative border.

Pleased with my craftsmanship when finished, I had a piece of the ship suitable for a cruise plaque. Setting off to find an engraver, I learned that such work was available onboard the ship but that work time had to be charged to W-Division. Even though machinists and their machines might be idle, none were permitted to do work for others without appropriate charge numbers. That concept was new to me, and I thought it strange that manpower and equipment could not be utilized during down time for whatever seemed appropriate, such as a commemorative plaque, and sat idle until another job with a charge number came along. I got the go-ahead and a charge number but was told to have all the names of SASS-Forward and SASS-Aft crewmen inscribed. With everything I needed, I set off to locate a nice walnut piece to mount my shield on, then gave everything and my list of names and cruise data to the machine shop. The next day, a machinist called to say that he could not inscribe all the information and names on the shield, it just wasn't large enough, so I envisioned making another one for SASS-Aft and told him to inscribe only the SASS-Forward list. That was a mistake.

Orders are orders to be followed, and I had not done so by making what I thought was a reasonable and justifiable decision on my own. Although the finished cruise plaque was a work of beauty that each of my SASS-Forward shipmates admired and congratulated me for producing, my senior who had authorized the work was highly perturbed that I had not followed his order. Even expressing my intention of making another plaque for SASS-Aft did not sooth his anger, and I was sternly ordered not to pursue such endeavors.

I mounted my plaque prominently displayed onto the bulkhead to the right of the SASS-Forward office entrance, the first such plaque to commemorate a cruise, listing crewmen by name. Afterward, I spent the remainder of my time reading rather than crafting.

I've often wondered what became of that plaque. When I left the ship following our return to the States, it remained in place, and I hoped that it would begin a trend of such things for each subsequent cruise. Years later, I learned that the ship was in port in Florida, and Mary and I drove to the Base only to be denied touring privileges. Unable to return to the ship since then, I can only recall those days of crafting memories in the quiet company of H-bombs and wonder if my plaque is still where I installed it.

The high traction decking our bombs sat on was raised from the ship's steel deck making an unused space about eight inches high between them. I used that space for my stash that was discovered in an ironic twist that I just could not believe. During the previous several years, I had acquired quite a collection of small bottles of booze, examples of various spirits similar to those served on airlines but difficult to find elsewhere back then. Why I was fascinated with these little bottles I don't know, but from port to port in the Mediterranean, I had acquired a couple of dozen more, each one an interesting bottle with labels denoting the country of origin and a product I had never seen in the States. I made careful selections thinking that they would make nice additions to my collection back home and interesting topics to talk about when recalling my Med cruise. I brought each bottle of highly contraband and forbidden spirits onboard and rolled each of them carefully with protective wrapping into a bundle. Looking for a hiding place where no one would find them, I selected a location at the edge of the raised decking adjacent to a hefty hull strut that rose up the steel plate making the starboard hull of our upper magazine. Sliding my package almost arm's length under the decking, I was certain that it was well hidden.... It was, until the ball game.

Being American boys well steeped in baseball, we were gathered one day in that very magazine when someone rolled a wad of masking tape into a ball and began batting it around hand to hand. Soon, all of us were playing hand ball with it, batting it here and there among the stacks of H-bombs when someone suggested that we choose up sides and have a real ball game. Heartily agreeing, we laid off the diamond in the open space between the two rows of H-bombs and made home plate with a piece of tape on the decking just in front of the hull strut. First base was the sharp nose of the upper B-61 in a selected stack. Second base was another piece of tape applied to the decking straight from home plate, and third base was the nose cone protector of the upper B-57 in a selected stack. The outfield was among the stacks of H-bombs, and our impromptu game got underway when teams were made. The pitcher performed outlandish windups prior to tossing the tape wad to which each of us in turn batted with our hands. The "ball" went flying with "hit" after "hit" requiring acrobatic fielding by dodging around and among the bombs. Several remarkable catches heightened competition and the game took on vestiges of a real challenge... until the "ball" did the most improbable thing I could imagine. It rattled down the narrow opening at the edge of the raised decking into the space underneath. When the catcher searched for it by hand, he discovered my stash.

"There's something under here," he said with surprise, and every gamesmen quieted in anticipation of the discovery. Out came my bundle, and I debated briefly about acknowledging ownership. If I didn't, it would simply be noted as left by a yard worker who forgot to recover his goods. But if I didn't acknowledge, I would lose the entire addition to my collection. If I did acknowledge, I ran the risk of severe repercussions. Hoping to recover at least some of my bottles, I strode over to the catcher and told the whole story, then realized that expecting each of my fellow crewmen to remain silent and assisting in my surreptitious activities with such contraband was too much to expect, especially when the novelty of each bottle and its strange contents raised questions like, "Wonder what it tastes like."

At that point the ball game was over, and the gathered teams turned to tasting the hootch. With one or more little bottle per player, the field of H-bombs became our lounges with sailors sitting on their carriages and talking about which bottle they liked best. In my case, being a non-drinker, I did not participate while collecting all the evidence for clandestine disposal, recognizing that I had lost my entire stash, but I also recognized that everyone's involvement insured silence.

We spent the low-key afternoon enjoying each other's company, exchanging stories about who we were and where we came from, and any other topic of interest. Since I was married and had a child, a question to me about women led to more about matrimony and fatherhood that evolved into a lengthy discussion about the whys and wherefores of female relationships. Only a few of my shipmates had met Mary, but she was known among them from the photos I had and was admired as a beauty.

She had also been the bride of the moment of another seaman, that occasion developing while on liberty in Barcelona. Among our first liberties, a fellow GMT and I were walking the Catalan city with him leading, pointing out the sights from having made the port on a previous cruise the year before. Everything was new and inviting to me, and his showing me around made for interesting introductions. One was in a spacious and up-scale bar where he met once again a fetching lady of the evening. Dressed in our blues, we were just a couple more sailors to walk into the bar, but his "lady" was still there a year later and recognized him. Knowing that the bar was the front for a brothel, I was intrigued to be in such a place and was impressed with this quite pretty and shapely "lady" and her profession. She was as close to an all-American girl as I was to see during the entire cruise, dressed in a nicely fitting sweater and skirt of high style, nice shoes, her stylish brown hair flowing freely to her shoulders, and with a welcoming smile as if seeing a dear friend after a long absence. I knew that each of us were just another "jack the sailor" to her, and my imagination percolated to find out more about her life. That opportunity arose when my friend had to make a pit stop, and she took up conversation with me.

I came right to the point, "You are a very attractive, woman," I said. "Why are you a prostitute?" She took no offense at my question and seemed to welcome the opportunity to talk to someone more interested in who she was rather than her body. She was just as quick to come to the point and told the tale that I recognized to be the source of the world's oldest profession, no means of making a living other than selling herself. I knew that was not the case because women had always found other ways to get through life, but I was surprised to learn that she was married with two small children. Her husband condoning her activities was an even greater surprise, justified by saying that she made far more money than he did and that she lived a comfortable life with fine clothes, noting with pride that she liked to dress like American girls because her mostly sailor patrons paid more for her services.

We sat at the bar talking until my companion returned, and that's when she began putting the mash on him. I was intrigued with her well honed techniques, but he was leery, having had to combat a bout of the clap after their previous escapades. She turned up the heat by stroking his hair, neck and back and rubbing her body gently against his while reciting her choice invitations. Being an old friend, she would be especially good to him and at reduced cost, but he remained standoffish.

     She must have thought that a drink would help soften her client, and while she stepped away further down the bar, I whispered to him that I had Mary's photo with Squire in my wallet and he could use it to excuse himself from her clutches. He agreed, and I slipped my wallet into his peacoat pocket. When she returned, he told of being married now and a father. Taking my wallet from his coat, he opened the tri-fold to reveal the first photo, a smiling Mary and infant Squire as his own. She complimented him saying "his" girl was beautiful and that she admired his devotion to her and "his" family, wishing happiness for him. He smiled and she backed off, and we left the bar to explore more of Barcelona.

Chapter 32

Pompeii

A most violent volcanic eruption nearly two thousand years ago preserved the culture that, although doomed, still endures. Spirits live in the ruins of Pompeii. They are the phantoms of our imaginations, so close to the touch, yet so far away in time.

In our mind's eye, we ponder the last moments of a doomed city, its people and all its life, while we feel akin to the rich beauty that remains. There should be Pompeiians here, merchants, citizens, and children, but there are none. Everywhere we see remnants of their lives, their marks of existence as clear as yesterday, but their last day was far in the past

Via di Fortuna is a quiet street now, but it is easy to imagine the clamor of ancient activity on it: carts of goods clattering along lava cobblestone; people going their way on raised walkways; everyone busy with the affairs of the day as had been carried on for centuries. Graffiti of another age remain plainly visible on the walls by the walks, and stone steps in front of doorways beckon for us to become Pompeiian, to transcend the barriers of time and feel as Pompeiians felt, to experience their lives within their homes.

Beyond the doors where they lived and into public streets that were once hectic with traffic, everything is still now: no clamor, no noise, the people are gone, the homes are empty. Yet, with the embrace of a gentle breeze, we turn, half expecting to greet one of them.

Multi-roomed and often storied, Pompeii's upper-class homes were built around a central, open atrium where family life centered. Flowers, statuary, fountains and pools were typical of finer homes whose atria provided fresh air, light and escape from cramped city life. Here, Pompeiians played, dined, and slept. Flowers bloom once again in their central gardens and long-dry fountains pour fresh water again. Their homes display the decorations they looked at so long ago, but they probably never thought that strangers from the future would one day stare at them with fascination and wonder about their meaning.

The marketplace, the focal point of commerce, is still a short walk up from the Porta Marina and its docks. Goods brought in by land and sea from all over the known world were traded in Pompeii, and images of local merchants and foreign traders haggling over prices produced a grin as I imagined them getting on with their business, imagery that I recall to this day.

Slaves laden with heavy burdens carry goods from the docks through the Porta Marina and up the wall-lined Strada di Marina to the marketplace. Along the Marina, I imagined galleys that sailed great distances to this city, for their captains knew that Pompeii was a rich and exciting port. Now far inland with no vestiges of waterways lapping at its stone docks, the marina of a seaport here does not seem possible.

The ancient Greeks were adventurers who founded trading colonies throughout the Mediterranean region. They also were admired for the quality and independence of life that their democratic form of government produced. Able seafarers as well, they plied their trade that flourished some five centuries B.C. among prosperous city-states and foreign ports-of-call. Pompeii, first Oscan, then Etruscan, was noted for its fine weather and rich soil that produced three crops a year and was the source of the Old World's famous Vesuvian wine. Life was good in Pompeii, but it came to a violent and sudden end.

Outside the walls of the city of some 20,000 inhabitants lay nearby Herculaneum, about one-fifth the size of Pompeii, and smaller Stabia on the opposite side, both destined to be Pompeii's companions in death. Together, the trio lay hidden and preserved in a haunting burial having to wait centuries for discovery. Doubts arose saying that, to have disappeared so completely, these towns must not have ever existed and were simply inventions of imagination. But records clearly stated that they had existed, but where? Meanwhile, new towns were built on top. The modern city of Resina stands on part of Herculaneum just a short distance south of Naples along the coast prior to arriving at Pompeii. Connecting them were well-built Roman roadways traveled by innumerable locals, roadways that remain buried to this day as modern life flourishes overhead.

Legend has it that Hercules founded Herculaneum, but even the strongest man in the world could not have prevented Mt. Vesuvius from covering it with 50 to 70 feet of volcanic rock, ash and debris from the bowels of the earth. Because of its volcanic cocoon, Herculaneum's buildings and wooden home furnishings, stairways, doors, cupboards, beds and tables and much more were well-preserved. Many works of art in bronze and marble, many sculptures and even a library of writings on Egyptian papyrus have been recovered. Herculaneum has come to be recognized as the most completely preserved glimpse of ancient life known, the old world's greatest gift to the new.

The tragedy of the three towns left us tables set for meals, shops displaying their wares, bakeries and wineries offering refreshments to passersby, all blanketed and sealed for centuries on end. Rediscovered streets are testament to children who played in them and wives who shopped alongside them for meals and kept homes while husbands carried on business that depended on them. The clatter of carts going to and fro, the buzz of life, of ships and trade, of Roman soldiers and citizens, playwrights and performers, athletes and musicians, rich man and commoner... all were hushed when Vesuvius roared. In less than three days, Pompeii and surroundings went from life to lost.

Throughout vast reaches of time, Mt. Vesuvius enriched the soil around its base, then provided a natural fortress location for early man's settling on fertile slopes and surrounding planes. Pompeii grew from those beginnings with the volcanic cone so dominating the view north that every Pompeiian and every visitor knew the mountain. Even in its sleep, steam vents within its gigantic crater say that the volcano is only sleeping. That vast cavity tells of the enormous amounts of volcanic rock, ash, and dust that were spewed out in tremendous explosions covering everything that lay close around. Under the debris, the hands of time were frozen as Pompeii and its neighbors lay buried in poisonous, sulfur-laden debris. All features of the area were obliterated, harbors were filled in and the land raised causing the sea to recede some two miles. Mt. Vesuvius had given prosperity to Pompeiians for centuries, gifts of bountiful lives that were suddenly eclipsed by the fury of raining doom.

The eruption spared almost no one in Pompeii. Earlier earthquakes had signaled the coming calamity, but the citizens just rebuilt their city. Then, during the afternoon of August 24, 79 A.D. the end came, and those who fled were eyewitness to the catastrophe. Those who stayed, perhaps most of the population, were encased in their doom.

Asphyxiated by the poisonous gases from the eruption, their bodies remained where they fell and were covered by tons of fine volcanic pumice. In time, all that remained were bones in a cavity exactly fitting the victim's final position. When first discovered, excavators wondered what the holes were and why they had bones in them. Then it was discovered that filling the hole with plaster resulted in a graphic form of a Pompeiian's last moment.

Trapped in an immense tomb of volcanic ashes, the lost city of Pompeii left a wealth of historical detail hidden well below the farm animals that later grazed on lush grasses above. People debated; Pompeii had been a well-known seaport, but there were no remains of such a large city on the coast. What had happened to it?

Those who wondered about Pompeii and looked along the sea for remains found nothing to argue that the city had existed, but could it have simply vanished without a trace? An entire city and its neighbors, too? Unrecognized was the change of terrain that had risen, pushing the coast further away. Pompeii lay buried well inland, not on the coast. In time, the lost city became the region's most celebrated mystery.

Some 250 years ago, a farmer digging a well unearthed unusual artifacts. Excitement about a great archeological discovery spread throughout the world. Pompeii had been found. Excavations began immediately with one exciting discovery after another.

Removal of immense quantities of ash slowly revealed structures and streets that prompted further inquiry into what was once a great and proud city. I came to see for myself and left with a more complete feeling for the grandeur that once was Pompeii and the works that made it grand.

Standing in the marketplace, the quiet was awe-inspiring. Under the prominence of Vesuvius, I knew that in this very place on that tragic day, different only in time, people from throughout the Mediterranean were carrying on their day's work, talking, arguing politics, perhaps discussing a recent performance in one of the city's theaters. I touched the stone columns their masons once admired as jobs well-done. Little did they suspect that a time-traveler would one day stand in the same spot and wonder about their work, the products of their lives become artifacts of antiquity. I quietly walked among the remains of buildings, homes, shops and temples as an intruder, and all conversation was in whisper. Why? Was it because I felt their presence?

The well-preserved craftsmanship, the artistry and creativity so abundantly displayed in dramatically colorful murals and mosaics in their homes, all spoke of a people full of vitality. They were cultured individuals who gathered the best of the known world about them. A large amphitheater that scholars consider the first of its kind was the arena for popular sporting events. Large theaters were the centers of cultural life, just as the marketplace was the center of daily life. Greek dramas and comedies of the time remain legendary, known to the modern world as some of the finest performances of all time. They were performed here. Prior to destruction, historians recorded Pompeii's existence and changes as it went from ancient Italian to Etruscan to Greek to Roman. Pliny the Younger saw the catastrophe and recorded the end of Pompeii, including the end of Pliny the Elder.

The magnificence of Pompeii is in many ways overwhelming. The extent of the ruins is far more than one person can grasp without considerable study, yet it speaks to everyone at every turn and evokes wonder, especially since so much of the site remained to be excavated. So overwhelming were the sights that I had difficulty organizing my thoughts in order not to miss important features, yet my short visit could only gather a smattering of what was there.

Pompeii and Herculaneum remain compelling because nowhere else in the world can so much of the details of the ancient world be seen, preserved in such intimate detail. Two thousand years ago is incomprehensible for most people and becomes noticeable only when we find ourselves yearning to pull a Pompeiian aside to talk about his city, to question him about the whys and wherefores of Greco-Roman life, wishing that we could get better acquainted.

There are wall paintings of Pompeiians, both men and women, who peer out at us from long ago and give us stunning color portraits of what they looked like, how they dressed, glimpses of their refined way of living, their learning and their art. Frescoes on walls and ceilings are as vibrant as if painted recently. Murals depict daily life, religious rites, favorite scenes, animals, sports and political events common in Pompeii to remain today's snapshots of what once was. They are displays of artistic beauty that tell us of ancient life as it was lived, what was felt and thought while the phantoms of our imaginations put together actions of Pompeiian life and catastrophic doom.

Pompeii is strangely quiet now, but I expected to encounter a child at play around the next corner, a shopkeeper busy at work in his street-side business, an ox-drawn cart loaded with farm produce going noisily by, the ruts still visible in the stones that the city's streets were paved with. My imagination would not let me really believe that an ancient city once so full of life could now be so completely empty. Amid these ancient ruins, whispers from the past reached me from the shadows. A movement caught by the corner of an eye caused an expectant turn to greet one. Was it the wind or a fleeting glimpse of a ghost from times long past?

In my mind, Pompeii was alive. I stopped to observe the busy ancients at work in shops now barren and empty; a stage comedy causing roars of laughter among the audience, the theater now silent and empty. Athletic games in the arena, or exhortations of a politician, or simply citizens going their way, they are not so different than me, yet nothing more than the spirits of my imagination. I saw life everywhere, but only a wisp in the wind and a rustle of dry grass remain. As I turned toward another of Pompeii's wonders, I felt a gentle breeze and smiled, a gift to my hosts of the past.

They are the ghosts of Pompeii plying silently, unseen, unrecognized, the phantoms of my mind brought alive before me in these ancient ruins. I had studied Pompeii back in high school, just dreams, yet here I was fulfilling the images seen in history book photos and making my own. Here I was communing with Pompeiians in their own city. I came from the far distant future to wonder, to walk in the past, to feel the spirits of long-forgotten ways, to be part of the world that speaks through tragedy, yet has given us the greatest of treasures, its very existence. There is no other place like Pompeii.

After standing transfixed at the museum displays showing the plaster casts of the death positions of Pompeiians, my imagination running rampant at the horrors they must have experienced, word spread to board the bus for the last leg of our tour, Mt. Vesuvius. Once there, we were again offered innumerable mementos to buy ranging from very expensive art to mass produced trinkets. Our tour included a gondola ride to the crest of the volcano, and some of us rode the lift high above the surroundings to exit at the rim. Our guide told us many facts about the crater and its steaming vents below us, but nothing of its size. I attempted to estimate width by timing echos and depth by throwing small chunks of lava rock and timing their descent; much wider and deeper than the crater appeared.

We were free to roam about a bit and as I studied the craggy, stratified wall on the east side across from me, I imagined the build-up of those layers over time that finally culminated in this enormous, hollow cone. As I walked up and down the crater and around a portion of its rim, the smell of sulfur permeated the air. From the volcanic gravel of black, grey and brown with shades of deep red, I chose a golf ball sized sample lying on the rim as my memento. When squatting to pick it up, I noticed the strangest thing: among the debris, rocks, boulders and steam that supported not a single blade of grass, a flower grew. Its green shaft and leaves rose from the dry volcanic soil about ten inches and ended in multiple pink blossoms in full bloom. The plant stretched toward the sun in this inhospitable place, life, arising from ground the closest to hell as is known on earth.

Chapter 33

Corfu

Corfu, Kerkyra in Greek, is an island of adventures, legends and surprises. Called the "Green Island" for its millions of olive trees, it was known in ancient times as Pheakon. It is the northernmost island in the Ionian Group of islands sprinkled along the western coast of Greece. Corfu lies at the entrance of the Adriatic Sea just off the coast of Albania. Thoroughly Greek historically and culturally, this small, leg shaped spit of craggy mountain ridge jutting up from the Mediterranean Sea is shaped rather like a reversed Italian boot in miniature. Although the second largest of the Ionians, Corfu is surrounded by just 135 miles of coastline. Small sandy beaches, mostly snug and golden, are among the best in the Greek world.

Mild winters with ample rainfall have given rocky Corfu lush vegetation, especially in the Ropa Valley. The island's chief products are olive oil, figs, a wide variety of wines and vegetables, and a unique type of kumquat fruit. Tourism has long been its main industry.

Other than the major Greek cities, Corfu is the most densely populated area within the Greek dominion, estimated at over 100,000 people. Why do so many people live on this island? Come and see it, and you will learn why. Warm, sunny summers; cool, mild winters; magnificent vistas everywhere; invitingly gentle Mediterranean surf in every direction; a slow-paced life with cosmopolitan flair; an ancient heritage with legacies grown of welcoming smiles, good cheer and great stories; and did I mention the magnificent land and seascapes? Corfu is a land of beauty and fun.

I learned these things about Corfu, and mythology tells that the island got its name from the daughter of the river god Asopos, the Nymph Korkyra, who was of such beauty that she was carried away by Poseidon. About 800 B.C. the Greek poet, Homer, wrote in his *Odyssey* that Odysseus found shelter here at the end of his wanderings where he received the care of King Alkinoos and his people, and the king's daughter Nafsika.

The western coast village of Paleokastritsa is bathed in the warm Mediterranean sun as one of the most beautiful of locations on the island. Its six small coves with clarity to the bottom rise up a jagged coastline along volcanic hills covered with olive, cypress and lemon trees. This is said to be the site of the fabulous palace of King Alkinoos, and the rock out in the sea, known as Kolovri, is said to have anchored the ship that carried Odysseus home.

Whether in search of myth or adventure, I found the natural beauty of Corfu to be inspiring, and its claim as "the island of song and music" to be one of lasting memories. It is known for being the island of cantatas, for stories sung but not acted that have become traditional Ionian Island love songs. Romance is easy on this island. My own adventures on Corfu began in Corfu City and became an unforgettable adventure.

Corfu City was Venetian until 1780 and lies on an eastern shore natural harbor with fortifications of the time built up from the seabed with stone that lies in abundance throughout the island. The expanse from the old fortress to the town is described as "the most beautiful esplanade in the world." Within this park-like arena lie walkways among stately trees, expansive flower beds, fountains and sculpture that speak of the deep legacies that have long resided here. Along this esplanade promenaders, paraders, marching bands, and festive regaliateers have celebrated untold occasions spanning hundreds of years. On the south end stands the Ionian Monument commemorating the island's reunion with Greece in 1864. The Liston Arcades border western reaches of the esplanade where many cafés and bars are just the beginning of the Campiello, the Old Town, that reaches inward in a fascinating maze of narrow streets and alleys, steep stairways and arches. Flowers and decorations were everywhere.

I was introduced to Ouzo here, that strange Greek drink of intense intoxication. Not only is its fragrance that of pine, this clear extract with anise flavor exhibits the same behavior as pine cleaners that turn milky when mixed with water. Ouzo is the national liquor of Greece and is a deeply felt libation so thoroughly entwined with the political history of the people that no other spirit can claim to rival it. I found it undrinkable.

Inland from Corfu City, modernity along the coast faded from village to village into old world ways marked by horse drawn wagons loaded modestly with goods bound for market. Housewives' search for firewood resulted in pack burros loaded with bundles of twigs and sticks. We met such a scruffy burro plodding blissfully along typically narrow roads with only the occasional passing car interfering with the slow pace of everything. There was no need to hurry anywhere on Corfu, and nobody did. The small size of the island means that anywhere is not far away, and light conveyance is all that's needed. A bicycle does well, and feet may be all that are required to arrive at innumerable resting places of blissful beauty. The small roil of the rich blue Mediterranean washing upon another small beach made day after day as peaceful as could be imagined.

While steaming during the spring, the call had been posted for ship's company who had interest in learning to scuba dive. A GMT among us was a highly skilled diver, and he coordinated us volunteers with the command to have additional auxiliary divers in the case of need. A contingent of US Air Force special forces stationed at Athens became our instructors for a week of intense training, and those passing the crash course received official certification along with a white stripe on red diver's patch displaying "Poseidon's People Athens, Greece," one of my favorite mementos from the cruise. The training was, however, very rigorous and exhausting because of the physical requirements that we had to demonstrate. After completing the equipment and techniques segment taught from manuals in a classroom, we went to a craggy spot on the Greek coast and jumped into the water.

With clarity to the bottom about a hundred feet deep, we could see all sorts of things including a small wreck that we were to dive on. Overlooking this rocky coast sat a pair of heavy walled pillboxes from World War-II, long since abandoned defenses that would have made improbable landings on the jagged shoreline even more difficult. As a final demonstration of our swimming endurance, each of us had to swim across the cove and back, a distance estimated to be a mile or more. Following my tendency to hold back and observe before jumping into something, I watched the first gung-ho volunteers leap into the surf and flail across the water until exhausting themselves, only to have the return ahead of them and no rest stops along the way. On my turn, I ran as hard as I could to the edge, took in a deep breath of air, flattened myself into extended arms and legs and did a belly flop to glide as far as I could on the surface. Conserving my energy as best I could with swim strokes I had learned before the Navy, completing the required distance, neveretheless, drained me to the bone. I was barely able to climb out of the water on hands and knees, and collapsed on the rock. A few minutes later I awoke with painful knees. Closer examination revealed why; I had climbed out over spiney sea urchins that had made pin cushions of both knees. Extracting them took some medical attention, but I had completed the course. My Poseidon's People patch was particularly rewarding.

Having completed our scuba training and wanting to use new skills, my diver friends and I requisitioned dive gear and pooled our resources to contract a taxi to take us to a recommended location on the western side of the island. We piled our equipment and ourselves into the dusty old car, and the driver set a leisurely pace suitable for sightseeing. Passing abundant greenery in the form of low olive trees in consort with the tall spires of evergreens, with modest to impressive villas here and there on elevations along the way, I recognized that the real Corfu remained mostly inland with infrequent resorts sprinkled along the shoreline as destinations for tourists. People of the interior looked to be of native persuasions while beaches were populated with vacationers who swelled the Island's population along its perimeter.

We arrived mid-morning at a stunningly beautiful cove that was a perfect setting for a spy thriller. The day was magnificent with a few fluffy white clouds lazily moving across the purest of blue skies and a warming sun that made the water even more inviting. Beyond the narrow entrance to our small cove, worn through soaring cliffs of black, volcanic stone on each side, the horizon met the deep blue Mediterranean beyond. I imagined that this gateway must have drawn untold generations of sailors out onto the sea. With only a small motel of perhaps a dozen modest rooms, commercialism had not found this cove. The motel held the choice ground with a view of the entire beach and across the cove through the cliffs to the sea beyond. Tiny waves gently lapped the golden arc of beach that curved into a semi-circle of soft strand ending with wooden piers at each extreme, each pier tucked into the base of the north or south cliff on either side of the gateway. Heaps of fishing nets and lobster cages spoke of the nature of the piers, along with a few small boats pulled up on the sand beside them. Inland from each pier stood a few modest, close-packed homes of faded white, each cluster a fishing village nestled into the lee side of abrupt crags that protected them from storms arriving from the west.

Those volcanic cliffs edging the open sea beyond provided the "pillars" on each side of our cove's entrance. High on the northern cliffs sat a villa of palatial proportions. Expansive rather than tall, I imagined it to be the get-away for a wealthy Greek family who came to this high ground for its spectacular views.

With our dive gear indicating our intentions, the proprietor of the motel trotted out to us to make a request. In his very broken English and our non-existent Greek, he offered a suitable number of drachmas for each lobster we brought him. We concluded that he had menu items in mind for his guests, and if we should happen upon such creatures, he would buy them from us. We nodded agreement, never suspecting that a different creature of the deep would become the focus of our attention.

We saw no other touristy types, and not even a skiff plied the waters. Nothing told of any takers for his rooms, but his interest in lobsters indicated tourists that we had not seen. The villages were quiet with only the occasional fisherman out on the low piers. The cove was ours, and when suited up and checked out, we were soon in the water.

As a novice diver with little time in the water, but one Poseidon's People, my partner and I spent the first hours in exploration that went progressively into deeper dives further out into and beyond the entrance to the cove. Once in the water, I noticed immediately that color faded away in the first foot or two of depth. All the yellow, orange and red bands that lay just under the surface quickly faded to monotone dark green. Water of light blue clarity permitted seeing the bottom of the cove with its lazily waving seaweed along with a few bottles and some debris lying on the sandy bottom that was slowly sculpted in the currents that flowed around rock tips. The center of the cove was a depression, and at its bottom lay a round black object that I assumed was a lost stone anchor.

Spear fishing was a technique that I was unable to master, even when targeting rather large fish. Why I was unable to make that arrow arrive at the point I thought I was aiming for still eludes me, and a slow moving, three-feet long fish did not appear to be a difficult target. Afterward, it was mentioned that had I speared such a large fish, I would likely have been pulled along on a frightening ride to who knows where, deeper for sure. The spear gun at the very least would have been lost.

Our in-water time was scheduled for periodic reunions to re-group and rest, and I had ample opportunity for reassuring myself that I was not the only ineffectual hunter. Some specimens I chose to avoid. Once while outside the cove I came up under a flotilla of Portugese Man-O-War. Carefully keeping my distance from their long tentacles dangling for food, the same that impart ferocious stings, I examined them in detail up to their surface bodies that looked like hat-sized blobs of translucent gelatin with a sail on top. I marveled at their long, deli-cate tentacles deep in the water just floating along, then turned to see a large, toothy black fish eyeing me. Lunch?

The thought of being a soon forgotten meal was a disturbing revelation when I recognized that I had no help at hand. Visions of being dragged into depths that I could not escape remain haunting. Dive masters say, "Never get out of sight of your partner" for good rea-son. As instructed in such encounters, I spread my arms and legs sufficiently that my size became daunting, and the thing ambled off.

After another rest, the caves along the entrance to the cove rose to be next on our list. Once again, gear on and checked out, we headed back into the water. My hazard warning system had been primed such that I declined to go very far into the caves' blackness, even with a flashlight and buddies nearby.

A day's worth of scuba exploring was near to exhausting, and our last outing was timed so that we could make it back to Corfu City about dusk. We were coming back in when the leader motioned down-ward toward the round black thing lying on the bottom. I arrived at it just behind him. When his hand reached out and touched it, I saw a motion that pegged my fright meter. We were upon a giant octopus.

A racing pulse and quickly withdrawn hand were accompa-nied by the imagined sudden onslaught of groping tentacles akin to Jules Verne's *20,000 Leagues Under the Sea*. A moment's hesitation lapsed into reconsideration, though, and we decided to capture the creature. The leader motioned me to the opposite side, and the two of us grasped the exterior surface, sticky, like cold tar, and we headed for the surface with all the speed that our fins could produce.

And there, on the beach of our magnificent cove, we dragged our broken amphora containing the slippery creature onto the sand, fighting us every step of the way. Our monster octopus, all of 24 inches from tentacle tip to tip, proved to be another adventure of unexpected drama.

Each of us held the octopus, feeling its suckers working along our hands and arms as it grappled us with its soft white undersides of slippery black legs. The creature's eight legs continually displayed cho-reographed attempts to get back into the water. On the sand, it "ran" in a leg-rolling fashion by extending its tentacles forward and rolling to their tips. Continuously repeating the cycle with pairs of tentacles flail-ing along, it moved surprisingly fast. Each time we laid our arm near the sand, the octopus leaped away and took off toward the water. We foiled each attempted escape, caught it, rinsed off the gritty sand in the water that also kept it moistened, and continued to get acquainted with the strange creature on our terms.

Our commotion attracted attention, and two tall, slender, blond women of mid-age walked over from the motel to see what we had captured. Their language indicated Swedish, and I assumed them to be tourists on Corfu as a reprieve from a frigid northern winter. Looking back, I suspect that subsequent events became the highlight of their vacation, a memorable story that I have since imagined to be wry tellings back home, sitting in a warm Scandinavian home with big-eyed children transfixed on the storyteller, snow piled deep outside, a howling wind whistling against every attempt to keep warm.

Like us, they gained the experience of feeling the octopus suckle along their arms and hands, though squeamish at first, but soon to become as fascinated as we were. The octopus moved rapidly, around the arm, up the arm, leaping off the arm to race toward the beach in repeated attempts to get back in the water.

Then, our group grew when a fisherman ran up to us. Ran! I was certain that he was a Greek fisherman. To this day the image I see when imagining a Greek fisherman is this lean and tanned, barefoot and beaming, unshaven man who approached us with uncommon excitement, a manner that took us by surprise. His dark blue fisherman's cap, set to his left and back on his head, looked like an afterthought on tufted, curly black hair that squiggled upward from around its worn band. Bare chested, with only a red and white bandana tied around his neck, he instantly became my model of the bronzed, hairy-chested Greek fisherman glistening in the Mediterranean sun. Loose fitting pants ragged below the knees, light blue in color with dark blue up-and-down stripes, were held low at his waist by a length of cord tied in a knot, its ends dangling unraveled in front. His bare feet sandy up to his ankles made him a perfect union of sea and seaman. He gestured excitedly with both hands as he talked, seemingly making an urgent request. Dark eyes wide and inquiring, with a big smile, he posed no sense of threat or fright. Speaking rapidly in a language none of us understood left us wondering what he wanted, so we stood there looking at each other wondering what he was talking about.

Our expressions must have indicated acceptance to him because he grabbed our octopus and ran over to the water, rinsed off the creature, punched his thumb through its sack, squeezed off the entrails and rinsed it again in the surf. He stretched a tentacle to its tip and bit it off at the sack just as another fisherman, almost a duplicate of the first but a little taller, ran up to him from the north end of the cove.

We had no intentions of harming our octopus and had been merely educating ourselves with our catch, but when the first fisherman turned toward us with a huge grin, a black tentacle held firmly in his teeth, its lashing about whipping around in the last throes of life, the spectacle was too much for one of our Swedish guests who peeled off in a faint and plummeted to the beach. Her friend gave immediate assistance while the rest of us, young, strong sailors mind you, grabbed our instantly queasy stomachs.

Our beautiful cove on such a magnificent day turned into an impromptu spectacle of watching two handsome Greek fisherman consume our fascinating octopus with the gusto of hound dogs. Between them they washed off pieces of the still alive animal and stuffed them into their mouths in such a way that the animal must have continued its squigglings down their throats and into their stomachs. None among my party moved a muscle as we stood transfixed, watching, over-whelmed with disbelief.

The two of them finished off what we learned first hand to be a much-prized delicacy, live, baby octopus. After their meal, turning to see our expressions must have presented a comical picture for both of them chuckled: US Navy divers dressed for the serious business of deep sea training, standing among tanks, masks, snorkels, and fins utterly dumbfounded.

The second fisherman walked back up the beach while the first fisherman came toward us, nodding, no doubt thanking us. With his broad smile, then touching his cap in such a gesture, he turned away and trotted off. Within a few steps down the beach he burst into a hearty laugh for what must have been his coup d'état over the bewil-dered tourists given an uncommon welcome to his island, a welcome that left a beautiful blonde out cold on the warm sand of the beach he knew well.

I imagine an old fisherman on the island of Corfu telling his grandchildren this story, laughing, slapping his leg, and describing how he left us with our mouths hung open and speechless.

MALTA
COAT-OF-ARMS

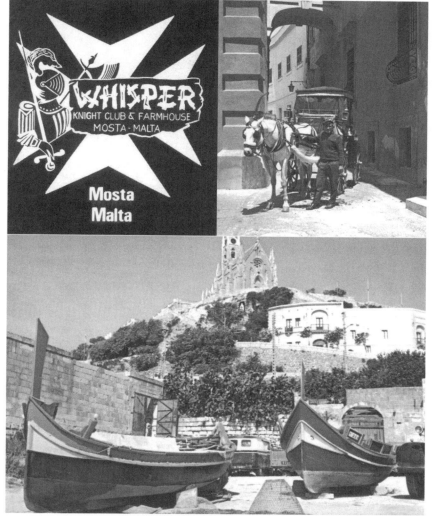

Chapter 34

Malta

Early one morning well before reveille, we were roused from slumber with BONG, BONG, BONG "General Quarters. General Quarters. All hands man your battle stations. General Quarters. General Quarters. All hands proceed up and forward on the starboard side, down and aft on the port side. General Quarters. General Quarters. All hands man your battle stations. General Quarters. General Quarters." If sailors could fly, we did in a flurry of jumping out of our racks and into our uniforms while on the run, then diving into our assigned battle station spaces. The prevailing sense was, "This is for real."

The afternoon before, we had anchored in a bay off the northwestern coast of Crete with expectations of liberty the next morning. As I walked the flight deck prior to sunset, I really looked forward to seeing the Palace of Minos and the labyrinth of the legendary half-man, half-bull minotaur. I took a few photos of the coastline and the flotilla of "gunboats" that circled our position. They were small, four-man fiberglass motorboats about twenty feet long, akin to our smallest Coast Guard close-in patrol boats. Dwarfed by the Forrestal, I suspected that they were our greeting party representing the Greek portion of the island.

I watched nightfall over Crete and wondered about the people of some four thousand years earlier who built the most advanced civilization the Mediterranean had yet seen, with only tiny fragments of their impressive achievements remaining. Then, around the time that mankind was learning to record existence with writing, the tiny island of Thira to the north of Crete blew up. It was just the top of a massive volcano that belched enormous quantities of destruction from the bowels of the earth. Quakes violently shook everything, and vast volumes of sulfur-laden dust and debris spewed out to rain down on the eastern half of the Mediterranean, including that portion of Crete. Left behind was acidic soil that ended the prosperous agriculture that the Minoans had developed over most of the island. The northern coast was crushed under enormous tsunamis that washed the coastline into heaped debris from giant waves that rocked back and forth within the basin of the Sea and its surrounding shoreline. Minoans were culturally advanced as illustrated in artifics of architecture and art discovered only within the last century, a people living in as ideal a location as the Mediterranean offered. Their flourish onto the stage of history ended with an eruption that destroyed much of their world on all fronts: land, sea and air. Theirs was a culture that had not needed fortifications because their mastery of the sea proved sufficient to control the region both commercially and militarily.

Centuries afterward, faint recollections of the Minoans and their destruction were told in the legends of Atlantis that were set in writing by Plato, well after the time of Homer who wrote of sea adventures among the first Greeks. Homer's works are considered the oldest of Greek writings, the product of a later culture who knew of Crete's destruction only in folklore, in tales passed down orally from generation to generation, stories told of the far distant past to illustrate the Greek notion of hubris: be humble or be struck down. What little has remained of the island's Minoans are the fragments of their civilization that was ancient to those Greeks, wonders that I hoped to see; but General Quarters early the next morning ended that prospect.

I walked the flight deck imagining what Crete was like those millennia past and wondered about the events that so drastically changed everything, setting the entire Mediterranean region on a different cultural track. Unlike Pompeii, just one city and surroundings snuffed out by a volcano, Minoan culture spanned the entire eastern portion of the Mediterranean. Then, a gigantic eruption far larger than Vesuvius so thoroughly destroyed their means of existence and protection on this long, finger-like island, followed by Mycenean invaders who completed their destruction, that the Minoans were almost entirely forgotten, surviving only in the legends of Atlantis, faint recollections of the wonders of the town of Santorini on Thira and the palaces and towns of Crete.

As daylight broke over the Med the next morning, the ship sat at anchor with the boilers up so that getting underway could be achieved quicker than having to bring power systems up from cold. I had seen this condition from shore on every liberty; the Forrestal sitting motionless at anchor but with a filament of smoke rising from the stack. When I watched the USS America depart for the States on the morning of my first Mediterranean sunrise, I saw the same image of an aircraft carrier at rest, then belching a plume of smoke as its signal for getting underway. On this morning, our ship turned up the wick fast and quickly put to sea. With General Quarters, we were soon locked down in Circle-W conditions and waited for word, each of us wondering what had caused us to go to battle stations.

No official explanation was given, but scuttlebutt said that a watchman manning the Big Eyes had seen a periscope eyeing us. I wondered about that, knowing that one nuclear torpedo amidship would have killed us all in an instant and ripped the ship in half, sending chard wreckage to the bottom in a mighty upheaval that would have left the giant ship a torched hulk surrounded by the blue waters of the Mediterranean, waters that had seen far greater destruction during the long lineage of man's quest for mastery of the sea.

Further wondering about how a foreign submarine could have

gotten so close to the ship, having had to sneak through the flotilla of outlying ships with their constant radar and sonar net surrounding us, I reasoned that no such thing had happened. I suspected that another cat-and-mouse exercise had been conducted by one of our own subs as training for getting into reconnaissance range of ships in harbors, torpedo firing range included. What seemed like a suicide mission by a foreign sub was, most likely, a test of our own Navy's submarine stealth capabilities. The Mediterranean's notoriously rocky shoreline and floor made any close approach undersea precarious at best, and doing so was a stealthy maneuver that I was sure the Navy and its sub commanders continuously perfected.

After securing from General Quarters, I went topside to see nothing of Crete. We were well out to sea and on our way to Malta again. After several days at sea, another stop at this strategically located, stony outcropping of nearly inhospitable Mediterranean rock controlled by the British would have to do. Liberty on far larger Crete would not be on this cruise, but we made port at Malta three times.

My first liberty in the old city of Valletta on the northern coast of Malta was another foot trek to interesting places. The ship's *Forerunner* told of sights to see, and like all tourists, the obvious sites included cathedrals and stately structures. On our first liberty, Jajinski and I strolled through some of the commercial sectors, sampled the cuisine here and there, and took in as much as footspeed permitted. Interspersed with miles of walking was sampling Malta's rather homespun pastries that turned out to be quite good.

Unlike the classy French pastries I had admired for their artistic flair, Maltese pastries were larger but far simpler in appearance and just as tasty. Typical was a sweet biscuit filled with a mixture of chopped nuts, honey and spices with dribbled sugar icing on top, a delicious local specialty for about ten cents. I had been introduced to baklava in Greece, an immediate favorite that I savor to this day, and although Maltese treats were similar, they were rather homey-looking sorts of flakey baked goods with various frostings and filled with savory fruit preserves or nuts and spices or puddings or dripping with honey.

Malta was the crossroads of the Mediterranean, and its breadth of cuisines was the product of peoples from diverse cultures who stayed, producing the most eclectic fare of all the ports we made. Because everything was both inexpensive and flavorful, I did my usual, sampling selected varieties of pastries during noon to early afternoon walkabouts, favoring apple turnovers, although I wasn't sure what the fruit was in most cases. When considering meals, though, I was less inclined to partake because of so many unknowns and potential complications.

That challenge arose when a group of us strolling rubberneckers in dress blues was approached by a street salesman who invited us to his "restaurant" with promise of wonderful steak dinners at cheap prices. "What restaurant?" was our immediate response because no such establishment was in sight, not even a sidewalk café. We were walking along a narrow street lined with shops and bars, but he assured us that his "restaurant" was the best on the island. None of us knew any better, and "cheap" was a good inducement. Although hesitant of venturing off into hidden recesses, I resolved that we were in sufficient numbers to defend ourselves and went along, too.

We followed our salesman beyond a door leading off the street up a narrow stairway. Dimly lit surroundings of chipped and scarred stucco walls were less than pristine, and I was immediately suspicious that we had gotten ourselves into something best avoided. Upon arriving at the second level, however, we were on an expansive flat with windows overlooking both the street we had walked and gardens behind that we didn't know existed. Brightly lit by daylight and spacious due to minimal furnishings, I surmised that the location was both a dance floor and a restaurant. Our salesman immediately turned to waiting on us and, with helpers in the adjacent kitchen, we were soon served sumptuous meals of fried steak, roasted potatoes, baskets of sliced dry bread with its thick, crunchy crust, all served to our satisfaction along with fresh vegetables cut into finger portions. My drink of choice was, once again, a cold bottle of 7-Up.

The friendly atmosphere and service-to-please at modest prices told me that this "find" was an undiscovered secret of Malta, a family restaurant that allowed us an insider's view of how the locals lived and how they did business. Street recruiting was the norm for the enterprising who did not have a street level store front. Such recruiting was employed for other endeavors as I learned during further walking tours of Valletta.

One sunny day while on foot, I happened upon Valleta's red light district as evidenced by the "ladies" standing in doorways offering themselves to every likely passerby. I was immediately intrigued by the culture that permitted and promoted prostitution as indicated by the "dog tag" each of the "ladies" had pinned just below their left shoulders. Each "lady" was assigned the number stamped on the brass "dog tag" that was used to both continuously track her medical condition and to display to potential customers that she was medically certified as free of disease. In addition to their physical appearances, displaying their stamps of approval was marketable, although I thought these "ladies" to be less than desirable on appearance alone, until I came to a rather striking young prostitute. Her tight fitting sweater conformed to her body in a most revealing manner, and her short skirt was just the right length for displaying her smooth, shapely legs. I concluded that this "lady" was new to the profession because she was noticeably younger than the others and, like them, she had her own methods to draw in customers. She ran up to me, grabbed my hat and stuffed it up under her sweater, then returned to her seductive doorway pose indicating "come and get it." I wasn't inclined to participate, but I needed my hat or risk being picked up by Shore Patrol for being out of uniform. She toyed with my requests for its return by encouraging me to come nearer. After several unsuccessful attempts to retrieve my hat, her compatriots weighed in with encouragements of every sort, but I stood my ground without resorting to aggressive actions or ill temperament.

Finally recognizing that I was hands-off, she relented and tossed my hat back to me, but in one last attempt to seduce me, she raised her sweater to her chin to display beautifully proportioned breasts and her smooth torso. I smiled and thanked her for my hat, then strolled on, to which she exploded with anger that I should not leave without rewarding her for her show, which I didn't.

Britain's Maltese holdings were at least three islands, the biggest being Malta, and Valletta was both the capital and largest city on them. Although the islands had been inhabited for thousands of years, evidenced by artifacts discovered in a number of natural caves along stony seacliffs, European occupation arrived during the 1500s when the Knights of St. John chose to make the islands their new home, having been pushed off the much more beautiful island of Rhodes by the Turks. On my first venture into the city, I found a book store and bought an excellent volume that told Maltese history in great detail, and by the time we made our second stop I was better prepared and sought particular locations, such as the fortifications that the Knights built to defend the natural harbor that they chose along Malta's rocky, northern shoreline. The book proved to be an informative choice, although I wondered why it was not available in the USA as noted on the cover. I read that the Knight's harbor selection steadily grew to become an active port, a location that proved pivotal during the Second World War as an Allied naval post centrally located in the Mediterranean. I marveled at the massive fortifications the Knights built on each side of the harbor and wondered how they managed to quarry and hew the vast number of huge stones comprising their works, and how they assembled everything with no machinery other than simple pulley systems and muscle.

As I stood on the massive wall and walked its ramparts, I envisioned the assaults that I read about, a war about five hundred years earlier that was brought by a huge invading force of Turks led by Suleyman the Magnificent. Their goal was, like Rhodes, to push the Knights off these islands as well. The Turks were the hated Saracens, infidels according to the Knights, inheritors of actions by their ancestors who rapidly spread Islam around the Mediterranean basin some eight hundred years before the Knights arrived on Malta. When the Knights began their new colony, Moorish Spain was the Saracen's European stronghold. As a major political and military influence in the region from the early 700s, their continual conflicts shaped the course of history in the Mediterranean region, spreading deeply into North Africa and then Europe.

Between portings at Malta and while upon my perch on the spud sponson, I had read the history of Malta as another stage in the long conflict between the Knights of St. John and the advances of Islam. Suleyman's conquests prior to invading Malta foretold the coming battles, and as I stood on the ramparts of the fortresses from which each side exchanged the heads of captives cannonaded through the air to deliver whatever insult value such an exchange was thought to have, I was aware that invaders and defenders alike resorted to whatever acts that warfare brought. Suleyman laid seige and the Knights successfully defended, ultimately to wear down the invader's will to continue prosecuting the war.

Because Malta was not a favored location for liberty, my fellow crewmen had little interest in hitting the beach after the first day or so in port. By late in our cruise, they were also less inclined to swap late watches for liberty. So, on the second and third of our stops at the island, I was limited to scheduled times ashore and went about seeing as much as my feet could endure. Since my interests were largely in different directions than my fellow GMTs, I was mostly on my own with intentions of seeing as much of Valletta's history and culture as I could. Having made a previous cruise, Jajinski proved invaluable for pointing out interesting locations that I would never have discovered on my own.

We walked for miles back and forth through the city until coming to a park where we rested. Children's swings and slides and whirl-arounds and monkey bars had attracted a few children and their mothers, and among them was a quite attractive young lady. Jajinski struck up a conversation with her. She was surprisingly responsive with a warm and welcoming demeanor that inspired him to ask her for date for the next evening. She accepted, surprising both of us.

I thought such a rapid unfolding of events to be unusual at best, and so did Jajinski. When I bowed out as a third wheel on his date, he insisted that I come along and so did the girl, another surprise. Mentioning that I was married and a father and not wanting a date, she suggested that the three of us take in a great place to go for food and entertainment. Well, OK, I resolved, thinking that I would be a third wheel who could take to foot when the need arose. There was, however, something unusual about this girl that both Jajinski and I just could not grasp; an American in her late teens or early twenties living on Malta and readily accepting dates with unknown sailors just did not compute.

The next day in port passed toward our late afternoon date with our mystery girl, and we walked from fleet landing to the park where our young lady was waiting as planned, a very attractive date that Jajinski found to his liking. As a resident of the island, she knew everything about it and told of this highlight and that location as someone well informed. We walked to the club that she suggested, an excellent choice as it turned out. Getting there, we walked along an ordinary Maltese street with stone buildings packed side-by-side, and got acquainted.

Our destination was the *Whisper,* as upscale as Malta had to offer, and both Jajinski and I wondered if our cash would be sufficient to cover this date. Upon entering the club, we were two sailors with a pretty girl arriving for dinner and ended up staying until the place closed. No other sailors told that this location had not been discovered by the Forrestal's crew, and we would not have known of it without our date.

In preparation and discussion for our outing, I offerted credit to Jajinski, if needed, and once perusing the menu, both of us recognized that items had to be selected carefully, although prices were more modest than the decor of the club suggested. Even a bottle of wine was within our means, and both of us deferred to our date for her selection. Perhaps it was the gentlemanly thing to do, but in my case, I didn't know one wine from another. She selected a bottle, and we made our dinner choices. In the getting-acquainted time before being served, we talked. Questions about who we were and where we came from and what we sailors did in the Navy were asked and answered with the Gunner's Mate cover story, then we inquired similarly of her. I was especially interested to learn what brought her, a pretty American girl, to Malta. She told of having lived on the island for some time, which seemed an odd choice to me, one that she did not seem to fully favor. Further chat about her life on Malta came to finally answering the question, why Malta?

She seemed reluctant to answer, then told us that she was the daughter of the American Ambassador to Malta. Talk about raised eyebrows, both Jajinski and I nearly choked, and both of us envisioned the repercussions for us if any bad tidings were relayed to Daddy. For the duration of the evening, we were on our very best behavior, although she assured us that she was pleased to be with us and welcomed the company of boys from back home saying that she was lonely for companions from her own country.

That was another revelation: I learned from her that living in Europe and touring it were quite different. In her case, while becoming culturally diverse and already the master of several languages, she missed her friends back home and the American way of life. Due to frequent travels to nearby countries and because of her high political standing, she was not stuck on the island, but Malta just was not fulfilling. She wanted to go home.

The evening progressed as a memorable outing that would not have been possible without Jajinski asking a total stranger for a date. The meal was excellent and affordable, the entertainment world class, and a superb group of musicians provided occasions for the two of them to dance. The headliner for the evening was a funny man who kept the audience rolling in laughter throughout his performance. Wearing sandals and dressed in a monk's hooded robe of brown cloth with cord ties around his waist, he was a famous European comedian who brought to Malta and the *Whisper* top drawer humor that was the best I had ever seen. His hilarious routines went on for a couple of hours, and I wondered why such a terrific act had not packed the joint. Noticing that everyone else was well dressed and civilian, I decided that the *Whisper* was not a club for locals and catered to the Island's elite. I wondered if it was connected with the various embassies and was, perhaps, a private club. All indications pointed to the *Whisper* being Malta's top club for dancing, food and entertainment.

That evening was among the best of my memories of the entire Med cruise, and after leaving the club and escorting our date home, the cool breeze and starlit sky could not have been more perfect, all because of a chance encounter with a pretty American girl whose name I did not get. Jajinski was so taken by her that he wondered how he might keep in touch, but being who she was and the two of us being just a couple of sailors on liberty, that prospect quickly faded as we made our way back to fleet landing.

Chapter 35

Trieste

When I looked at the map of the Adriatic Sea well north of Corfu, I thought the location of Trieste rather odd: an Italian port on a thin coastal strip of land almost completely surrounded by Yugoslavia. I wondered what events of history had kept such a far-flung Italian holding under the belly of the communist world. I was sure that, for the Slavic government, the USS Forrestal steaming along its coast was certainly not a welcome sight; but for Trieste, the influx of American dollars was a shot in its economic arm, probably why the city was selected as a port-of-call, and a statement of the free world's intent to operate within international waters and make port wherever welcome.

"The history of Trieste is long and complex, due to its location in a harbor area where Latin, Teutonic, and Slav influences converge. Trieste was an outpost of the Roman Empire, and subsequent conquerors and numerous changes of authority have given the city a cosmopolitan flavor that is unusual for such a small population."

That's what the ship's *Forerunner* said in addition to describing the city's location as further confined by a range of nearly bare, rocky hills that rise to heights of over 1,000 feet just to the east, Yugoslavia at their crest and the plateau beyond. A siege from that line of hills seemed an inviting and highly defensible position for an invading army, and I wondered why the city had not fallen to Slavic invaders long ago. Yet, Trieste remained in Italian hands, the crossroads of east and west, the result of convoluted politics that included being Austria's sole seaport during that country's imperial age. When declared a free port by Austrian emperor Charles VI in 1719, independence was just what the Triestines had always hoped for. Later, a post-World War-II peace settlement created the free territory of Trieste, but years passed and the "free" status had not materialize by the time the Forrestal dropped anchor during our 1970 Med cruise. The city had remained under post-war British-American jurisdiction while surroundings were under Yugoslavian military control well into the 1950s. With the "free territory" status still unresolved, the area remained an Italian holding as long as the peace settlement remained pending.

Rather like Monaco in location but much larger and a concentration of far less wealth, Trieste was new to me. As I read more and learned of its long history, I came to realize that this location was another of the ancient Mediterranean Sea colony sites at the mouth of a river bringing fresh water to the locals while also providing an outlet to the Sea. It was a port already with a lengthy history when captured by the Romans in 178 B.C. during the Empire's conquest of Istria. The Istrian locals pushed back, and Rome recognized that a fortified buffer zone along the empire's frontier was needed. A Republic named "Republica Tergestina" was formed, from which the name Trieste is derived, and the Triestines were compelled to serve the Empire's defense and expansion in the Apollinare Legion. This Legion distinguished itself early on, then was exterminated in battle against the Parthians during a Persian expedition.

So, from times before and after the Romans, Trieste was continually on the front lines of human conflict. Fifteen hundred years later during the Renaissance, its citizens were still pursuing their long quest for independence while striving to become a commercial rival of Venice, but they did not succeed. The city's holdings were no more than a thin strip of coastline to the north and down from the Yugoslavian hills, coastline that was successively cleared of swamps and backwaters and filled with earth to secure small measures of prosperity gained from both the sea and the soil during times of peace. My visit was during one of those times and into a city built upon limited land and spanning a long history of conflict, elements of Triestine character that I found intriguing but lacking in an outgoing, welcoming demeanor that I interpreted as a city and its people who maintained themselves just above the level of exhaustion.

Our ship anchored in the Bay of Mugia, and crewmen motored to fleet landing by liberty launch as usual. We stepped ashore into the heart of the old city, and simply by walking from one interest to another, Jajinski and I stumbled along seeing the sights as they presented themselves: sites one after another that had been preserved from times of olde amid a continually growing and modern commercial seaport.

A tour to Venice was offered during this port-of-call, but neither of us had the money, so Trieste was our liberty location, and once again, we hoofed our way up and down narrow streets that were Medieval in character and laced with fascinating histories that could only be imagined among interesting remains.

We climbed toward the most prominent feature of the city, the citadel of San Giusto (St. Just) and its fortress, and made our way over the remnants of defensive walls built during the time of Caesar Augustus around 33 B.C. On the slope of the fortress hill in a beautiful location overlooking the bay, Jakinski and I walked into the first century Roman theater, nicely restored and once again used for outdoor performances. It had been discovered under modern construction that was cleared to reveal a theater capable of seating about 20,000. My imagination played our walk into a fascinating twist in time as we strode among the roaring crowd laughing at a comedy performed some two thousand years ago. We were visitors from the far distant future wandering unseen among them, separated only in time. Silent now, this stone edifice knew them well, and as I wondered what stories this work of semi-circular seating carved into the hillside could tell of these people and their times, I once again recognized that the progression of time washes over all things to leave only the artifacts that succeeding generations consider important enough to save. My imagination wandered freely over the expanse of time to include the coming of the age of knights and walled cities that passed some centuries later with the emergence of gunpowder and bombardment from a distance.

During the fourth century, the magnificence of prosperous times quickly faded under Emperor Constantine, who deprived Trieste of her territories and sent the city into poverty. He split the Empire and moved its capitol from Rome to Bisantio, renamed Constantinople in his honor (modern Istanbul), initiating a rift between east and west that resulted in collapse of the western Roman Empire within two centuries. Trieste was in the eastern half and only barely survived repeated barbarian invasions. Completely destroyed, rebuilt, then repeatedly pillaged again and again, Trieste's sad story is one of a beautiful location continually being the envy of the next invader's eye.

Vestiges of the glory that was once Roman lay long past as Triestines continually struggled amid their rubble of war. Unlike Venice that grew and prospered to become the rich and powerful commercial seafaring hub of the Mediterranean, Trieste's meager wealth had to be continually expended in defense and reconstruction. The city's wealthy neighbor repeatedly came to its aid as evidenced by the Venetian castle of San Giusto perched on the citadel, but rather than independence, Trieste found itself increasingly bound to Venice. This uneasy alliance resulted in the construction of the Castle in 1508, the means by which Venice strengthened its hold on Trieste while also improving defense against invasion.

The fortress location on high ground held a commanding view of the entire city and bay, and, as we approached it, Jajinski and I came upon the reconstructed remains of a Roman basilica adjoining an expansive esplanade with a tall stone pillar prominently positioned so it could be seen from all around. On top was a bigger-than-life bronze of men in combat, commemorating Trieste's World War-I dead.

I stood looking at it, snapping a photo or two, and had the same thought when looking at similar works seen elsewhere. As in every country visited with their monuments to fallen sons, this monument spoke of immense loss and grieving resulting from another unnecessary war that grew from leaders committing their country's youthful manpower and resources to causes that, after the fact, proved tenuous, elusive and unjustifiable. I recognized that this monument repeated the sad tale told everywhere; war's huge cost in manpower and energy would have been better spent in construction rather than destruction.

In time the rubble of war is cleared, the destruction is rebuilt to await the next war, and monuments are unveiled to tell of the sorrow of war expressed in hindsight. Trieste's troubled past resulted from the long and deep-rooted Triestine desire for independence, to seek its own way in the world, while its geographic location made it an easy target for invaders who came from all directions.

Imagining the somber moment when this large bronze statue was dedicated, when memories among the gathered throng sadly recalled their own losses, I recognized that whatever their nationality or faith, fallen sons were commemorated everywhere in nothing more than monuments that a generation or two later had little, if any, recognized connection with. The passage of time reduced the dead to forgotten souls who lost their lives in battle, lives that would have been long and productive had they not been cut short by war, war begun by politicians at the expense of the young.

As I looked at the bronze, behind me stood the old fortress dedicated to that very cause, now obsolete because of man's development of gunpowder and the new dimenions to warfare it brought, seige at a distance. Out in the bay sat my ship from half a world away with enormous firepower that I knew well, firepower that caused the world to shudder in fright whenever the words "nuclear" and "war" are combined. The interplay of the ancient and modern on the ends of recorded time spanned innumerable wars on this ground, and I concluded that throughout time, mankind has learned nothing from history and repeatedly demonstrates lack of foresight from lack of hindsight. When history is studied the lesson is abundantly clear, mankind has continually waged war with ever-broadening destruction brought by increasingly destructive weapons. In the twentieth century, we arrived at a time when nuclear war became increasingly possible and makes no sense at all.

Touring the fortress was another study in how such a huge complex was constructed with the simple tools available at the time, an enormous work that spoke of man's will to build because of the lingering conviction that dedicating vast resources for defense is necessary. Jajinski and I walked its walls and toured the interior learning more about how soldiers fought man-to-man, hurling weapons of wood, stone, metal, and themselves against foes whose only goal was plunder and glorification of their own success over the defeated, knowing that a single air burst from my arsenal of H-bombs could destroy Trieste and any other city beyond anything ever imagined.

After a morning of hiking, we came upon a pizza shop and thought the establishment to be our chance to experience real Italian pizza. Since English was common though not the local's first language, we had no difficulty in making our selection. Then, served hot from the oven, our order came to us swimming in oil, the most uninviting pizza I have ever eaten. But eat it we did, and never before or since have I had indigestion like the bout that pizza gave me. Never again would I try "real Italian pizza," and I stuck to my usual of sampling pastries. But that day, even pastries did not sit well, and I was left with walking off the gassiest gut bomb of my life.

I remember Trieste well.

Chapter 36

Return to Norfolk

The Forrestal's command knew who we were as shown by our being detailed to the Master-At-Arms, the ship's police force, on our return to Norfolk. Our eight month long cruise of the Med was about over, and a sweep of all compartments was made to locate and retrieve any and all contraband. Every inch of the ship outside of personal lockers and off limits areas was searched during our week long crossing back to Norfolk. For me, seeing portions of the ship that I had not been in broadened my perspective of how a giant aircraft carrier was constructed and operated.

My group was assigned to the extreme forward portion of the ship, and I noted the narrowing of the ship's construction toward the bow, steel girders, ribs, and supports with welded on steel plating that made the hull. The bow was heavily constructed to handle all the loads inherent in repeatedly crashing into waves throughout the lifetime of the ship and to handle tons of steel in the anchors and their chains. In the forecastle (pronounced foke-sul) lay those massive chains that hauled up the anchors. I marveled at the anchor chains whose links had a cross-section of steel bigger than the diameter of my thigh and the enormous size of the capstans and winches used to haul everything aboard. The forecastle was normally off-limits to all personnel but was unguarded. This area of the ship was supposed to be rarely visited and only then for purposes of inspecting the equipment or repair work. It was, however, used by crewmen seeking privacy and seclusion as evidenced by the debris they left behind, debris that we bagged for removal during checking every nook and cranny for contraband.

Near the narrowest point of the ship, I came upon a plastic bag hidden in a recess. It contained about a pint of white powder. I didn't know what was in the bag and made no attempt to find out, but I suspected that the bag had been hidden for a reason, its contents likely to be the sort that was worth far more on American streets than the price paid in Europe. Turning it over to the Master-At-Arms, nothing more was said, and our search continued.

Our return crossing was made with a completely different demeanor among the crew; we were going home, and everyone was happier than usual. The thought had not occurred to me that some crewmen would "lift" whatever they thought would be a desirable memento of the cruise, such as pieces of aircraft or anything that would fit within a duffle bag when leaving the ship. I also had not thought that those who did not like their time in the Navy might do whatever they could to sabotage the ship or planes.

Unlike the sour grapes among us, I had made the most of my cruise and thoroughly enjoyed all the experiences it provided. I now had many tales to tell of wondrous places visited and sights seen. So, when I was detailed to watch a portion of the hangar deck, I took along coursework to study for advancing in grade. I was facing a decision in a few days. If I chose to re-enlist, I would be taking examinations for First Class within a couple of months, and further study would be helpful since I wanted to have my prospects of a career in the Navy in the most advanced position I could produce. Then, while sitting on an aircraft tractor in the hangar bay, the Chief came by saying that I had been reported for reading on watch. When he saw that I was actually studying for advancement in grade nothing came of the incident, other than being told that I should watch for clandestine activities around the planes.

Once my study books were back in my locker in SASS-Forward, I returned to the hangar deck and stood watch by strolling around. The planes were aligned with folded wingtip-to-wingtip along the perimeter of the hangar bay leaving the central portion of the deck open, and a roll-around basketball goal had been set up. Two teams had faced off, and I watched a bit of their game while marveling that nothing about their play indicated that we were at sea, no pitch, no roll, no movement at all. The deck was as stationary as any gymnasium floor.

Trying to do what I thought watch was for, I walked among the planes and equipment that had put in many months of duty on station in the Med and used the occasion to renew my acquaintance with the undersides of Skyhawks and Phantoms that made up the bulk of the Forrestal's assignment of jet fighters and fighter-bombers. I looked them over well, while keeping an eye out for clandestine activities, although observing nothing suspicious. When I came to mounting points for attaching bombs onto a Phantom, I immediately associated them with Chop Sticks operations. Down below in our magazines sat every one of our H-bombs, none having moved any further than to one of our shops for some attention, then back into place. Thousands of flight hours had been logged by these aircraft with no munitions expended other than during the search-and-destroy exercise told of earlier, bomb training conducted by smoke bombs dropped on a bouy towed behind the ship, and, perhaps, additional munitions training as well. But not one of the plane's bomb mounts had been fitted with one of our H-bombs. So far as most of the crew knew, no such weapons were onboard, although I suspected that rumor had told of them. Our entire cruise had been conducted with no interface whatever between us and either the ship's crew or air crews.

Later while off duty and strolling the hangar deck I was amazed to see entire tool chests along with electrical hand tools and equipment being shoved out to the edge of the elevators and tossed over the side. All that equipment had made the cruise and was, presumably, in good working order as used extensively when servicing the aircraft. Why was it being dumped, I wondered? When I happened upon a couple of seamen who had just pushed a large roll-around, multi-drawer chest filled with tools over the side, I inquired why. They explained that to do the jobs of aircraft maintenance, they continually needed good tools and equipment that required no maintenance or repair. Used hardware often failed and impacted the ability of the flight crews to keep planes in the air. Properly functioning tools reduced aircraft down time, and, when allotments for new hardware was not spent, subsequent budgets were reduced. New equipment was always purchased for the next cruise to keep good tools on hand and to maintain their budgets.

That made sense in a way, but I still could not justify disposing of so much equipment that could be sold as surplus once back in the States. I reasoned that all of this equipment strewn across the floor of the Atlantic served no purpose to anyone, but who was I to question such enduring Navy traditions.

Another tradition, return to port, grew into an effervescent atmosphere when we arrived back in Norfolk. Pier 12 was clogged with welcoming families, everyone waving and yelling happily back and forth. I walked the flight deck among my shipmates thinking that Mary might be there for me, but I knew she wasn't. In our letters we had agreed that I would make my way back home on my thumb. I had not mentioned to her that I was contemplating a career in the Navy and that with each exit interview the inducements to re-enlist had been sweetened. I was offered a Variable Re-enlistment Bonus (VRB) of $8,700 and NESEP. I would be going to the University of Colorado for three years of college on a 12-month rotation or four years with summer semester assignments somewhere, then Officer Candidate School afterward if I successfully completed the program. I planned to follow that with the Navy post-graduate school at Monterey, California when the first opportunity arose.

As inviting as the offers were, I had difficulty with the provision that each year of college required eighteen months of sea duty, even though some of that duty would be shore assignments at weapons facilities. By then, I knew that H-bomb depots on foreign soil were few, submarine bases mostly, and that surface ships contained their own arsenals of nuclear weapons onboard in special magazines that I knew well. I had further difficulty with the lack of written commitment to Nuclear Power School. Even if I met all qualifications by successfully completing college and OCS under the stated goal of becoming a surface fleet nuclear power officer, my detailer could not guarantee that I would be anything other than a weapons officer for the duration of my career. He explained that the Navy had far too much invested in me to have all that investment turn to power plants rather than H-bombs for which I had received extensive high level training with skills already demonstrated. That reasoning was the final stumbling block that swayed my decision to leave the Navy. Soon to be out of uniform, I turned to investing in me through college using the GI Bill benefits of a Viet Nam era veteran.

Mary and our Alpine Mk V, SN B395003153, sold on May 6, 1966 for $2,833.33. With trade-in, tax and financing; $72.79 for 36 months.

Chapter 37

Our Alpine

Winning the WTOB radio contest by discovering the villain's hideout in Winston-Salem was how Mary and I were able to put a down payment on a brilliant red Sunbeam Alpine Mk V roadster. The time was the Spring of 1966, and being newlyweds, we had made round after round of the sports car dealerships in town dreaming about which car to buy, though we could afford none. With our winnings, the dream became a reality at the Sunbeam dealership. The floor model Alpine was beautiful and beckoned to be soaring along the curvy rural roads we liked to drive. Drawn aside, I kept looking at the white Tiger sitting next to the Alpine, but with its plain wheels and "police" car hubcaps, it was not at all captivating, as long as I didn't think about roaring along those rural roads to the tune of V-8 power that gave the Tiger its growl. I was certain that the Tiger would really be FUN, but it wasn't nearly as appealing visually as the classic red Alpine with its wire wheels. Mary liked the Alpine, and it was nearer to what we could afford, not counting the $1250 special on a "bottom beetle" at the Volkswagen dealership. No fun!

The deal was made, and we immediately began enjoying our first new car. We drove it through city streets, along back roads all around, entered it into gymkhanas and had many pleasurable hours just driving, even when given a speeding ticket. On that occasion, I was well beyond being caught, but the free flowing exhaust pipe I had installed was loud enough to lead the "boys in blue" straight to the car while I was stopped at a traffic light far from the scene of out-running a 6-cylinder Mustang.

Cars and racing were enormously popular in the mid-1960s, and we were often at one of the nearby drag strips, five of them within easy driving distance for a day at the races, along with the Virginia International Raceway for sports car road racing. The color, noise and competition kept us in the fun of cars all the time. Mary became quite good at winning with the Alpine and soon became the "drag-on queen" of O/Stock class. Our Alpine posted a succession of 75 mph, 17-second runs in the quartermile. Since it was "her" car, we agreed that, if she won her class, then I could drive in the eliminations. That day came; she won a trophy as class champion, and I got to drive.

The day was a clear and sunny September Sunday. The week before, I had gotten my draft notice and resolved that I would be sent to Viet Nam and never return. Some of my friends had made a similar exit. Late one night while on the way back from being examined for the draft, Mary was driving when a large dog leaped in front of the car. The front bumper of the Alpine was seriously bent, and I took it off the next day, then reinstalled the bumperettes. When we arrived at the drag strip ready to race again, the tech inspector motioned for me to drive the car up on the scales. This was not the usual for a stock class car. He said the car was being put in Gas class.

"This is not a gasser!" I protested. "It's stock, except for removal of its front bumper!" Nothing would change his mind, and our less than 100 horsepower Alpine, with no more than its exhaust pipe uncoupled, was classified F/Gas. Our shiny red Sunbeam was pitted against fully prepared drag race cars, but Mary performed the miraculous: she won her class! I think it was her long blond hair that competitors noticed just before being flagged away. However she did it, she won, and I got to drive. The first round of Competition Eliminator disposed of half the cars, and I was still in it. I made another run and won again. Now I was just one race away from scoring a huge victory and taking home the Competition Eliminator trophy.

In those days, drag strips had a flagman, the "christmas tree" of yellow, green and red lights yet to come, and for this last race the flagman kept motioning me further and further out into the lengths painted on the edge of the strip to make up for differences in performance among cars in different classes. I counted twelve lengths... Gasp! My little F/Gas Alpine was up against an A/Gas car.

While I sat on the strip plotting my strategy to win, the announcer gave the last call for my opponent. I noticed that the crowd was cheering wildly, and I hoped that my adversary would not show up so that I would win by default. Then the earth shook. The din of the crowd was overwhelmed by big cubic inches brought to life to wage war. It was the B&M Drag Team '41 Anglia from Atlanta, Georgia, a beautiful car I had admired earlier. Its race prepared fuel injected 426 Hemi engine was a jewel; the car was magnificently prepared, a professional drag racing car. My Alpine now seemed less than diminutive, 99 horsepower against about 600.

I craned my neck to look back at the flagman and watched the Anglia roll into the staging lane. A helper sprinkled BX-10 rosin powder in front of its huge slicks. The driver then rapped the gas peddle; the Hemi belched smoke from its exhaust pipes flaring out from under the car just behind the front wheels, the blast echoing off the trees; the body flexed; the tires bit and boiled into clouds of smoke. Goliath was ready.

Meanwhile, I sat about one-fifth the way down the strip. My strategy was to shift at my 4-banger's torque peak, and starting with such a lead ahead of the Anglia, I planned to beat the car. A tense moment followed as Goliath eased up to the line. Then, with the motion of the flagman, we were ready. The needle of my tach rose steadily to 5500 rpm. He flagged us away, and my Alpine's little engine pulled hard to red line. I speed shifted to second and was winding up when the Anglia rocketed by me like I was going backwards. Undaunted, I ran the quartermile with every ounce of power the Alpine could muster. Goliath was out of sight.

Once through the traps, I slowed and circled onto the return lane. Goliath was parked on the side up ahead. I stopped and offered to help, but the driver declined. He said his crew and tow truck would be along shortly. Going on, as I approached the timing tower, I noticed the crowd cheering and clapping. I waved. Had Goliath been disqualified, I wondered? No, as it turned out. I was being cheered as the underdog. Goliath had won for sure. I stopped at the timer's window to get my timing slip; 55 mph.

"What did he do?" I asked the timer.

"155; set a new North Carolina A/Gas record against you."

I just smiled.

The story of our Sunbeam Alpine is told among the recollections in this book as an integral part of our young lives. From the mountains of North Carolina to Chicago to Albuquerque to Clarksville and on to Norfolk, our little red roadster rolled as our wheels of freedom. From frigid winter to southwest sun, our Mk V Alpine took us to all sorts of places, and we especially enjoyed New Mexico. The beautiful weather and low humidity made mid-day heat comfortable while cool mornings and evenings were daily delights. One evening we drove the car to a three-screen drive-in theater on base and watched a young actor by the name of Clint Eastwood play a nameless but likeable bounty hunter in *A Fist Full of Dollars*, a movie that was talked about for days afterward.

On another evening while inside the Kirtland Air Force Base movie theater with friends, I heard the unmistakable roll of thunder and darted outside to witness one of the torrential rain storms New Mexico is known for. Our Alpine sat at our apartment with its top down. "Ruined," I thought as I ran several blocks back to salvage as much as I could. Soaking wet, I stopped short of the car; I could not believe my bad luck. I had parked at the corner of our two-story apartment building near a downspout, and a broken joint above the car was clogged such that collected runoff from the roof was spraying from it directly into the cockpit. I looked into the car to see water up to the seat bottoms. When I opened the door, collected rainwater gushed out onto my feet. I shook my head in despair, then raised the top to enclose the soggy interior and scurried up to our apartment to change into dry clothes. With a cup for bailing and an armload of towels for drying, I returned to mop out the interior sufficiently to get Mary and our friends back home for the evening.

The next morning was another magnificent day, cool and crisp with deep blue skies. I laid the canvas top of the Alpine across the trunk lid and opened everything I could in hopes that the car would dry out. When I came back that afternoon, I was amazed to discover that the interior wasn't wet anywhere, even the foam in the seat bottoms was dry! I was certain that the drenching would ruin the car, costly to repair at least, but no ill effect ever materialized. Our Alpine was simply a one-time fish bowl that dried out, bone dry.

After months of training in North Chicago, then Albuquerque followed by assignment to Clarksville Base for two year, then Norfolk, our Alpine was our conveyance to many sites wherever we were. While living on Virginia Beach near the Navy base, just as I arrived at our apartment one afternoon, a loud BANG in the engine compartment got my immediate attention. A severe vibration shook the car, and I was certain that the engine had blown, imagining that an over-stressed part from drag racing had let go. Steam belched from under the car, and I suspected that the engine block had a giant hole in it. If the Prince of Darkness was paying me another visit, it was huge this time.

I immediately turned off the engine, darted into a parking lot, and coasted to a stop. Dreading to look under the hood, I was relieved to discover that the problem was simple; one blade from the 4-blade fan had broken off, causing the BANG and the sudden vibration. The broken blade sliced through the inlet hose from the radiator to the engine unleashing the gush of steam. Everything was a quick fix once I got a new fan and hose from the auto parts store just a few doors down the street, and we were on the road again.

While I was at sea for a year, Mary moved back home and kept the Alpine running as best she could, considering that no one in the mountains of North Carolina had ever heard of a Sunbeam car, much less knew how to work on it. Sunbeam bread, Sunbeam toasters, Sunbeam shavers, yes, but a car...? She got lots of snickers and an occasional offer to buy our Alpine, but it wasn't for sale.

By the time my stint in the Navy was over, "the Fast Tomato" was four years old and had been our regular, often frustrating, transportation throughout that time. Upon exiting the Navy, I returned to college on a budget that did not permit maintaining a British sports car. With no money or time to keep it going, we chose to park the car, and it took up residence in my grandfather's barn. Our Alpine, being our youthful companion during our years of adventures, had come to the end of its roadworthiness. But having owned it from the beginning, our old friend just wasn't for sale, and we never considered any of the many offers from would-be buyers. It sat in the barn collecting dust for several years until post-college employment returned us to Tennessee, and our Sunbeam Alpine still sits in our garage awaiting restoration and the day when the three of us will, once again, motor along the rural byways and recall fond memories of our lives together.

About the Author

Alex Gabbard is a widely published author of fiction and non-fiction whose work has received international acclaim resulting in two books receiving Book of the Year awards in their field. His photography has received a similar award and has illustrated hundreds of magazine and newspaper features over the past quarter-century. Among many published features on topics of US and European travel, available on the Internet, the author received the year 2000 IAMA Silver Metal Award for travel writing. Following that award, the International Society of Poets bestowed upon him the Poet of Merit Award for the year 2002. Among more than a dozen books, a previous work of fiction based on a true and tragic story, *Blood of the Roses,* was a Freedom Book of the Month selection. *Return to Thunder Road* and *Checkmate* are also currently available where books are sold, Amazon.com, alexgabbard.com, and GPPress@att.net. Order author signed books from:

GPPress
P.O. Box 22261
Knoxville, TN 37933-0261

Blood of the Roses
A Novel
by Alex Gabbard

Based on a True Story
An Epic Tragedy

ISBN: 0-9622608-7-8
Casebound
  with dust jacket
248 pages, 3 illustrations
$22.95 + $3.50 S&H
Signed and numbered 1st editions, 1st printing available while they last.

Freedom Book of the Month
December 2002

"*Blood of the Roses* deserves to be widely read solely on the basis of its wonderful presentation of an inspiring story of freedom... The story of the White Rose and its principals, Hans and Sophie Scholl... Gabbard weaves a slow, inexorable magic... skill, that he can portray 'foredoomed' characters so convincingly...."

- *The Freedom Network*

"Very highly recommended reading from cover to cover."

- *The Mid-West Book Review*

"...gave me nightmares..." - *Reviewer*

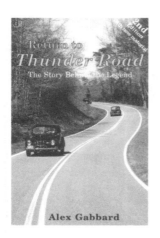

ISBN: 0-9622608-3-5
240 pages with index
Trade Paperback
57 illustrations
$11.95 + $3.50 S&H

Read the real-life story of moonshining as a way of life in the southern Appalachians. This is the story of backwoods survival the way it had been taught for generations, handed down from father to son. Ride with the moonshiners as they tell their stories from corn mash to car loads of "mountain dew." Listen to the U.S. Treasury Agents who were sent to stop them. This is the way is was, told in these pages by the men who live it! A powerful saga of an age gone by when making whiskey grew from "nuthin' to do but hoe corn and make moonshine" to a massive effort to shut down the multi-million dollar trade with a manhunt that put most moonshiners out of business, and many behind bars.

"Your knowledge of American and Automobile History is incomplete until you've read *Return to Thunder Road*."
                    - *Southern Wheels Magazine*

"A darn good book." 5-stars
                    - *Amazon.com*

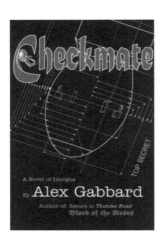

ISBN: 0-9622608-9-4
294 pages
Trade Paperback
$15.95 + $3.50 S&H

Award winning author, Alex Gabbarad, thrusts you into lives of government secrecy, with assassins lurking about, a day-dreaming scientist, a frightened bomb builder, wantabe rock stars, an enterprising computer jock, a bungling secret agent, a failed concert pianist, Beethoven, da Vinci, and "The Babe," all wrapped in the sinister cloak of intrigue.

"*Checkmate* is tremendously imaginative, and it features some wonderfully off-beat characters and colorful dialogue... an awfully fun read."
                    - *Red Wagon Entertainment*